14.99

City and Islington Sixth Form College
Library
The Angel 283-309 Goswell Road
London EC1V 7LA
T: 020 7520 0652
E: sfc.lib@

Book of Literary Non-Fiction

Writing about travel, nature, food, feminism, history, sexuality, death and friendship

Sally Cline and Midge Gillies

Series Editors: **Carole Angier and Sally Cline**

B L G

City and Islington College

SFC25934

Bloomsbury Publishi

First published in 2012

Bloomsbury Publishing Pl
50 Bedford Square
London WC1B 3DP
www.bloomsbury.com

CITY AND ISLINGTON
SIXTH FORM COLLEGE
283-309 GOSWELL ROAD
LONDON EC1V 7LA
TEL 020 7520 0652

Copyright © Sally Cline and Midge Gillies 2012

The authors have asserted their rights under
the Copyright, Designs and Patents Act, 1988,
to be identified as the authors of this work.

A CIP catalogue record for this book is available
from the British Library.

ISBN: 978-1-408-13123-7 (paperback)

Typeset by Country Setting, Kingsdown, Kent CT14 8ES, UK
Printed and bound in Great Britain by MPG Books Ltd,
Bodmin, Cornwall

This book is sold subject to the condition that it shall not,
by way of trade or otherwise, be lent, resold, hired out, or
otherwise circulated in any form of binding or cover other
than that in which it is published and without a similar
condition, including this condition, being imposed on the
subsequent purchaser.

This book is produced using paper that is made from wood
grown in managed, sustainable forests. It is natural, renewable
and recyclable. The logging and manufacturing processes conform
to the environmental regulations of the country of origin.

SFC25934
808·85 CLI
3 Wks

Sally would like to dedicate this book to Ba Sheppard
with much love.

And this book goes with many hugs to Marmoset,
Theo and Arran.

Midge would like to dedicate this book to Sarah
Mnatzaganian, poet and soulmate.

Sally Cline's previous books
Biographies and books about life writing
The Arvon Book of Life Writing (with Carole Angier)
Dashiell Hammett: A Brief Life (forthcoming, Arcade Publishing, USA, 2013)
Lillian Hellman and Dashiell Hammett: Memories and Myths
    (forthcoming, Golden Books, 2012)
Zelda Fitzgerald: Her Voice in Paradise
Radclyffe Hall: A Woman Called John

Literary non-fiction books
Couples: Scene from the Inside
Lifting the Taboo: Women, Death and Dying
Women, Celibacy and Passion
Just Desserts: Women and Food
Reflecting Men at Twice their Natural Size (with Dale Spender)

Edited books
The Arvon Book of Crime Writing (Michelle Spring and Laurie King)
Memoirs of Emma Courtney (Mary Hays)

Midge Gillies' previous books
Biographies and literary non-fiction books
The Barbed-Wire University: The Real Lives of Allied Prisoners of War
    in the Second World War
Waiting for Hitler: Voices from Britain on the Brink of Invasion
Writing Lives: Literary Biography
Amy Johnson: Queen of the Air
Marie Lloyd: The One and Only

Books contributed to
How to Write by Philip Oltermann

General non-fiction books
The Wedding Book
Business Writing

Contents

Part Three: Write on

Foreword

by David Kynaston

Welcome to this exhilarating, wonderfully readable *vade mecum* of suggestions and warnings, of anecdotes and reflections, created and assembled by
Sally Cline and Midge Gillies. 'Literary non-fiction' may be an unavoidably
awkward portmanteau term, but it encapsulates the crucial point that this is
something different in its ambitions from purely functional non-fiction. The
critic Cyril Connolly long ago offered the helpfully implacable dictum that it is
only if a book is still being read ten years after publication that the author has
succeeded. Almost always it is the literary dimension – one of sensibility as
well as style – that will largely determine that outcome.

There is, though, perhaps something else involved, and I think the word is
distinctiveness. My own career as a self-employed historian since leaving
university in 1973 has had its share of wrong turnings and dead ends; but
looking back I can identify two fortunate moments when I realised that
potentially it lay in my grasp to tackle a particular subject in a way that marked
a break from previous approaches. The first was in the early 1980s: I knew I
wanted to undertake something ambitious about the City of London, and it
suddenly struck me that here was a subject that could be treated as a social
anthropologist studies a village, albeit a rather important village. The second
was some twenty years later, when coming across a mixture of diaries and
Mass Observation material jolted me into a conception of my history of post-
war Britain in which the experience of everyday life, as told by those
experiencing it, would be at the very heart of my treatment and not just a
pleasantly diverting adjunct. We need to be alert to these epiphanies and
their possibilities: for most people, myself included, they don't come along
very often.

But, of course, there is not just the 'how' question but also the 'why'.
Specifically, why should one want to devote a sizeable chunk of one's life to
attempting to write literary non-fiction? I sometimes find this an uncomfortable
question I try to bury, but do have a couple of positive thoughts.

It may sound Victorian, but I believe that we are all trying, however fitfully and unsuccessfully, to improve ourselves as human beings; that part of this improvement is becoming less solipsistic; and that being engaged in some form of literary endeavour (whether non-fiction or fiction) has the enormous benefit, quite apart from its other satisfactions, of enabling us to get – or start to get – inside other people's heads. The novelist Richard Hughes once remarked that if Hitler and Stalin had read novels they would not have been the monsters they were, and I suspect he was right. Literature probably does not make us nicer people, but it does enhance our imaginative sympathies.

My other thought relates to being a historian, but not exclusively. I was recently in Sheffield, looking at the vast Park Hill estate that looms above the railway station. Built in the late 1950s, it promised a 'streets-in-the-sky' vision of the future of public housing that captured the imagination of a generation. In the event it failed, for many reasons, and much is now derelict and abandoned. As I walked round, I found myself wondering about the hopes and lives of the families who had lived there – all now gone and largely irrecoverable. Yet if we can recover *something*, whether of those lives or of millions of others, and if we can tell their stories truthfully and without sentimentality, then that is our small cry of defiance, on behalf of the forgotten, to time's relentless, devouring bulldozer.

Good luck, and as Clark Gable says to Marilyn Monroe at the end of their last film, *The Misfits*, 'Just head for that big star straight on – the highway's under it.'

Preface to series

by Carole Angier and Sally Cline, Series Editors

The Arvon Book of Literary Non-Fiction is the third in our bold new Arvon series of books on writing.

Like the others, it is dedicated to a form less commonly studied than traditional ones such as poetry and the novel (though the novel will be included as well, later in the series). And like the others too, it is intended for a wide range of readers – from emerging writers to professionals considering a new genre, from critics to practitioners, and from Chattertons alone in their garrets to groups working together, with a tutor or without one.

It is written by two distinguished writers and experienced mentors of literary non-fiction. And it includes – again like all the books in the series – a central guest section, in which many of the most famous exponents of the genre offer brilliant brief glimpses into their practice.

In fact, literary non-fiction is not a single genre, but many: travel writing, food writing, nature writing, history writing, memoir writing; writing on culture, on feminism, on sex and death, on countless mental, physical and spiritual aspects of being human. So our authors' first question is – what *is* literary non-fiction? And then – how is it done? Of all our Arvon books, this one enters the most unmapped territory. It is a journey of discovery into a fascinating and multifaceted form of writing. *Bon voyage.*

Part 1:
Literary non-fiction

1: Introduction

by Sally Cline

The plan of this book, like the plan of each book in this series, is based on the model of the UK's Arvon Foundation for Writing.

Courses at Arvon traditionally have two established writers working together as mentors with both emerging and experienced writers, with many different writing genres ranging from short stories, through novels, poetry, TV and radio writing, biography, and memoir to general non-fiction.

Similarly, all the books in our series will have two writer-tutors and an exciting range of topics. The first two volumes (published 2010 and 2012) covered life writing and crime writing. Those that follow will include children's fiction, historical fiction, short stories, television and radio, and novels.

In this volume on literary non-fiction, we have brought our different writing experiences and our complementary voices to the subject of literary non-fiction in its many forms. Among the areas we have chosen to cover are social and cultural history, nature, landscape, food, feminism, travel, social history, neuroscience, sexuality, death, and the mysteries of mind and body.

At the Arvon Foundation, the two tutors invite a guest midweek to add another voice to the writerly conversation. Again following the Arvon model we have invited thirty guests, each of them distinguished in their own area of literary non-fiction, to contribute their experiences and their talents in their own voices to our book.

Thus, we have travel writers, historians, landscape and nature writers, feminist philosophers, psychotherapists, novelists who write non-fiction and non-fiction authors who write novels. They will expand the conversation that is about to take place between the authors of this book and the readers and the guest writers participating in it.

Our book has the same three-part structure that all volumes in this series will have. Part One is devoted to the history, definitions and philosophy of literary non-fiction as well as to the challenges of writing it. Part Two is our

Guest Section, where we can hear a wondrous variety of different voices. Part Three is practical, active and very much the readers' section. It is a hands-on approach to planning, researching and writing literary non-fiction.

Part One: Literary non-fiction

We begin the first part of this section with several key questions: what does the term literary non-fiction mean? How does this genre differ from any other mode of non-fiction and especially from the prose called creative non-fiction? What is fascinating about genre-bending books? Why is it important that literary non-fiction writers show a respect for truth in its many forms? We then discuss how the concept of excellence lies at the heart of the mysteries of literary non-fiction. This is of course subjective, yet it contains essential elements many can agree upon.

We then move to an analysis of the challenges of literary non-fiction and how they can be overcome. We discuss the structural and ethical difficulties of this kind of writing, in particular the problem of who owns the lives of its subjects.

We ask questions about the re-creation of the past, how it can be achieved accurately and where it may lead. We are interested in the kinds of imaginative explorations needed to make familiar subjects jump up and seem strange and wonderful. Then we try to analyse the attraction and the difficulties of blurring the edges between non-fiction areas (for instance, books that are part autobiography, part travel, part philosophy). Having tackled the theory and the thorns, we then turn to non-fiction subjects which we find exciting. Midge explores in detail travel writing, nature and landscape, history in several forms; Sally immerses herself in feminism, food, friendship, sexuality, death and in parts of neuroscience and psychology that analyse the strange behaviour of our minds and bodies.

Part Two: Tips and tales

In Part Two of the book, our guests talk directly to readers. Thirty top non-fiction writers provide pithy, provocative and thoughtful pieces about their own craft. All thirty authors are among the very best and best-known writers in their field. They offer helpful hints on the writing game, their own despairs and joys, and the challenges that face us all.

Our contributors include those who enjoy the delights of nature and place, such as Richard Mabey, Jennifer Potter, Robert Macfarlane and Barry Lopez. We have biographers such as Philip Hoare and Diana Souhami, who stretch the boundaries of non-fiction in diverse directions to weave together fact, fiction, autobiography, history, literature, natural science, humour and danger. We devote a whole section to food writing and have invited, among many possible food writers, the historian Lizzie Collingham to talk about the complexities of her craft.

We have gathered feminists from across the globe to challenge received opinion in their writings. Australia's Dale Spender joins the UK's Susie Orbach, Natasha Walter and Bidisha, who use their individual expertise in psycho-therapy, analysis, broadcasting and digital media to throw light on contemporary sexual politics.

Travel authors form a strong part of this section. They range from Colin Thubron to Sara Wheeler and Rosemary Bailey. Yet none of them is a straightforward travel writer: their books are also memoirs, or philosophical essays, or even dramas with foreign characters and strange riveting plot lines.

The genre of literary non-fiction is home to a number of diverse modes of scribbling,, and we have novelists who write non-fiction and non-fiction writers who write novels. Siri Hustvedt, a witty and revelatory novelist, writes an equally powerful neurological memoir.

If the quintessential element of literary non-fiction is the mixture of originality and imagination, then writers Francis Spufford and Dava Sobel beautifully embody it. Both endow their works with significant themes and a happy fusion of styles. And we have the wonderful storyteller Simon Winchester, whose subjects have included a book about a madman, a publisher and a dictionary, and a biography of an ocean in *Atlantic*.

Part Three: Write on

Here we stop talking and invite you, the readers, to participate in some hands-on work. We offer a selection of chapters containing creative exercises alongside practical advice. We have divided the section into three parts: planning, researching and finally writing the book.

Under Planning, we look at structure, format of books, prologues, prefaces, bibliographies and indexes, as well as how to use and indicate referential material.

Under Research, we talk about internet research, libraries, archives and interviewing, and wrestle with that tough question of when it is time to stop researching and start using the keyboard.

The Writing section includes exercises, illustrations and top tips for most of the points given in the book: for instance, on interviewing; on description, quotes and dialogue; on the use of fictional techniques; on how to achieve a balance between facts and artistic truths.

2: What is literary non-fiction?

by Sally Cline

What is literary non-fiction? It is rainbow-hued and many-splendoured. It can be a book about the Arabian Desert or the exquisite sluggishness of the sloth. It can be a book devoted to the differences between shaved ice and hot oatmeal in this culture or another far away. It can express feminist excitement and rage or it can be about understanding badgers or standing up to sharks. It can help us understand the wonders of neuroscience or the history of antiquities.

It can be about anything writers of non-fiction can dream of, but it has to have the stamp of literature.

Any non-fiction book will contain one riveting element to pull readers in: the fact that it is about something that actually exists or actually happened. Readers want to know about real lives and real events, especially those that are not our own, indeed are unlike our own. They want to know about other places, foreign travel, different landscapes. Readers want to know which trees grow where, what happened in a particular historical period, how we can unearth the mysteries of body and mind. Non-fiction books can provide fascinating information on social or political groups, cultures, philosophies. What is Buddhism? How does feminism work today? Why do we eat what we eat, whereas people in other lands eat unbelievably different foods? I remember feeling queasy when my friend told me she had been served goat stew at a British dinner party. If she had said she had eaten it in Morocco or the Caribbean I would have been less surprised, though I would still have felt peculiar. I have to say that I am a long-time vegetarian, so English Sunday roasts, American chilli hotdogs, barbecued alligators or Texas turkey turnovers do not thrill me. But they do interest me, because they are not matters of invention but matters of fact.

The importance of non-fiction to readers is exactly that. We do not need to suspend our disbelief; what we are being told is true. Or so we hope and believe. The version in print or on our Kindles may not be totally accurate, but generally readers assume that non-fiction authors believe their accounts are true, or at least were at the time of writing. Most writers also believe that, indeed strive towards that. If we are invading the territory of the family, ours or other people's, we need to be even more careful. One area of literary non-fiction, that of life writing, is particularly vulnerable to this problem. The challenge of what is ethical as well as what is 'true' is always there.

Often the non-fiction material most of us write will include a clear and balanced argument. Traditionally, our general purpose is to be simple, clear and direct. There are some non-fiction writers who use supposition or their imagination to smooth out their narratives. On occasion I have done this to good effect; but for many non-fiction readers brought up to respect a straightforward classical style and tempo, the use of literary techniques in fiction may appear inappropriate. This certainly has been true in the past, although today matters are changing.

There have always been genre-bending books in literary non-fiction, such as A.J.A. Symons's *The Quest for Corvo* and the works of W.G. Sebald, which successfully blur the boundaries between fact and fiction.[1] Jonathan Raban's *Coasting: A Private Voyage* about a voyage round Britain in a two-masted sailboat, partly a seafaring tale, partly a memoir, partly a novel, successfully blends a journey-narrative with a discussion of the history of the sea. Another exceptional example is *Leviathan* by one of our guest writers Philip Hoare, an amazing feat which blends memoir, social history, biography, literary criticism and nature writing.[2] These are all works of imagination and indisputably works of non-fiction literature.

We would suggest that a non-fiction work is creative if it conforms to the fundamental requirements of respect for truth, but also results from originality of thought and expression. To be considered, in addition, literary, the work must possess the key characteristic of literature, which is writing that has permanent worth through its intrinsic excellence.

Central to the concept of excellence is the use of fine and polished language, which will show mastery of imagery, texture, colour, word choice, rhythm and voice. Literary non-fiction writers will also offer a way of looking at the world, as well as serious research, which makes the content credible and helps shape the material.

Useful examples of what is literary non-fiction and what is not can be found in food writing, as I show in a later chapter in this book. I single out the differences between engaging but non-literary food writers who offer good recipes and anecdotes about culinary procedures, and imaginative literary food writers – for example Muslim or Jewish writers who imbue their material with the culture, religion or ethics of the society from which that food stems. Their research offers us a new world in which to feast, in which to delight.

Sometimes excellence in non-fiction literature can include the management of fictional devices such as suspense, a compelling narrative or a story arc. Where this takes place the writer deploys description, conflict, change and resolution in the manner of the classic short story. The challenge for these writers is that, while using the relevant fictional tools, they must always remember that at the heart of their prose must be truth.

The best literary non-fiction dwells among lasting themes, and offers a sense of the profound in which the subject stands for more than itself.

A good example is Barbara Ehrenreich's witty and thoughtful *Smile or Die: How Positive Thinking Fooled America and the World*. On the surface this is a sharp, often brutal attack on the 'have-a-nice-day' greeting which has permeated American life.[3] Ehrenreich's style is not dissimilar in places to that used in the later New Journalism and in the best creative non-fiction. What separates this book from those earlier modes is its sagacious theme, its originality and its intellectual acuity.

For underneath the humour is an explosion of intellectual wrath about the marginalisation of critical thinking in the United States. Ehrenreich exposes crucial flaws in this kind of upbeat philosophy in the areas of health, academia, the economy, politics and war. The book is serious, sane and utterly unfashionable. That is why it is important, and that is why it is a book of literary consequence.

In my own work as a literary non-fiction writer with a keen interest in social and cultural history, I have tried to engage with subjects whose own lives stood for more than themselves and who reflected significant themes or historical shifts in their own period. In writing about Radclyffe Hall, the British novelist, I was keen to explore the ways in which her life had value outside itself, as well as being specifically rooted in the early twentieth century, when the concepts of 'Englishness' and 'normative sexuality' were starting to alter.[4] Hall had individual significance as a pioneering lesbian writer standing up to legal challenges against her book *The Well of Loneliness*,[5] but she also had considerable cultural importance as a leading figure in the changes that took place in twentieth-century society.

Studies of marital couples can become windows into a wider world. In my book *Couples: Scene from the Inside*, underneath what appeared to be a simple study of the benefits and costs of coupledom, I explored how intimate partnerships can enhance or destroy not only the life of the couple but also a great many lives outside.[6] Another of my aims in the book was to reinterpret and enlarge definitions of heterosexual and gay relationships, while exploding the myth that traditional partnerships are necessarily an ideal way of life.

Similarly, my biography of Zelda Fitzgerald tried to go beyond one famous marital pair's destructive relationship. It explored an unjust period in history for women who wished to achieve something for themselves.[7]

In the book I am now writing about the first American woman publisher Blanche Knopf, I point to her literary and historical significance as the one small American woman behind the twentieth century's most famous writers, and how she directed the way Western writing developed. But more significantly my goal is to show that the history of her tempestuous marriage to Alfred Knopf, set against the history of the Knopf firm, is also the history of twentieth-century publishing.

The key to our definition of writing literary non-fiction is imagination. This can invite questions such as: Should the author become part of the story? Can a first-person perspective illuminate the material in ways that a third-person viewpoint may do less well? Is there something in the writing of the text that could open up the minds of readers, reinvigorate them, even change them? Imagination in our view is an integral part of excellence in writing.

Relative positions and reputation

Non-fiction books can be distinguished according to genre (history, travel, social science, nature, landscape, etc.), but in addition can be accorded a different prestige, status or standing according to whether we term them, for example, academic or creative or literary. Although these are merely labels and it is possible to argue that labels go in and out of fashion, they nevertheless signify some important criteria.

It is useful to compare this to a similar process that goes on in fiction, where the gradings are between what is called genre fiction (which includes mystery, horror, fantasy, sci-fi, crime, romance, children's literature, gay and lesbian fiction, historical fiction) and what is called literary fiction. Many universities with modules in short fiction deploy precisely these dividing lines in their courses. Even then the lines, as with non-fiction, are often blurred. Helen Dunmore's children's books are all termed literary rather than genre; Jeanette Winterson's *Oranges Are Not the Only Fruit*, Michael Cunningham's *Flesh and Blood* and Alan Hollinghurst's *The Line of Beauty* are seen as examples of literature, not of gay genre fiction. Similarly, Willa Cather's *Death Comes for the Archbishop* and Hilary Mantel's *Wolf Hall* both grace shelves marked literary fiction, not historical fiction.

Although the term literary non-fiction is relatively new (though excellence in non-fiction literature is certainly not new), it builds on older prose forms, such as the New Journalism and creative non-fiction, sometimes called narrative non-fiction or documentary prose. It is useful to look at these early forms as they show not only where literary non-fiction's techniques have come from but also its varying levels of reputation.

The New Journalism

The New Journalism sought to communicate facts through narrative storytelling and fictional techniques. Tom Wolfe, author of *The New Journalism* (1974), popularised this style in the hope that he and others would be able 'to write journalism that would . . . read like a novel'.[8]

Wolfe wrote an investigation into the custom-car world, *The Kandy-Kolored Tangerine-Flake Streamline Baby*, which was published as the title story of his first book of collected essays in 1965.[9] With its flamboyant language, shifting scenes and realistic dialogue, it became almost a manifesto of the style if not the themes of the New Journalism. Though New Journalists were broadly interested in culture and politics, there were no special unifying subjects. What did unite them was their writing style, the way their work was formatted, the bold staccato rhythms, the interrogative methods.

New Journalists rejected the standard facts-only approach taught in newspapers, and focused instead on dialogue relevant to the events they described, sometimes also including scenarios that the author had experienced. Exhibiting subjectivity became a feature of the New Journalism, so that truth and reality were seen not through a third-person neutral narrator but through the author's eyes. The writer then had the creative freedom to blend elements of fiction, fact and opinion. The journalist's voice became critical to readers in forming their own opinions of the work.

Tom Wolfe collected a series of articles written by himself, Truman Capote, Hunter S. Thompson, Norman Mailer, Robert Christgau and Joan Didion in *The New Journalism* (1973). He codified the term and set out certain principles of the language associated with it, which he discussed in an article in *Esquire* (December 1972), where he hailed the replacement of the novel by the New Journalism as literature's 'main event'. He suggested several points of similarity between the novel and New Journalism. All New Journalists in his view employed four realistic techniques once the prerogative of fiction writers. These were: first, scene-by-scene construction as a way to tell a story rather than historical narrative; second, using accurate dialogue in the form of conversational speech rather than quotations and statements; third, inserting a point of view so that different scenes could be presented through the eyes of different characters; fourth, using concrete descriptive details (such as behaviour, possessions, relationships with others in the story) to round out 'characters'. Using such techniques, he decided, meant that the form that had originated with the novel was now mixed with many other prose devices. In addition, the new style had an extra powerful element: readers knew the story had in fact happened.

Although New Journalists employed fictional tools such as symbolism, cadence, irony and tension, they always maintained that New Journalism was not fiction. It kept steady the elements of reporting, including strict adherence to factual accuracy where the writer is the primary source. It was meant to be as reliable as the most reliable reportage, although New Journalists sought what they saw as a larger truth than was possible through the mere compilation of verifiable facts, use of direct quotations, and adherence to the rigid organisational style of the older form. To get 'inside the head' of a character, journalists used standard interview techniques to establish how subjects felt. They did not use their own powers of invention.

Wolfe held to the principle that reportage was the great unexplored art form, that a factual work could explore whole new dimensions in writing that would double the effect fiction had, because every word in the book would be true.

As a genre, New Journalism was a fresh and creative reporting form, but the term itself was not new. The label had been used with widely different meanings throughout the history of American newsprint. Robert E. Park, 'for instance, in his 'Natural History of the Newspaper', referred to the advent of the Penny Press in the 1830s (so called because it cost only one cent per newspaper) as 'new journalism'. Later, in the 1880s, when certain newspapers – such as Joseph Pulitzer's *New York World*, which used eye-catching headlines and sensational news stories to improve sales – became known as the Yellow Press, pundits and historians suggested that another kind of 'New Journalism' had been born.

During the 1960s and 1970s, the label took on its more recent meanings when investigative journalists, social activists and humanist writers, including Gay Talese, Terry Southern and George Plimpton, used some of these stylistic techniques. Most of them wrote features, essays, articles or short prose booklets. Few wrote book-length prose, such as all the literary non-fiction discussed in this Arvon book. There were, however, some interesting exceptions.

Hunter S. Thompson moved from features to book-length prose with his first book *Hell's Angels: The Strange and Terrible Saga of the Outlaw Motorcycle Gangs* (1966), a ruthlessly honest look at the Hell's Angels club. This book has the embryonic beginnings of a more memoir-based approach to reportage.

Some writers engaged in traditional fictional modes switched to writing in this experimental style. Two of the best known were Truman Capote with *In Cold Blood* (1965), about the murder in their own home of a Kansas farm family; and Norman Mailer with *Armies of the Night* (1968), the Pulitzer Prize-winning 'non-fiction novel' whose subtitle *History as a Novel/The Novel as*

History gives a clue to the narrative split into fictional and historicised accounts of the October 1967 March on the Pentagon.

However, despite the New Journalism label fixed to their work by fellow writers, the two authors separately and loudly decided that they were not writing like journalists but like 'non-fiction novelists'.

In the 1980s, New Journalism seemed to be in decline. A few rather staid elderly writers, who were once young hippy trailblazers, still used fictional techniques in their non-fiction books. However, younger writers in *Esquire* and *Rolling Stone*, where the style had flourished in the two earlier decades, shifted so far away from the New Journalism that Pulitzer Prize winner Thomas Powers asked in a 1975 issue of *Commonweal*: 'Whatever happened to the New Journalism?'. Writers speculated about the reason for its final illness, but what was certain was that less than a decade after Tom Wolfe's 1973 *The New Journalism*, the consensus was that New Journalism was dead.

Creative non-fiction

Running alongside the New Journalism, then succeeding it, was the genre called creative non-fiction.

It arose partly from a dissatisfaction among certain non-fiction writers who were not journalists with the cultural situation in which they found themselves. In the early 1970s risk-taking non-fiction writers who were not reporters were rare. Few, for instance, used such tools as scene-setting, dialogue, description or first-person viewpoints to enhance their truthful factual prose. They left those to fiction writers. Experimental non-fiction writers wanted an outlet.

In America the category creative non-fiction was formally established in 1983 specifically to deal with the problem posed by America's National Endowment for the Arts, which had not yet found an answer to what to call a genre of non-fiction that was factually accurate about people and events, yet was told in a bold, arresting manner more like that of fiction. The NEA, established by Congress in 1965, is an independent agency of the USA federal government which has so far awarded more than 4 billion dollars to support artistic excellence, creativity and innovation.

In 1983, they needed a named category for applicants to submit what they hoped would be prize-winning prose to the board to obtain what became known as Creative Non-Fiction Fellowships. Members of the NEA English Departments campaigned for the use of this term to represent a method that utilised the tools of literary craft to present non-fiction.

The basis of this category was that creative non-fiction writers did not make up anything; they merely made existing ideas and information more exacting, more accessible.

The American Creative Non-Fiction Foundation, supported by both public and private funds, was incorporated in 1994 to pursue educational and publishing initiatives in high-quality non-fiction such as literary journalism, memoir and personal essays. It supports a popular journal founded and edited by Lee Gutkind, Professor in the Hugh Downs School of Human Communications at Arizona State University. The journal's dedicated regular writing team encourages guest contributions as well as online courses.

So what did the Foundation mean by creative non-fiction? They saw it as a genre which fuses literary styles to factually accurate accounts. The goal is to communicate information, but to shape it in a way that reads somewhat like fiction. Literary critic Barbara Lounsberry in her book *The Art of Fact* (1990) suggested four elements should be present in creative non-fiction. The first was documentable subject matter chosen from the real world rather than invented by the writer. The second was exhaustive research. The third was 'the scene', by which she meant a detailed description of the context of each factual event. The fourth element was fine writing dependent on narrative structure and form.

Some writers who used certain stylistic techniques from both the New Journalism and/or creative non-fiction transcended those genres because their aims, philosophy and imaginative writing were those of literary non-fiction. Literary non-fiction writer Joan Didion is a powerful example. She writes in the moment, often about the moment, but with reflective undercurrents that are perennial and humane. Initially seen as a major proponent, even pioneer, of the New Journalism, she used that writing style to explore the cultural values and experiences of American life in the 1960s.

Whereas many New Journalists focused only on the 'now' and offered an incisive comprehension of a particular event or situation and its meaning at a particular time in history, Didion used similar techniques to explore long-term human themes. Her interest from her earliest years was in the profundity of experience and its universal meanings.

How she looked at language changed with her literary development. Early in her career in a 1976 *New York Times* article called 'Why I Write', she said that the structure of each sentence was essential to the subject and meaning she was trying to convey in her work. 'To shift the structure of a sentence alters the meaning of that sentence, as definitely and inflexibly as the position of a camera alters the meaning of the object photographed.' Her interest was in the arrangement of words. 'The arrangement you want can be found in the picture in your mind.' That picture, she believed, helped her arrange the words 'and the arrangement of the words tells you, or tells me, what's going on in the picture'.[10]

In an interview in 2005, nearly thirty years later, when she had radically changed her literary stance from that of the incisive young journalist to that of the reflective critical literary non-fiction writer, she talked about the changes in how she used words and sentences. These alterations became most obvious when she discussed the nature and style of grief in her extraordinary study of bereavement following the death of her writer husband John Gregory Dunne.[11]

'I found it amazingly easy to write . . . It was me sitting down and crying. I didn't even have the sense that I was writing it. I'm usually very conscious of the rhythm of sentences and how that is working. I didn't even give that any thought.' The conscious stylist was now the unconscious literary writer.[12]

One thing remained stable throughout her writing life. In 2005, as in 1976, Didion still felt that: 'I write entirely to find out what I am thinking, what I'm looking at, what I see and what it means.'[13] Every first-rate literary non-fiction writer or novelist whom I have met says they too believe that.

Exclusions: What literary non-fiction is not

For the purposes of this volume, we have made several decisions as to what literary non-fiction is not.

It is not print or web journalism. It is not what has been called the New Journalism, such as that written by Tom Wolfe, Norman Mailer or Lillian Ross. It is not the Literature of Reality, such as Truman Capote's *In Cold Blood*. It is not academic writing. It is not diaries or letters. It is not technical writing, nor collections of scientific papers, nor user manuals, how-to guides, travelogues, handbooks, text books, nor literary criticism. A great deal of life writing (biography, autobiography and memoir) is literary, but some examples are not. Sometimes this depends on the author's intentions. If a biographer wants to write a completely factual book or has a star of entertainment or celebrity as its subject – or, in the case of autobiography, where the author focuses not only on a sporting star's life but wishes to concentrate a great deal on the technicalities of the sport – by their nature these non-fiction books would not have the imagination, word choice, rhythm or profundity to be termed literary.[14]

Originally we had not included standard non-fiction on social science, politics, psychology, psychiatry, medicine, pure science, art history or history, where the language is not literary, or where there is insufficient imagination brought to the subject, or where the themes are too ephemeral. However, to our delight we discovered from our guest section that many fine writers do indeed write non-fiction books relating to historical, political, neuroscientific or medical matters, which are without doubt literature.

Short literary non-fiction

Although some essays and belles lettres stand as examples of literary non-fiction, we have largely excluded very short pieces from our analysis, partly because many, due to their circumscribed length, favour style over substance. We decided to concentrate almost entirely on book-length prose with substantial content and rich and memorable writing that also maintained a stance of unflinching accuracy.

Miniature prose can, however, be a good diving platform for writers of literary non-fiction. Worth reading and learning from is the short prose in an American online literary magazine called *Brevity* edited by Dinty W. Moore. Here you will find Pulitzer Prize finalists, Pushcart winners, authors published in *Best American Essays* and writers from India, Egypt, Spain and Ireland. English writers are especially encouraged to submit work. It is often easier to expand than to cut, so in terms of learning the craft of writing literary non-fiction, short prose is an excellent starting place.

Notes

1. Peter Ackroyd, *Dickens,* Sinclair Stevenson, London, 1990; HarperCollins, New York, 1990. A.J.A. Symons, *The Quest for Corvo,* Penguin, London, 1966; New York Review, New York, 2001. W.G. Sebald, *Vertigo,* Vintage, London, 2002; New Directions, New York, 2001. W.G. Sebald, *The Rings of Saturn,* Vintage, London, 2002; New Directions, New York, 1998. W.G. Sebald, *The Emigrants,* Vintage, London, 2002; New Directions, New York, 1996.

2. Jonathan Raban, *Coasting: A Private Voyage,* Vintage, London and New York, 2003; Philip Hoare, *Leviathan,* Fourth Estate, London, 2008.

3. Barbara Ehrenreich, *Smile or Die: How Positive Thinking Fooled America and The World,* Granta, UK, 2009; Picador, New York, 2010 (under the title *Bright-Sided*).

4. Sally Cline, *Radclyffe Hall: A Woman Called John,* John Murray, London, 1997; Overlook, New York, 1999; Faber Finds, London, 2010.

5. Radclyffe Hall, *The Well of Loneliness,* Virago, London, 2008.

6. Sally Cline, *Couples: Scene from the Inside,* Little, Brown & Co., London, 1998; Overlook, New York, 1999.

7. Sally Cline, *Zelda Fitzgerald: Her Voice in Paradise,* John Murray, London, 2002; Arcade, New York, 2003; Faber Finds, London, 2010.

8. Xiaocong He, 'A Masterpiece of Literary Journalism: Joan Didion's *Slouching Towards Bethlehem*', *Sino-US English Teaching,* Vol. 3, No. 2 (Serial no. 26), February 2006, ISSN1539-8072, USA.

9. The story was originally published in 1963 in *Esquire* magazine.

10. Joan Didion, 'Why I Write', *New York Times Magazine,* 5 December 1976.

11. Joan Didion, *The Year of Magical Thinking,* Harper Perennial, London, 2006; Vintage, New York, 2007.

12. Joan Didion, interview with Jonathan Van Meter, *New York Books,* 2 October 2005.

13. Joan Didion, 'Why I Write', p. 13.

14. In this volume we have mentioned biographies and memoirs where relevant but have not dealt in detail with life writing as Volume 1 in this Arvon series is devoted to it: *The Arvon Book of Life Writing* by Sally Cline and Carole Angier.

3: Challenges of literary non-fiction

by Midge Gillies

Whose story is it?

Sometimes writing literary non-fiction can seem too challenging. When you are writing about the past, how do you re-create it honestly and with imagination when you weren't there? How do you write about travel in a way that obscures the inevitable tedious aspects of a journey or makes a virtue of them? Is it ever possible to write about something as familiar as a flower or an animal so that the reader sees both in a different light? What do you do when different accounts of the same event don't quite tally? Wouldn't it be simpler – and less demanding – to turn everything into fiction?

Writers of literary non-fiction face ethical and structural dilemmas at every turn, but it is precisely because they walk this tightrope that the genre is so satisfying for both authors and their readers. When Rebecca Skloot started researching the story of a Petri dish of cancer cells that had once belonged to a poor black woman from Virginia called Henrietta Lacks, she plunged into a hotbed of ethical issues. In her book *The Immortal Life of Henrietta Lacks,* she tackled the morality of medical research and racial attitudes – but she also had to confront her own ethical dilemma. In much the same way as a biographer, she was forced to think about exactly who owned Henrietta's life, how she as an author related to it, how much to include the Lacks family in the book, and how much of the author should appear. She faced the structural challenge of telling a complex medical story in a compelling way, while also including the other strands that are intrinsic to it.

And then there is that whole fraught area of who owns the story in the first place. It can feel reassuring to write about the dead – after all, you can't libel them. But it is surprising how once you become wrapped up in someone's story they often nag at you from beyond the grave, so that the responsibility for representing their life accurately feels as pressing as if you were sitting interviewing them in your front room.

Unlike fiction, writing about the truth is rarely neat. Plot lines can only be smoothed out by omission rather than invention, characters sometimes refuse to be 'fleshed out' or remain elusive despite exhaustive research. Writers are forced to make decisions that can seem like playing with the past: giving more credence to one account of an event over others, or dismissing a version from someone who cannot answer back.

In her 2009 book *The Suspicions of Mr Whicher, or The Murder at Road Hill House,* Kate Summerscale is as anxious to uncover the truth about who really killed the three-year-old Saville Kent as Jack Whicher, the celebrity detective who tried to solve the murder in 1860. Because she cares about the characters, so does the reader.

The same is true of the travel writer. An author like Colin Thubron respects the people and landscape he encounters. He is more likely to poke fun at himself as the 'foreigner' than at the local people. In *To a Mountain in Tibet* he describes how his guide, Iswor, says grimly, in his troubled English: 'You will die here'.

> A faint alarm. 'Die here? Who will kill me?'
> He laughs curtly. 'Not "die here". I said "You will diarrhoea." These people dirty.'[1]

In an earlier age and with a less skilled writer, Iswor might have been the butt of the joke.

Nature and landscape demand a similar respect, and writers can face a similar ethical dilemma: if they write too compellingly about a place, they risk destroying the very essence of what they are describing. They shake up the snow dome and the flurries land in a way that alters the landscape for ever. John Berendt's evocation of the strange, whimsical world of Savannah, Georgia – with a cast that includes a foul-mouthed drag queen called The Lady Chablis and a voodoo priestess – brought curious visitors flocking to the city. A year after his book was published tourist numbers had doubled. But while the local economy delighted in *Midnight in the Garden of Good and Evil,* most nature or travel writers would feel queasy at the thought that they had destroyed the remoteness of a place, or the seclusion of an animal's habitat. Some manage to disguise locations just enough to put off all but the most dogged acolyte.

The elusiveness of literary non-fiction

Although literary non-fiction covers such distinct genres as travel writing and writing about nature, history, feminism and landscape, often the very best literary non-fiction blurs these distinctions.

Footsteps, Adventures of a Romantic Biographer by Richard Holmes has been described as 'part biography, part autobiography', because Holmes retraces the journeys of his biographical subjects. He sleeps rough to follow Robert Louis Stevenson's journey through the Cevennes; in the 1960s, he witnesses the Paris riots, but also explores Mary Wollstonecraft's experiences in the city; and in the 1970s he traces Shelley's travels to Italy. The book is certainly both biographical and autobiographical, but I would add a third category of writing – travel.

Leviathan or, The Whale by Philip Hoare notches up even more genres. It is part memoir, part natural history, part travel writing, and in its assessment of the work of Herman Melville, part literary criticism. *What I Talk About When I Talk About Running* by the Japanese novelist Haruki Murakami is a series of essays about his preparation for different marathons held around the world. But it is essentially a book about the art of writing, as well as a memoir, a travelogue and a training log. His publishers classified it as 'memoir/sport'.

As Murakami says in the Foreword to the book: 'One thing I noticed was that writing honestly about running and writing honestly about myself are nearly the same thing. So I suppose it's all right to read this as a kind of memoir centered on the act of running.'[2]

That a book cannot be neatly pigeonholed is often a sign of good literary non-fiction, although this can make it harder for a publisher to grasp or a bookseller to know which shelf to put it on. *Bomber County* by one of our guest contributors, Daniel Swift, is ostensibly about the author's search for the grandfather he never met, a Second World War pilot with the RAF's 83 Squadron. He dredges civilian and military archives, interviews survivors and revisits places significant to his grandfather with the tenacity of a seasoned historian. But it is his intimacy with the literature of the period that allows him to make the connection between poetry and the bombing campaigns of that war, and thereby to make his book so much more than a history book.

Telling the story

It is this multilayered approach that allows non-fiction to be literary: Kate Summerscale's ability to give the reader the context of the period in which she is writing, to probe the development of the detective and his use in literature; Daniel Swift's account of what it means to be bombed or to bomb, and of the morality of aerial warfare; Philip Hoare's ability to use his lifetime obsession with whales to explore *Moby-Dick* and environmental issues.

The complexity of non-fiction presents one of its greatest challenges – how to tell a compelling story, but at the same time to put it in its historical context, and to address some of the larger philosophical questions that arise from it. Writers of any kind of literary non-fiction face many decisions when building the structure of their book. Should they tell their story in a chronological order or a thematic one? Should they follow one person's story? Or should they use a mixture of all three? If the latter, when do they decide to break off from the main narrative to put their story into context?

Or maybe the author has found a more ingenious device that tells the story through a different medium altogether. The art historian Carola Hicks, for example, took iconic objects such as the Bayeux Tapestry and the stained-glass windows of King's College Chapel in Cambridge, and revealed both their life stories and their cultural afterlife.

James Shapiro's *1599: A Year in the Life of William Shakespeare* adopts the clever tactic of following the playwright through one year that was highly significant for his artistic output, but also reflected great political uncertainty. It was the year in which he completed *Henry the Fifth*, wrote *Julius Caesar* and *As You Like It*, and drafted *Hamlet*. Around him the court struggled with an ageing queen, unrest in Ireland, intrigue at court and the threat of invasion. The device is obviously artificial (Shapiro starts his book in the winter of 1598 and it covers more than the year of the title), but by focusing on a distinct period he sheds a particularly sharp light on the influences on Shakespeare's work.

Rebecca Skloot spent years researching Henrietta Lacks, writing scenes here and there, before she fixed on a structure for the book. Eventually she decided to 'braid' three narratives together and to jump around in time.[3] She said later that if she had decided to stick to a strict chronological timeline it would have been 'a little off' in terms of character balance. She mapped out the whole book using different-coloured index cards – one for each thread – and then pinned them on to her wall. Next she asked her local bookshop to order her every novel they could find that contained multiple characters and jumped around in time. One of the most useful in the early stages was *Fried Green Tomatoes at the Whistle Stop Café* by Fannie Flagg.

At first Skloot thought she would cover the scientific aspects of the story by writing news stories: then she started to watch movies for inspiration about structure. She found *Hurricane*, about the boxer Hurricane Carter, particularly useful because it has three stories. She unpicked the structure of the movie by 'story-boarding' it and comparing it to her own colour-coded system. This made her realise that some of her chapters were too long, and that what worked best in the film was its fast pace. She moved sections around several times, and said her final structure evolved from 'a combination of fiction and movies'.

When I wrote about prisoners of war in the Second World War in *The Barbed-Wire University*, I felt overwhelmed by the prospect of ordering my material in a coherent way that still allowed the prisoners' voices to be heard. I was concentrating on the creativity of POWs – how they took up art, performed plays and concerts, learned languages, made objects and took exams. Should I arrange my material thematically, chronologically or even by camp? In the end I followed a chronology, but broke the book into geographical sections. Part one started in Europe because the war started there; the Far East followed because Japan entered the war in late 1941; then it was back to Europe and finally the Far East (where the war ended in August 1945). My last section dealt with what happened to the POWs after their release and how their experience of captivity shaped their careers and lives.

Within this chronological and geographical framework I wove in themes such as 'art' and 'sport' and followed the stories of men I had interviewed, and in particular my own father's story. I tried to vary the pace by introducing three very short chapters called 'Uses for a Red Cross Parcel Number 1 – String . . . No 2 – Cigarettes . . . No 3 – Tins'.

Once I had started writing the book I felt like a cross-Channel swimmer who has lost sight of land but has to keep ploughing on, just hoping that they are heading in the right direction. Several times I was concerned that I might have veered wildly off course, and might be far out in the Atlantic rather than on my way to France; at other moments I had the unnerving impression I was about to be mown down by a super-tanker. But I kept going until I was safely on the other side, and could reflect on the course I had taken and whether anyone could follow it.

The slippery truth

The writer of literary non-fiction soon discovers that there is usually more than one version of the truth. My father liked to tell a story about the birth of his younger sister, Ruby. During her pregnancy their mother, who ran a small grocery shop in Scotland, had a craving for porridge oats, and every time she went into the shop could not resist scooping out a handful from the barrel where they were stored. As a result of her ante-natal indulgence the baby was born covered in oatmeal . . . or so the story went in my family.

Obviously, from a medical viewpoint the notion of a mother's food being passed, undigested, into the amniotic fluid is ridiculous; and yet I have always been fond of this story. The oats reflect my family's Scottishness, the gorging my grandmother's zest for life. When I mentioned the anecdote to a writers' class as an example of a story that was obviously untrue, most of the group nodded in sage agreement. But one student pointed out that the strange whitish coating my family had noticed could well have been 'vernix' – a secretion babies produce as a way of protecting their skin during their stay in the womb. It was a timely reminder that the writer does not have a monopoly on the truth.

It is important not to dismiss out of hand stories from the past, or from people who seem less sophisticated – no matter how outlandish their tales appear. This is as true in travel, nature and science writing as it is in history or life writing. When I was researching how it felt to live in Britain under threat of invasion by Nazi Germany, I became fascinated by contemporary accounts by pet owners and farmers who were convinced that their animals and birds could predict a bombing raid. I could believe that a pheasant or a collie dog might show distress long before the human ear was able to detect the drone of a bomber, but it seemed fanciful to credit them with the ability to distinguish between one that was about to drop its load and one on its way to inflict destruction on Germany. However, what was important was that people at the time believed it, and that watching for signs of anxiety among their pets became part of the daily routine of that tense summer. What is more, the vigilant pet owner may have been right all along, and there may be some physiological trait that gave the animals advance warning of a raid. In recent years, scientists have started to study whether animals such as elephants can hear the approach of a tsunami, or can detect it in other ways, such as through changes in barometric pressure.

In Baltimore in the 1930s and 1940s, poor black families were convinced that 'night doctors' from the Johns Hopkins medical school snatched black people from the streets and used them for medical experiments. The hospital, so they believed, was built in the heart of the poor black neighbourhood in order to provide a ready supply of bodies.[4] This legend could not have been further from the truth. The hospital was set up in 1889 by a wealthy banker and grocer, Johns Hopkins, with the aim of helping those who could not afford to pay medical bills, and with the specific remit that patients should be treated regardless of their colour. This was the reason why the hospital was built where it was.

But in this example, as in the others, what people believed to be true is as important as the truth itself. The story of my aunt's oatmeal-covered birth became part of my family's history. Using animals as early-warning devices was one way, like studying the skies for a clear 'bomber's moon' that would guide destruction to Britain, in which people weighed up their chances of survival in 1940. Fears of 'night doctors' made the black population of Baltimore fearful of seeking out help in the very place that could do most for them in those years of racial segregation.

Writers of non-fiction must, of course, search for the truth, but it is often their interpretation of the many layers of truth that gives their writing depth and makes it literary.

Reader, meet your author

Roger Deakin's *Waterlog, A Swimmer's Journey through Britain* starts with a mesmerising description of the author in his element:

> *The warm rain tumbled from the gutter in one of those midsummer downpours, as I hastened across the lawn behind my house in Suffolk and took shelter in the moat. Breaststroking up and down the thirty yards of clear, green water, I nosed along, eyes just at water level. The frog's-eye view of rain on the moat was magnificent. Rain calms water, it freshens it, sinks all the floating pollen, dead bumblebees and other flotsam. Each raindrop exploded in a momentary, bouncing fountain that turned into a bubble and burst. The best moments were when the storm intensified, drowning birdsong, and a haze rose off the water as though the moat itself were rising to meet the lowering sky. Then the rain eased and the reflected heavens were full of tiny dancers: water sprites springing up on tiptoe like bright pins over the surface. It was raining water sprites.[5]*

Deakin introduces himself in this very first paragraph and establishes an image that drives the book. As he explains in the second paragraph, in 1996 he wanted to swim through Britain, taking as his inspiration John Cheever's short story 'The Swimmer', in which the hero decides to swim the eight miles home from a party on Long Island via his neighbours' swimming pools. Instead of backyard pools, Deakin travelled across the country via rivers, lakes and quarries in a celebration of what is now known as 'wild swimming', viewing the landscape from his watery perspective.

The use of the first-person pronoun is unavoidable in travel writing and in most nature writing. The reader is interested in the author's experience of the journey and his reaction to wildlife. Another guest contributor, Robert Macfarlane, starts *The Wild Places* with a description of retreating to the top of a beech tree that he called his 'observatory'. The first line is: 'The wind was rising, so I went to the wood.'[6] As in *Waterlog*, the author is our guide, and he makes immediately explicit what his book will do.

In *Arctic Dreams*, Barry Lopez, another guest contributor, manages to fade in and out of his narrative. In the preface, he sets out the inspiration for the book, a camping trip with a friend in the western Brooks Range of Alaska. In the rest of the book, he deftly explores the wildlife and history of the Arctic, occasionally popping up to remind the reader of his passion for the area and to illuminate it with his own experience of the particular Arctic conditions. Two-thirds of the way through, he calmly recounts how he and a group of scientists were caught in a storm that threatened to trap their boat in ice, a very long way from help. The description adds an exquisite point of drama to the book but also reminds the reader of Lopez's intimate knowledge of his subject.

Historians and biographers can find it harder to justify the use of 'I' in their writing. After all, they have presumably decided to write about other people rather than themselves because they think other people's stories are more interesting. I have always tried to avoid putting myself in my books. The only exception was when I was writing about prisoners of war and even then it took an astute editor to nudge me in that direction by convincing me that, as the daughter of a POW, I was justified in putting my own observations about my father in the first person. Other writers have not been so coy. In Peter Ackroyd's monumental biography of Charles Dickens he actually invents meetings between his subject and himself in which they chat about the art of biography. The book was a commercial success, but several critics had their doubts about this technique.

The main danger in introducing yourself into your narrative is that readers might not like you. If they find you patronising or annoying, they are likely to feel the same about your book. It is hard not to like our guest contributor Dava Sobel at the start of *Longitude*, her book about John Harrison who invented an instrument that allowed sailors to navigate round the world. On the first page, she describes a collapsible beaded wire ball her father bought her when she was a little girl, and how its hinged wires traced a pattern of intersecting circles that reminded her of the lines of longitude and latitude she knew from the globe in her classroom. As her father strode up Fifth Avenue with her on his shoulders they would pause to stare at the statue of Atlas carrying Heaven and Earth. Here again she could see the imaginary lines.

The description of the young Dava is so appealing because it simplifies what is a complex subject. It reminds us that the author was once a child who was fascinated by the world. We can relax, knowing we are in the hands of a skilled storyteller.

Like any kind of writing, the success of literary non-fiction depends on the relationship between reader and writer. If the reader has confidence in the writer, they will allow themselves to be taken anywhere. And one of the joys of non-fiction is that it can lead anywhere.

Notes

1. Colin Thubron, *To a Mountain in Tibet*, Chatto & Windus, London, 2011, p. 37.
2. Haruki Murakami, *What I Talk About When I Talk About Running*, Vintage, London, 2009, p. vii.
3. Youtube, presented by Live Wire! Radio and The Woodstock Book & Literary Festival.
4. Rebecca Skloot, *The Immortal Life of Henrietta Lacks*, Pan Books, London, 2011, pp. 190–91.
5. Roger Deakin, *Waterlog, A Swimmer's Journey through Britain*, Chatto & Windus, London, 1999, p. 1.
6 Robert Macfarlane, *The Wild Places*, Granta, London, 2010, p. 3.

4: Reflections on travel writing

by Midge Gillies

The writer who travels

I am someone who reads travel writing to escape. Most often I enjoy reading about places I would never visit – because they are too frightening, too hot or too cold, too primitive or too modern. Travel takes time, and I prefer others to do what I cannot and report back in a way that transports and entrances me. I love the idea of the intrepid traveller setting off – Laurie Lee on a journey that would take him from the Cotswolds to Spain, a country on the brink of civil war; Patrick Leigh Fermor leaving a drizzling 1930s London; Paul Theroux glancing through his train window as images of Kent fly past, one showing: 'the perimeter of a housing estate with lots of interesting clothes on the line: plus fours, long johns, snapping black brassieres, the pennants of bonnets and socks, all forming an elaborate message, like signal flags on the distressed convoy of those houses.'[1]

For me, it is not the destination that is important but the writing: whether the author can describe the landscape and his or her encounters with its inhabitants; whether he or she can make me laugh, move me or shake my prejudices. I rarely read books about a place I am visiting when I am there, preferring to form my own impressions. When I do, however, I am most impressed by the travel writer who can make me see things I would otherwise have missed. When I visited Northern Ireland for the first time, I read Colm Tóibín's *Bad Blood, A Walk Along the Irish Border*. As he travelled along what was at the time one of the most dangerous stretches of land in Europe, he exposed the rituals and deep-seated hatreds that had formed the landscape in a way that, several years later, I had no hope of detecting without the guidance of someone who knew the country as intimately as he did. It was Tóibín's skill as a writer that brought the country into focus for me.

Sara Wheeler – who was the first woman writer in residence at the US South Pole Station, and who has travelled throughout South America, Bangladesh, India, Nepal and parts of Europe – is clear about what comes first:

> I'm a writer who travels, rather than a traveller who writes. I'm a non-fiction writer – I think people are born one thing or the other. I wake up every day and thank God that I've never wanted to write a novel . . . travel just loaned me the perfect vehicle. It gives a structure into which I can smuggle ideas and other stuff I want to write about. All I really want to write about is what it is to be human. What else is there?[2]

Bill Buford, in his introduction to *Granta Travel Writing,* agrees about the malleability of the genre: 'Travel writing is the beggar of literary forms: it borrows from the memoir, reportage and, most important, the novel. It is, however, pre-eminently a narrative told in the first person, authenticated by lived experience.'[3]

Travel writing has had a chequered history. William Dalrymple, another highly successful practitioner of the art, traces its lineage back to ancient writings such as the *Epic of Gilgamesh,* the wanderings of Abraham in the Old Testament and the travels of the Pandava brothers in the Sanskrit poem *Mahabharata.*[4] The genre's detractors, however, draw attention to travel writing's less attractive past, most notably periods when it appeared to be denominated by well-to-do, mostly male writers such as Peter Fleming and Evelyn Waugh, who sometimes viewed the lands they visited through a patronising, colonialist sheen.

Recently, some commentators have asked whether the instant information available from the internet has made travel writing redundant – a question that misses the point altogether. Travel writing is as different from a travel guide as Nigel Slater's description of an Arctic Roll in his memoir, *Toast,* is worlds apart from a magazine recipe for the perfect pavlova. Travel writing has very little to do with the practicalities of buying the cheapest train ticket from Agra to New Delhi, but everything to do with the experience of queuing up to try to buy the ticket, encounters with other passengers and the sensory punctuation marks of the journey: the smell of the train and its occupants, the food for sale and the landscape through the window.

Some critics also like to point out that the world has shrunk to such an extent that there is no need for travel writing. In an age when satellite tracking devices make it difficult to lose one's way, why would readers want to accompany a writer to a part of the world that they can view for themselves on Google Earth? Again, the criticism misses the point.

As Colin Thubron points out: 'A changing world invites constant reinterpretation. Places that were once easily accessible on the ground – Kashmir, north Pakistan, Afghanistan – transform into forbidding challenges, while old terra incognita – China, the ex-Soviet Union – fall temptingly open.'[5]

The best travel writers provide a multidimensional description of the place they are visiting – not just what it looks like, but how it has been shaped by history, art, religion, trade, war, climate, ecology; and, above all, how the journey is shaping the traveller. Writers such W.G. Sebald, Bruce Chatwin, Jonathan Raban, Paul Theroux, Sara Wheeler and Barry Lopez reveal a place through encounters – with other human beings, with landscape and wildlife – and in many cases their writing refuses to be bound by the conventions of one genre.

William Dalrymple considers Bruce Chatwin's description of Buenos Aires at the beginning of *In Patagonia* as one of his favourite evocations of place. He also admires Patrick Leigh Fermor's description of walking through a German winter in *A Time of Gifts* – 'as wonderfully purple as Chatwin is sparse'; and Leigh Fermor's description of Melk cathedral in the same book is, according to Dalrymple, 'one of the most amazing pieces of architectural description I know of'.

For Dalrymple, John Berendt's description of Lady Chablis in *Midnight in the Garden of Good and Evil* is one of the finest examples of bringing a character to life in a single page. He points to other skilful evocations of characters: Chatwin's hippy miner and Scottish farmer in *In Patagonia,* and Eric Newby's description of the explorer Wilfred Thesiger in *A Short Walk in the Hindu Kush.*[6]

In the developed world most people have the opportunity to travel beyond their immediate town or village; a few even see foreign travel as a right. But mobility and exposure to new places are not enough to create a writer capable of acute observation. Anyone who has sat in a class where the teacher has told the group to write about 'What I did on my holidays' will know that in the hands of an unskilled writer the most exotic destination can become dull, but a perceptive traveller can turn a voyage that – on paper at least – sounds dreary into a funny, fanciful or poignant chronicle.

London Orbital by Iain Sinclair is an example of the latter. In it Sinclair writes about the 127-mile stretch of motorway that most drivers see as a necessary but ugly and stultifying asphalt loop. Sinclair takes a year to walk round the M25, joining up with different companions, and interweaving the history of London with the stark reality of modern politics and urban planning. At the start of his book, in 'Prejudices Declared', he describes the road as:

> *a dull silvertop that acts as a prophylactic between driver and landscape. Was the grim necklace, opened by Margaret Thatcher on 29 October 1986, the true perimeter fence? Did this conceptual ha-ha mark the boundary of whatever could be called London? Or was it a tourniquet, sponsored by the Department of Transport and the Highways Agency, to choke the living breath from the metropolis?*

His style is all the more surprising because he is describing a motorway that for most of those who use it has a numbing effect on the senses. *London Orbital* is proof that a writer does not need malaria tablets or the latest survival gear – or even a passport – to launch their reader into a new world.

Voyages of discovery

The earliest examples of English travel writing emerged from the adventurers who set out to discover new lands. Sir Walter Raleigh (1554–1618) and Sir Francis Drake (?1540–96) swashbuckled their way around the Americas and the West Indies trying to please Elizabeth I, and left behind vivid accounts of their experiences to inspire later writers.

Authors such as Daniel Defoe (1660–1731) and William Cobbett (1763–1835) found their inspiration closer to home, and were often motivated by a desire for social and political change. Defoe – who visited France, Spain, The

Netherlands, and possibly Germany and Italy – was a prolific writer whose eye for detail and rich imagination led to his famous novels *Robinson Crusoe* and *Moll Flanders*, as well as *Tour through the Whole Island of Great Britain* (1724–6). Between September 1822 and October 1826 Cobbett rode his horse round south and south-east England to see for himself the effects of the Napoleonic Wars, and to gauge whether measures to alleviate poverty had worked. In *Rural Rides* (1830) he vents his anger against groups such as tax collectors and landlords, but also celebrates the English landscape.

James Boswell (1740–95), the son of a Scottish judge, is best known as a companion of Doctor Johnson and for the biography that emerged from that friendship. But Boswell was also a travel writer. Like many well-to-do men of his time, he indulged in a leisurely Grand Tour of Europe to sharpen his knowledge of its classical past. He wrote about his travels, in particular in Corsica (whose claim to independence he endorsed, to the extent that he shocked polite society by appearing dressed as a Corsican), but his most lasting contribution to travel writing is *Journal of a Tour of the Hebrides* (1785), based on his tour of Scotland with Johnson.

In the Victorian and Edwardian era, travel writing began to take a distinctive shape. David Livingstone plunged into darkest Africa, driven by missionary zeal; whereas the thick-skirted Mary Kingsley could only take to her canoe after her parents died and left her, at the age of thirty, free to pack her bonnet and head for West Africa. The race to discover the South and North Poles produced travel writing as bitingly intense as the conditions experienced by the explorers. Apsley Cherry-Garrard (1886–1959) wrote *The Worst Journey in the World* while recovering from injuries sustained in the First World War. The journey in question was a five-week struggle with two companions over 140 miles to fetch emperor penguin eggs. Ian Jack later described the book as among the best descriptions of cold ever written,[7] and Paul Theroux said it was the book that most inspired him, 'for its quiet power to evoke a time and place, for its correction of history (for the unsparing portrait of Captain Scott), most of all for its heroism'.[8]

Cherry-Garrard was the son of a major-general and studied at Oxford University. He was undeniably upper class, but the extreme physical suffering he endured allows him to avoid the label of 'gentleman traveller'. Patrick Leigh

Fermor (1915–2011), who travelled mainly by foot and produced his books at a languid rate, has been tagged with the same label, but for many he is the travel writer's travel writer. In 1933, he took a year to walk from Holland to Constantinople, but the first part of his projected trilogy only appeared as *A Time of Gifts* in 1977; *Between the Woods and the Water* was published nine years later, while the final volume remained unpublished at his death. Throughout his travels, he was able to take shelter in castles or palaces owned by rich and titled friends and relatives scattered throughout Europe – although he also stayed in police cells and beer halls.

Leigh Fermor set off on his travels rather than go to university, and his writings are full of the fruits of his autodidacticism. They contain the dry wit associated with someone of his background, a wry humour similar to that of Evelyn Waugh and Eric Newby. Newby, whose most famous book is *A Short Walk in the Hindu Kush* (1958), liked to show himself as a bumbling Englishman abroad. In my opinion, however, one of his best books is also his darkest: *Love and War in the Apennines* (1971), in which he remembers his time on the run as a prisoner of war in Italy. As someone who has read countless POW memoirs, I can recommend it as one of the most authentic and moving accounts of wartime captivity. His description of the landscape and people of that part of Italy is insightful and vivid, and all the more powerful because of its setting of wartime occupation.

By the second half of the twentieth century, writers such as Bruce Chatwin, Colin Thubron and Jonathan Raban were finding new ways of describing a world that was no longer closed to most people in developed countries. The familiar became the focus of many travel books: Raban explored the British Isles from his boat in *Coasting,* and the American Bill Bryson wrote as an outsider with an insider's view in *Notes from a Small Island* (1995), in which he toured Britain before returning home. Humour in travel writing became more sardonic and sharply observed, perhaps because the writer was less vulnerable to accusations of colonial smugness.

The female traveller

Women have always had fewer writing opportunities because of their limited access to education. When it comes to travel writing, they have been doubly cursed, as, until the twentieth century, most were forced to stay at home. Jane Austen confined her fiction to domestic settings, despite living through the Napoleonic Wars that claimed her cousin. Charlotte and Emily Brontë both spent time abroad, but it was their Yorkshire home that provided their greatest inspiration. George Eliot, who travelled widely in Europe, was more concerned with events in Britain – as seen in the subtitle of her novel *Middlemarch: A Study of Provincial Life.*

As Mary Morris says in her introduction to *The Illustrated Virago Book of Women Travellers,* even those women who were in a position to travel did so in a different way from men – usually with an escort, chaperon or husband: 'While the latter part of the twentieth century has seen a change of tendency, women's literature from Austen to Woolf is by and large a literature about waiting, usually for love.'[9] She adds, perceptively, 'I find it revealing that the metal bindings in women's corsets were called "stays". Someone who wore "stays" wouldn't be going far. Nor would a woman with bound feet.'[10]

She suggests that women travel differently from men and have different fears, most obviously the fear of sexual assault. In many parts of the world a woman who travels alone is still seen as an aberration, and will experience the discomfort that that position often brings.

And yet the fact that *The Illustrated Virago Book of Women Travellers* can exist at all proves that women's travel writing has a distinguished past. Contributions from the eighteenth century include Lady Mary Wortley Montagu, who travelled to Turkey with her husband, and Mary Wollstonecraft, author of *A Vindication of the Rights of Woman,* who described Scandinavia in letters home. The most startling writing from the Victorian era emerges from women who were freed from their domestic lives by a twist of fate. Yorkshire-born Isabella Bird (1831–1904) was able to take flight after doctors urged her to recuperate abroad following a spinal operation. Rarely can a bad back have been put to such good use as in her vivid accounts of journeys to Japan, Malaya and the Rocky Mountains.

Mary Kingsley (1862–1900), niece of the novelist Charles Kingsley, was largely self-taught and stayed at home to nurse her parents, until their deaths in 1892. She made her first trip to West Africa the following year and wrote about her wanderings and ethnological research in *Travels in West Africa*

(1897). Her writing has a refreshingly modern tone in its admiration for the people she encounters and her call for a greater understanding of African culture. Above all, her style is deliciously witty and self-deprecating, as in this description of a crocodile:

> On one occasion, the last, a mighty Silurian, as The Daily
> Telegraph would call him, chose to get his front paws over the
> stern of my canoe, and endeavoured to improve our acquaint-
> ance. I had to retire to the bows, to keep the balance right, and
> fetch him a clip on the snout with a paddle, when he withdrew,
> and I paddled into the very middle of the lagoon, hoping the
> water there was too deep for him or any of his friends to repeat
> the performance. Presumably it was, for no one did it again. I
> should think that crocodile was eight feet long; but don't go and
> say I measured him, or that this is my outside measurement for
> crocodiles. I have measured them when they have been killed by
> other people, fifteen, eighteen, and twenty-one feet odd. This was
> only a pushing young creature who had not learnt his manners.[11]

Kingsley is an early example of how an affinity with the people among whom she was travelling, combined with an academic knowledge of their land, helped to produce a new kind of travel writing. The travels of Gertrude Bell (1868–1926) were shaped by family connections: in the late nineteenth century, she visited her stepmother's relations in Bucharest and Tehran. But it was her intellectual grasp of each region's language and history that gave her writing its vividness and authority, while her physical stamina allowed her to discover parts of the world seen by few Westerners.

Bell was the first woman to obtain a first-class honours degree in history from Oxford University and later taught herself Persian. She was interested in archaeology and became famous as an Alpine climber in the early years of the twentieth century, then worked for the Red Cross during the Great War. But it was her passion for the Arab world that brought her her greatest influence, when she provided intelligence for the British government in their efforts to persuade the Arabs to fight against Turkey. Like her friend T.E. Lawrence, she campaigned for independence for the Arabs, and advised the British and the new regime in Iraq in the 1920s.

Freya Stark (1893–1993) came from a more Bohemian background: she was born in Paris where her parents were studying art. Like Bell, her knowledge of the Arab world allowed her to provide intelligence to the British government – this time in the Second World War. Her book *A Winter in Arabia* was published while she was working as Southern Arabia Expert for the Ministry of Information in London. Unlike Bell, she also travelled and wrote about her experiences beyond the Arab world. Sara Wheeler recently cited *A Winter in Arabia* as the book that most inspired her, adding: 'She [Stark] did not try to be an honorary man in a field still woefully dominated by that species.'[12] In the same article, about travel writers who inspire the present generation, Colin Thubron highlighted another Stark book, *Ionia: A Quest*: 'It persuaded me, at the start of my career, how richly landscape and history may interfuse, and how deeply (and sometimes dangerously) a quiet attention can fire the imagination.'[13]

Rebecca West's sensitivity to the culture of the Balkans between the two World Wars gave her a similar understanding of that region, which she visited with her banker husband and later wrote about in her two-volume *Black Lamb and Grey Falcon* (1941). She was also a successful novelist and skilful reporter, who wrote about the Nuremberg trials in a series of articles commissioned by *The New Yorker* and published as *The Meaning of Treason* (1949).

The novelist Rose Macaulay (1881–1958) only wrote one travel book, *Fabled Shore,* about a journey by car along the Spanish coast in 1948, but it proved so powerful that some have claimed that it was instrumental in creating the Costa del Sol as we know it today. Her account was so compelling that thousands followed her lead and set out to discover a new holiday destination.

Macaulay was on the cusp of a different type of travel in which car, train and plane allowed the writer to venture further afield. Pioneering pilots such as Amelia Earhart, Beryl Markham and Amy Johnson (for whom I have a special affection, since I wrote a biography of her) were forging new routes around the world, and in doing so making it a smaller place. Many of them wrote about their experiences in a way that embraces the romance, danger and – above all – the freedom that this new form of transport gave them. Beryl

Markham's *West with the Night*,[14] which was published in 1942, is the most famous. The title is an allusion to her record-breaking solo trip across the Atlantic, but most of the book describes Kenya, where she grew up, trained race horses and became the first woman to receive a commercial pilot's licence, which allowed her to run a business with Denys Finch Hatton, the lover of Karen Blixen, author (under her pen-name Isak Dinesen) of *Out of Africa* (1937). The two books are often compared, although the latter is much more disciplined and tightly structured. Markham, however, has a talent for describing the mystical dimension of a long-distance flight fraught with danger.

> It is dark already and I am over the south of Ireland. There are the lights of Cork and the lights are wet; they are drenched in Irish rain, and I am above them and dry. I am above them and the plane roars in a sobbing world, but it imparts no sadness to me. I feel the security of solitude, the exhilaration of escape. So long as I can see the lights and imagine the people walking under them, I feel selfishly triumphant, as if I have eluded care and left even the small sorrow of rain in other hands.[15]

Beryl Markham wrote with little awareness that she was wandering through male domains – in her case, aviation and horse racing – but for many female travellers their gender plays a part in their experience. Most of the time Sara Wheeler takes a wry view of her minority status among the 'frozen beards', as she likes to call them, of Antarctica, but in a chapter headed 'One of the Boys' she describes a drinking area festooned with postcards of bare bottoms, where a man was telling a joke about periods: 'It was as if I had entered a time capsule and been hurtled back to an age in which Neanderthal man was prowling around on the look-out for mammoths.'[16]

Archaic views on gender can sometimes work in favour of the female traveller. When Jan Morris found she had locked her keys in the boot of her car in a small town in Texas, the occupants eased themselves out of their chairs, tipped their Stetsons over their eyes and strolled into the car park to help by levering their way into the car. When she discovered that she had in fact left them on the Dairy Queen counter they were not disconcerted. They undid their work and retired to their previous positions, muttering, 'You bet, lady, any time.'[17] Would the experience have been different if the traveller had been a man?

Reporting the big picture

Wheeler has described American journalist Martha Gellhorn as one of her favourite writers, because she was 'pitch perfect' and 'brilliant at moving from the detail to the big picture'.[18]

It is no coincidence that many fine writers of literary non-fiction – Simon Winchester, Sebastian Junger, Jan Morris, John Berendt and Rebecca Skloot, for example – started their careers in journalism. This is particularly true in the USA, where magazines like *Rolling Stone*, *Vanity Fair* and *The New Yorker* provide scope for longer, more thoughtful pieces. Journalism demands an eye for detail and a nose for a good story that are both invaluable in travel and history writing. But good travel writing needs something more.

In his introduction to *Granta Travel Writing*, Bull Buford observes that pieces by writers such as Gellhorn, Chatwin and Thubron succeed 'not by virtue of the details they report – exotic as they are – but by the contrivance of their reporting. They are all informed by the sheer glee of story-telling, a narrative eloquence that situates them, with wonderful ambiguity, somewhere between fiction and fact.'[19]

Buford, who wrote his introduction in 1984, adds that travel writing has some similarities to the New Journalism of the 1960s and 1970s (discussed earlier in this book). From the perspective of the early twenty-first century, it appears that some travel writing has found a new energy by dwelling on subjects that have otherwise been reduced to sound bites and tweets.

Rory Stewart, one of the new generation of travel writers, believes travel writing provides the space to explore complex issues:

> In an age when journalism is becoming more and more etiolated, when articles are becoming shorter and shorter, usually lacking all historical context, travel writing is one of the few venues to write with such complexity about an alien context.[20]

While it is true that travel writing – more than other forms of literary non-fiction – can provide what Buford describes as 'armchair-emancipation',[21] which is particularly welcome during times of economic turmoil, it need not always provide easy reading. Travel writing faces up to difficult truths such as bigotry, environmental concerns and religious fundamentalism. There are still places in the world where the ordinary traveller may not venture.

For a long time the polar regions would have been included in that list, but now it is even possible to take an Arctic or Antarctic cruise. War zones, however, remain closed to all but the accredited reporter. This may be where a new form of travel writing will emerge, written by authors describing lands that will remain, thankfully, foreign to most of us. Geoff Dyer believes that some of the greatest books of our time are being written about 'the big story of our times'[22] – the al-Qaida attacks on America and the wars in Iraq and Afghanistan. As examples of this excellence he points to David Finkel's *The Good Soldier*, the result of eight months spent with the US 2-16 Infantry Battalion in Baghdad, and Sebastian Junger's *War*, based on the author's time embedded with an American platoon in Afghanistan. Dyer observes that both have the storyline and character development of a novel. Finkel uses the third-person, near-omniscient narrator to be found in many novels; Junger writes in an unobtrusive first person.

Dyer cites Martin Amis's essay *The Moronic Inferno,* in which Amis claims that the 'non-fiction novel', as written by authors like Norman Mailer and Truman Capote, lacked 'moral imagination', because the facts cannot be arranged to give them 'moral point'. Dyer believes this view needs updating. We are moving beyond the non-fiction novel to different kinds of narrative art, different forms of cognition. Loaded with moral and political point, narrative has been recalibrated to record, honour and protest the latest, historically specific instances of futility and mess.

Battlefields have their own landscape, and describing them may become part of a future travel writing. The genre will always offer 'armchair-emancipation', but in future the armchair may not be quite as comfortable as it became in the late twentieth century.

Notes

1. Paul Theroux, *The Great Railway Bazaar*, Penguin Books, London, 1977, p. 13.
2. *Woman's Hour*, BBC Radio 4, 6 April 2011.
3. *Granta Travel Writing*, Penguin Books/Granta, London, 1984, p. 7.
4. 'Home Truths on Abroad', *The Guardian*, 19 September 2009.
5. 'Author, Author', *The Guardian*, 28 May 2011.
6. By email, 14 September 2011.
7. *The Guardian*, 9 January 2010.
8. *The Guardian*, 17 September 2011.
9. *The Illustrated Virago Book of Women Travellers*, Virago, London, 2006, p. 8.
10. *The Illustrated Virago Book of Women Travellers*, p. 8.
11. Quoted in *The Illustrated Virago Book of Women Travellers*, p. 47.
12. *The Guardian*, 17 September 2011.
13. *The Guardian*, 17 September 2011.
14. Markham's third husband Raoul Schumacher may have helped her to write parts of *West with the Night*.
15. Beryl Markham, *West with the Night*, Virago, London, 2001, p. 284.
16. Sara Wheeler, *Terra Incognita: Travels in Antarctica*, Vintage, London, 1997, p. 200.
17. Jan Morris, 'Interstate 281', in *Granta Travel Writing*, p. 197.
18. *Woman's Hour*, BBC Radio 4, 6 April 2011.
19. *Granta Travel Writing*, p. 7.
20. 'Home Truths on Abroad', *The Guardian*, 19 September 2009.
21. *Granta Travel Writing*, p. 7.
22. Geoff Dyer, 'The Human Heart of the Matter', *The Guardian*, 12 June 2010.

5: Reflections on food writing

by Sally Cline

My two passions are writing and food. I can't get enough of either. So writing about food or reading exquisite prose about food is almost as fulfilling as a Cordon Vert meal.[1]

Inside a simple snack or an elaborate five-course meal lurk history, geography, a different culture, a different time period from the one in which we are currently feasting. The great food writer, like the doyenne M.F.K. Fisher, needs to be, in John Updike's phrase, a poet of the appetites. Fisher's books are a mixture of sardonic yet warm autobiography, insights into the author's love of friendship and food, and a feast of wit and wisdom. Occasionally artless, often esoteric, the books are witty yet scholarly investigations into words and language. Inside *With Bold Knife and Fork* lurks a description of how the sound of avocado echoes that of deep bells ringing. There is a hymn to Vichyssoise which at all costs must not be strained, so that the potatoes melt somewhat stubbornly into the creamy stock while delicate shreds of the onions still wander through.[2] W.H. Auden said M.F.K. Fisher was as talented a writer as she was a cook, and he knew no one in the United States who wrote better prose.

This kind of food writing has a literary quality that may contain descriptions of a dish or a memory of a food occasion but imaginatively transports the reader somewhere else.

Nigel Slater's memorable *Toast* is a humorous yet inspiring memoir seen through food. Listen to him describe his mother's cake-making activities: 'She never quite got the hang of the mixer. I can picture her now, desperately trying to harness her wayward Kenwood, bits of cake mixture flying out of the bowl like something from an *I Love Lucy* sketch. The cake recipe was written in green biro on blue Basildon Bond.'[3]

Loving meticulous details such as blue Basildon Bond and the wayward Kenwood sum up an era, and show the writer's understanding of a woman who couldn't cook in a period when she jolly well had to.

When I read *The Realm of Fig and Quince* by Ria Loohuizen, one of many food historians, so alluring were the descriptions that I lost myself inside Mesopotamia and the Maghreb, picking figs warmed by the sun and trying out quinces which for years had been mere literary allusions. Remember quince as the mythical golden apple of the Hesperides? Now at last I tasted the bumpy pear-shaped fragrant fruit and found I had to eat it as fast as possible as it turns brown as soon as it is cut open. Only when I had learnt to put it in lemon juice and water to save the colour was I able to make a starter pot of quince jam.

Literary food books may sometimes look like simple cookbooks but they are in fact works of literary consequence. John Wright's *Edible Seashore: A River Cottage Handbook* is a small writerly miracle about gathering wild foods from the sea and what to do with them when they are caught.[4] I learnt about dulse, a blood-red seaweed which hangs like huge red rosettes with finger fronds, and also that Wright believed H.G. Wells had dulse in mind when he wrote in *The War of the Worlds* of the tumultuous 'red weed' that the Martians brought with them on their ill-advised excursion in Surrey. If you look closely at the thick carpet of veinous foliage that covers the lower shore at low tide, you'll see it does have an alien appearance.

The Irish and the Canadians eat it more often than the rest of us, dried, as an on-the-move snack like a crisp. It's much tastier with far fewer calories!

My dining room is stuffed with books like these. When I am cooking a dish from one of them, my breaks are spent cross-legged on the floor, luxuriating in their prose, stirring their adjectives, adding white sauce to their verbs, anticipating their next suggested meal. Anticipation is the key, an essential component of fine food writing.

Passion should underline good food writing, which, however enhanced by literary imagination, must be founded upon a deep devotion to and understanding of food. The starting point is taste and touch. A desire to sing about the way bread from a hot oven feels in your hand. An awareness that the moment before you bite into the soft curd cheese filling of your first cheesecake is like the moment before you open the bedroom curtains and see the first crocuses of spring. Heady expectancy then absolute fulfilment.

The prose should convey joyous gratification. It should be evocative, exhilarating, abundant. It should allow mundane beasts like poultry to transcend themselves. Here is Nigella Lawson on one such animal: 'I have long been an excitable fan of turkey . . . I like the contrast of its mild meat to sharp, pungent flavourings . . . The saltness of the anchovies and the sharpness of the gherkins give the timid turkey real bite.'[5] The phrase 'timid turkey' stayed in this vegetarian's mind for days.

Food writing can be adventurous and wide-ranging, like that of Claudia Roden and Madhur Jaffrey, who offer readers their encyclopaedic knowledge yet never use a dull word. Here is Jaffrey in Bali: 'I have sat barefoot on the veranda of a seaside villa and dined on the most magnificent greens that have been cooked very simply with a mound of shallots and a touch of garlic.'[6]

Staying in a royal Hyderabadi household, Jaffrey describes the sweet-and-sour stuffed aubergines. As I read I felt that I held those aubergines in my own hands, as I mopped up the stuffing with soft split pea and rice pancakes. It comes as no surprise when Jaffrey says with deep contentment, in her book *Eastern Vegetarian Cooking*, 'I love vegetables.'[7]

Love for vegetables is on every page. Love for home-grown tomatoes off the vine, upstanding white heads of cauliflower cooked with fenugreek seeds, crisp Hong Kong asparagus tinged with sesame oil, and Japanese cabbage seasoned with umeboshi plums.

Jaffrey is also a practical food writer. This is important, for, if food writers do not encourage us to cook and eat as well as celebrate food, they are not doing their job properly. Jaffrey makes sense when she writes about nutritional values. Vegetarians and meat-eaters alike will appreciate knowing that, if we combine soy or mung beans with grains such as rice or wheat and then add any dairy product (her favourite is yoghurt) to a meal strong on vegetables, our protein needs are taken care of. She reminds us that in India and China cooks have been following that theme for thousands of years. Indians traditionally eat cumin-flavoured mung beans with whole-wheat griddle breads, accompanied by a glass of buttermilk. Chinese dine on bean curd spiced with garlic, spring onions and red pepper, served with rice and hot-and-sour soup which contains an egg. Jaffrey describes the South Indian Uppama dish which is a tangy pilaf, semolina based, filled with diced vegetables: 'It starts the day on a very perky note.'[8]

Jaffrey is herself a perky writer, who shows us how food from every country can be perked up, transformed and made helpful. Mint kills germs, ginger makes split peas easier to digest, cumin and green cardamom are cooling, so put them in summer drinks. Cloves are warming, so suffuse your winter tea (or red wine) with some. Black pepper livens the appetite. Each time I read her books they are like black pepper: I have an appetite for more food. More of her food writing.

Claudia Roden relies on fragrant memories and evocative smells, rather as Proust does. She is a culinary historian, ethnographer, anthropologist and memoirist who treats foods as if they were poems, and the poetry of her food writing is richly sensuous.

Roden embarks on her odyssey to discover old and new Jewish dishes around the globe from Samarkand and Vilna. Because Roden is a social and cultural historian, when she reaches the Sephardi world she offers us an insider's view of the four different styles of Sephardi cooking. There is Judeo-Spanish, which is Turkish and Balkan, learned from Iberian ancestors who went to live in Ottoman heartlands. There is Maghrebi, North African cuisine which includes Moroccan, Tunisian, Algerian and Libyan. Thirdly comes Judeo-Arab cooking from Syria and Lebanon, and fourthly the Jewish cooking of Iraq and Iran. Roden describes Sephardi food as sensual, aromatic, colourful. It uses anything that can produce a flavour: seeds, bark, pods, resin, petals, pistils, even flower waters. The flavours are related to the sunny hedonistic Sephardi nature. Breezily she summarises their views: 'They [the Sephardim] were less concerned with the inner, spiritual life than the Ashkenazim, more sensitive to beauty and pleasure; and good eating has always been part of their traditional Jewish life.' Their cooking, she says, 'is of a kind that lifts the spirits'.[9]

Roden's writing is also of a kind that lifts the spirits.

Food writing can be original, funny and deeply shocking, like that of Anthony Bourdain. Bourdain says he started his food career with 'a significant event'. 'I remember it like I remember losing my virginity – and in many ways, more fondly.' It was eating his first oyster. It was 'the proudest moment of my young life . . . that unforgettably sweet moment . . . that one moment still more alive for me than so many other "firsts" which followed – first pussy, first joint, first day in high school, first published book . . . – I attained glory'.[10]

If we are lucky the food writing we pounce on in a library or bookstore might be heady and glowing like Nigella Lawson's. When talking about an Irish Cream tiramisu she calls it an 'elegantly buff-tinted, creamy-toned variant of the punchy, if comfortably clichéd, original'.[11]

This is how she described routine jar-filling:

> It's scarcely strenuous, deeply enjoyable . . . I fill a jar with golden
> sultanas, pour Grand Marnier over them and let them steep . . . I
> put morello cherries and cherry brandy in a jar, and – a very
> recent innovation and rubily gorgeous – mix dried cherries and
> berries . . . with a pomegranate liqueur called Parma. Any of these
> are exquisite tumbled over ice cream.[12]

Whoever said filling jars was dull? And rolling 'rubily gorgeous' around the tongue is a heady experience in itself.

Here is an author who is possessed by food. She yearns to write about it. That yearning must be discernible in fine food writing. Readers must be knocked back by the tastes, the smells, the colours, the memories, the dreams and the desires. For writing about food is a sensual act. An exquisitely set dinner table is a seductive place. A picnic cloth spread on a beach is tantalising. Food is as much about expectations of the future and evocative memories of the past as it is about ingredients. And so with the writing.

Christopher Hirst, author of the irresistibly funny *Love Bites: Marital Skirmishes in the Kitchen*, sees literary food writing as a love story, a romance that blossoms at the stove. The book is dedicated to Mrs H, whose real name is Alison. It starts with their first meeting. 'Given our common interest, it was appropriate that Mrs H (as she then wasn't) and I met in a kitchen.'

Hirst tells us that when 'one thing happily led to another, food emerged as a joint passion. The first meal I ever made for Mrs H was a giant pile of smoked salmon sandwiches.' The first meal Alison made for him was a Mongolian hotpot. This is a great plate of raw titbits (ranging from mange-touts through prawns and sliced scallops to slivers of chicken breast and broccoli florets) which you cook piecemeal in a large pot of stock simmered over a methylated spirit burner. When you have simmered a piece you eat it. Hirst writes: 'Mongolian hot pot is an ideal dish for a couple in the exploratory stages of courtship. Because you use chopsticks to fish out the various items, there is plenty of scope for intimacy.' He confesses that 'the meal was a revelation. My passion for food began when I became passionate about Mrs H.'[13]

The reverse can also be true. My passion for certain women and men in my life has often begun over food. Being Jewish, I was forbidden certain foods (such as shellfish and pork), and once I had tried them I knew the taste of sin. In the 1960s, I had a male lover, a church-going Christian (another sin), a fellow journalist on a rival newspaper, whom I only ever met at airports and hotels abroad. I would fly in. He would already be in the airport bar. At our table would be the forbidden prawn cocktails. Was it the excitement of breaking one set of rules that enticed me as a married woman to break another? Looking back, I see he was a very dull fellow, so the seafood must have had a lot to do with it.

A more significant example came in the 1970s when I first met the love of my life, a young woman, another Christian, a single mother with several children, and a heady way of frying bacon on a Sunday morning. The smell of the bacon and the beauty of the cook could never be untangled.

Nor indeed could my devotion to first-class cooking.

Food is my beloved. But we have a very simple romance. My appetite can be tempted by anything on toast. Anything with chips. Anything on a cheese board.

Not of course burned toast, or over-crispy toast, or even toast made from soft brown bread. The bread must be crusty white, toasted to a pale golden shade, and the butter, unsalted, Danish, must be placed on it at once so that it melts immediately. Then it is ready for its perfect partnership with egg. Listen to Nigella Lawson on the theme:

I have one rule and it's simple enough to adhere to: it's never worth cooking anything for supper unless it can stand on equal footing with one of life's great and simplest gastro-delights: boiled egg on toast (the best Italian eggs, soft boiled, rapidly peeled and squished . . .). Of course, I don't want that every day, but nor do I want to settle for anything less.[14]

Having read that, I won't settle for anything less, unless it be for chips.

Chips must not be sturdy, like the thighs you don't sigh for. They must be well-proportioned, slim stylish straws. They must never look clumsy or fall over each other. I need hardly say, if you can't make home-cooked chips, make creamy mash instead, or gently boil new potatoes, then decorate with parsley or mint, but never debase your meal with plastic oven-ready chips.

As for cheese, some professionals might say it must not include Cheddar or Laughing Cow or anything ordinary. But a cheese addict, like an alcoholic, cannot rule out any form of her addiction.

How reassuring to know that, as far back as archaeology can reach, there has always been evidence of cheese. Check out, for example, Trevor Hickman's absorbing book on the historic cheeses Leicestershire, Stilton and Stichelton.[15] I learned that cheeses have probably been made in England for over four thousand years.[16] Hickman takes us through the history of Midland cheeses from the Roman occupation until the present day, offering us a startling new view of the familiar slice stuffed between hearty white or thin brown, which we often unthinkingly snatch up at railway station buffets.

I do much of my writing about food, in both fiction and autobiography, in Sennen, a small village in Cornwall where my displacement activity centres on spreading Cornish Pepper on to circular water biscuits, then munching them as I sit and write on the cliffs.

In a village in Crete where in past years I spent many weeks writing about food, for breakfast I drizzled honey on Manouri goat's cheese that had the light creamy texture of childhood cheesecakes. No wonder it percolated my stories. Often at lunchtime, hot, lazy and unimaginative, I headed for the local baker's and bought a spanakopita filled with Manoypi, another goat's cheese.

If you are crazy about food and crazy enough to be a writer, your madness may spread into your books. When I look back at my own writing, I notice that I devoted a whole book to food: *Just Desserts: Women and Food*. In this book, I looked at shopping, cooking, food disorders, sexual battles, media messages and literary images to show up the fraught and the fearful versus the passionate and pleasurable about every relationship to food.

Many of my other books, ostensibly about topics such as the process of writing, versions of reality, women's relationship with men, sexuality, celibacy, dying, illness, politics and memory, have been infiltrated by descriptions of dishes or flights into food fancies. Again and again I return to my Jewish upbringing, where all rules and all activities were centred on food. Food for the men first, then food for the rest of the family.

In my biography of Radclyffe Hall[17] I was mesmerised by Hall's obsession with the idea behind her award-winning novel *Adam's Breed*, the story of a waiter who becomes so utterly sick of handling food that he almost lets himself die of starvation. Hall herself was fascinated by food and deeply immersed in its symbolism. I found myself drawn to her through our shared devotion long before her writing and her sexual stance caught my attention.

Similarly when I wrote the biography of Zelda Fitzgerald,[18] I was captivated by her romance with her Southern birthplace, especially by her attachment to Southern food. In New York's magnificent Plaza Grill, Zelda sips tea from tiny teacups surrounded by the smell of creamy sweet butter. But it is for Montgomery that she is homesick. It is Alabama's peaches and biscuits for which she hankers. At a London lunch hosted by Lady Randolph Churchill, Zelda samples dessert strawberries as large as tomatoes, but it is Montgomery cuisine, Montgomery's method of dealing with tomatoes, she desires. Her dreams are of Alabama fried green tomato sandwiches, conch chowder, Key lime pie, collard greens, blackened elk with blackberry port, even goo goo clusters.

In my biography of playwright and memoirist Lillian Hellman and crime writer Dashiell Hammett, Lillian, like Zelda, comes from the Deep South. Her birthplace was New Orleans, home of exotic foods. Even when unwillingly transplanted to New York, she insisted on cooking New Orleans dishes for her celebrity guests. Even when she is almost blind and dying, it is the cookery of her birthplace that she recalls as she struggles to write her last memoir, unsurprisingly a book about food and memory.[19] She returns to the South. To

Southerners she had loved. To Southern food she had cooked for them. With her odd brilliance she evokes the tastes and smells of boiled short ribs for Max her dad, lobster salad and ice cream for Julia her mum; shrimp gumbo for her nurse Sophronia and crayfish bisque and clams à la oregano for her beloved aunts, Hannah and Jenny.

Lillian Hellman used her playwright's skills to become a magnificent, even lyrical food writer. Until the end she held the strong belief that there is always a correct place and a correct time for the correct food. She would never cook curry on a hot July afternoon, or serve chilled watermelon at Christmas. She felt the seasons and the locale should dictate the foods eaten. Nigel Slater, one of our finest food writers, feels the same.

> *Right food, right place, right time. It is my belief – and the point of this book – that this is the best recipe of all. A crab sandwich by the sea on a June afternoon; a slice of roast goose with apple sauce and roast potatoes on Christmas Day; hot sausages and a chunk of roast pumpkin on a frost-sparkling night in November . . . There is something deeply, unshakeably right about eating food in season.*

Slater goes on to say that our culinary seasons have been blurred by commerce; today it is too easy to lose sight of food's natural timing and, worse, to miss it when it is at its sublime best. 'Hence my attempt,' he tells readers, 'at writing a book about rebuilding a cook's relationship with nature'.[20]

His *Kitchen Diaries* are packed with delicious dishes, but also fragrant with the scent of paper-white narcissi in a bowl on his table, which fills his kitchen with a gentle vanilla smell. It is a literary food book.

Notes

1. Cordon Vert diplomas are similar to Cordon Bleu but for vegetarian cooks and chefs.
2. M.F.K. Fisher, *With Bold Knife and Fork* (with Introduction by Prue Leith), Vintage, 2001, pp. 44, 45, 41.
3. Nigel Slater, *Toast: The Story of a Boy's Hunger*, Harper Perennial, 2004, p. 2.

4. John Wright, *The River Cottage Edible Seashore Handbook*, Bloomsbury, London and New York, 2009.

5. Nigella Lawson, *Nigella Express*, Chatto and Windus, London, 2007, p. 12.

6. Madhur Jaffrey, *Eastern Vegetarian Cookery*, Jonathan Cape, London, 1983, p. ix.

7. Jaffrey, *Eastern Vegetarian Cookery*, p. ix.

8. Jaffrey, *Eastern Vegetarian Cookery*, p. x.

9. Claudia Roden, *The Book of Jewish Food: An Odyssey from Samarkand and Vilna to the Present Day*, Penguin (new edn), 1999, p. 182.

10. Anthony Bourdain, *Kitchen Confidential. Adventures in the Culinary Underbelly*, Bloomsbury, 2001, pp. 13, 14, 16.

11. Lawson, *Nigella Express*, p. 135.

12. Lawson, *Nigella Express*, p. 109.

13. Christopher Hirst, *Love Bites: Marital Skirmishes in the Kitchen*, Fourth Estate, London, 2010, pp. 1, 2.

14. Lawson, *Nigella Express*, p. 3.

15. Trevor Hickman, *Historic Cheeses: Leicestershire, Stilton and Stichelton*, DB Publishing, 2009.

16. The first cheeses were almost certainly made by the early farmers of the Neolithic period between c. 4000 and 2400 BC. On leaving school, Hickman started his adult life by becoming apprenticed to a printer and bookbinder who also ran his own subscription library, a haven for a young man who wanted to become a local historian.

17. Sally Cline, *Radclyffe Hall. A Woman called John*, John Murray, London, 1997; Overlook, New York, 1999; Faber and Faber, London, 2010.

18. Sally Cline, *Zelda Fitzgerald: Her Voice in Paradise*, John Murray, London, 2002; Arcade, New York, 2003; Faber and Faber, London, 2010.

19. Lillian Hellman and Peter Feibleman, *Eating Together: Recipes and Recollections*, Little, Brown, Boston, 1984.

20. Nigel Slater, *The Kitchen Diaries*, Fourth Estate, London, 2005, p. vii.

6: Reflections on nature and landscape

by Midge Gillies

Nature has crept up on me. Until a few years ago I was suspicious of anyone who took too great an interest in the nesting habits of birds or the foraging patterns of small mammals; it all seemed a bit cultish.

I have always had friends who love birdwatching, and others for whom the ideal way to celebrate their child's birthday was to go pond-dipping on a dank piece of National Trust land – while my daughter spent her special day in a darkened cinema with her hand deep in a bag of sugar-rush E numbers. Whenever these friends happened to be together the conversation would always at some stage drift off into – for me – mysterious realms: rumours about the sighting of a bittern, or the work of *Alice in Wonderland*-sounding organisations like the Dormouse Captive Breeders Group. This was a world apart; but it was a world where its followers showed the sort of zeal I had only ever previously seen among football supporters.

I first encountered the eloquence of nature writing, and how nature is inextricably bound up with the human psyche, while researching the summer of 1940, when people were so fearful of invasion that they resorted to atavistic instincts they probably did not even realise they possessed. Reading contemporary reports, I was struck by how the threat of bomb attack had made city dwellers more attuned to nature: studying the moon to see whether it could guide a bomber to its target; hearing for the first time the eerie hoot of owls, whose numbers grew in a blacked-out London.

One of our guest contributors, Daniel Swift, in his book *Bomber County* explores how nature adapts to human folly. In it he quotes the naturalist R.S. Fitter, who at the end of 1945 published a study of the wildlife of London, *London's Natural History*.[1] Fitter pointed out that the Second World War created large areas of waste ground in the centre of built-up areas, which plants such as rosebay willowherb, which had previously been found only in gravel banks and woodlands, quickly colonised. As Swift says, this plant is 'curiously well adapted to modern aerial warfare', since it flourishes in well-lit areas, and can cope with soil that has been subjected to heat. Fitter recorded 126 species of flowering plants and ferns on bomb sites, and noted how the black redstart benefited from the holes and crannies created by bombing, which made ideal nests for the birds.

The redstart also proved the inspiration for what has been described as 'the best single species study ever written',[2] Before the war John Buxton was a poet and Fellow of New College, Oxford. When he was captured in 1940 and held in various officers' camps in Germany, he began to study the birds, enlisting the help of a team of observers who spent nine hours a day recording their movements. Captivity gave Buxton the perfect setting for his obsession, while his skill as a poet allowed him to write a book that was far from a dry ornithological study, and which found a resonance with his own plight. He was enchanted by the redstarts because they

> inhabited another world . . . They lived wholly and enviably to themselves, unconcerned in fatuous politics, without the limitations imposed all about us by our knowledge. They lived only in the moment, without foresight and with memory only of things of immediate practical concern to them.[3]

His research, based on the painstaking notes he'd written as a prisoner, was published after the war as part of Collins's prestigious New Naturalist series. Buxton retreated into academic life, but *The Redstart* is still viewed as a classic; the former Poet Laureate Andrew Motion has described it as a 'masterpiece'.[4]

Nature writing demands and deserves poetry. Describing an object such as a flower, a waterfall or an eagle is challenging, because the object is both beautiful and familiar to the reader. It takes a poet, or a poetic turn of phrase, to make the reader see it for the first time. In *Pilgrim at Tinker Creek* (for which she won a Pulitzer Prize), Annie Dillard explores the unknowing, mystical side of nature. We still cannot be certain why birds sing; and how can we explain why birdsong is beautiful?

'Beauty itself is the language to which we have no key; it is the mute cipher, the cryptogram, the uncracked, unbroken code,' she writes. 'And it could be that for beauty, as it turned out to be for French, that there is no key, that "oui" will never make sense in our language but only in its own, and that we need to start all over again, on a new continent, learning the strange syllables one by one.'[5]

It is no coincidence that some of the most remarkable descriptions of nature have been written by poets, Ted Hughes, of course, being a fine example. Richard Mabey, the contemporary nature writer (and one of our guest contributors), says that the poet John Clare (1793–1864) is one of the few writers to have 'created a language that joined rather than separated nature and culture'; and he quotes Clare as saying that he 'found his poems in the fields'.[6] Mabey begins his memoir *Nature Cure* with an extract from Clare's poem 'The Flitting'.

Clare, the son of a labourer from Northamptonshire, has long been overshadowed by the poetic giants of Romanticism: Keats, Byron, Blake, Wordsworth, Coleridge, Shelley. Now, however, he is increasingly celebrated for his genuine links to the landscape he describes, whereas many more famous poets were simply passing through.

Gilbert White (1720–93) has influenced many modern nature writers. According to Richard Mabey, whose biography of White won the Whitbread Biography Award in 1986, his four essays on 'hirondelles' (swifts, swallows and martins) are regularly cited as the 'prototypes of "objective" nature-writing'.[7] White was born in Selborne, Hampshire and spent most of his life there as a curate. In 1751, he started to keep a 'Garden Kalendar', and then a 'Naturalist's Journal'. His letters to two established naturalists, Thomas Pennant and Daines Barrington, formed the basis for his famous *Natural History and Antiquities of Selborne* (1788). It reveals his love of nature, what Mabey calls a 'real respect for our fellow creatures',[8] and his detailed observations of the wildlife around him. It is unusual among nature books for appealing both to scientists and to the lay reader, and was one of Charles Darwin's favourite books as a boy.

On the other side of the Atlantic, Henry Thoreau (1817–62) has provided similar inspiration to modern nature writers. Indeed, he is one of those thinkers who appear so far ahead of their age that they seem to be time travellers. Like White, who was a Fellow of an Oxford college, Thoreau was a scholar; he studied at Harvard, and became a friend of the philosopher and poet Ralph

Waldo Emerson. Emerson had developed a mystical reverence for nature after meeting Wordsworth, Coleridge and Carlyle in England; he then settled in Thoreau's beloved hometown of Concord, Massachusetts. Thoreau published only two books: *A Week on the Concord and Merrimack River* (1849), which described a canoe journey he took with his brother, John, and *Walden, or Life in the Woods* (1854). His second, and now much more famous work, describes the two-year period in which he built a single-room cabin on Emerson's land near Walden Pond, a mile south of Concord village, and, aged twenty-seven, tried to live a self-sufficient life. In it he describes his attempts at farming, his visitors, the wildlife around him, and his awareness of the land's Native American past. Some of his themes appear starkly modern: his unease with the materialism of nineteenth-century life, and the unrelenting pressure to harness oneself to work. His lyrical writing is remembered through lines such as 'The mass of men lead lives of quiet desperation' – a thought that has spoken eloquently to subsequent generations.

But it is not just his memorable style and his keen eye that ensured the growth of his reputation and influence after his death. Thoreau was a deeply principled man, not merely prepared to spend two years experiencing a different way of life, but also willing to face imprisonment (albeit for just one night) in protest against the Mexican war and slavery. His essay on Civil Disobedience of 1849 expresses sentiments that would ring true to protesters against racial discrimination a hundred years later, and it was Thoreau's idea of passive resistance that inspired Gandhi.

As John Updike wrote: 'A century and a half after its publication, Walden has become such a totem of the back-to-nature, preservationist, anti-business, civil-disobedience mindset, and Thoreau so vivid a protester, so perfect a crank and hermit saint, that the book risks being as revered and unread as the Bible.'[9]

Literature of Place

Some of my favourite books are those that describe landscape so perfectly they make you reluctant to look up from the page: Thomas Hardy's Wessex novels, Bruce Chatwin's *On the Black Hill*, Graham Swift's often dark description of the fens in *Waterland*, Ronald Blythe's history of a Suffolk village, *Akenfield*,

Roger Deakin's damp travelogue, *Waterlog*, Laurie Lee's description of his Cotswolds childhood in *Cider with Rosie*, and Flora Thompson's intimate observations of the late nineteenth-century Oxfordshire countryside in *Lark Rise to Candleford* – this cornucopia jumps from genre to genre, taking in fiction, travel, history, life and nature writing.

In his essay 'A Literature of Place' (an extract from which is included in our guest section), Barry Lopez says that writing about the impact of nature and place on culture is 'one of the oldest – and perhaps most singular – threads in American writing'. He mentions, of course, Thoreau – but also Hermann Melville in *Moby-Dick*, and novelists such as Willa Cather, John Steinbeck and William Faulkner. Lopez says that he turns to geography himself, as writers of another generation once turned to Freud.

On the back of my battered edition of *Akenfield* (price 75p), I am shocked to discover that the publishers, Penguin, have categorised it as 'Sociology & Anthropology'. Perhaps they simply had no idea how to market such a fresh and original approach to non-fiction in the 1960s. I usually think of *Akenfield* as social history, and, when I bumped into Ronald Blythe at a publishing event, I plucked up courage to shake his hand and tell him that his book was the reason I studied history at university. White-haired and on the cusp of ninety, he was too charming and modest to be startled; besides, he is probably used to the adulation of strangers. It was gratifying to discover recently that a modern edition of *Akenfield* has been reissued simply as a 'Penguin Classic'.

In his *Who's Who* entry, Ronald Blythe lists his recreations as 'walking, looking, listening'. It seems to me that these are the essential pastimes of any writer of non-fiction, particularly if they want to write about nature or landscape. Barry Lopez and Annie Dillard are geniuses at all three.

Robert Macfarlane describes Lopez's *Arctic Dreams* (1986) as 'in many ways the founding text of contemporary nature writing in the States'.[10] *Arctic Dreams* was a *New York Times* bestseller and won the American Book Award. I cannot think of anything that compares to it in Britain.

What makes the book such a joy to read is that Lopez takes what appears to be a blank, monotone landscape, and weaves into it history, natural science, ecology, anthropology and memoir. The book's structure is a master-class of careful blending and pacing. It is full of astonishing facts – on the different ways, for example, that Arctic animals conserve heat (the Arctic fox can reduce the temperature of its footpads to near 32 degrees Fahrenheit) – and compelling stories. Yet the narrative never feels 'fact-heavy', nor does it allow any one story to dominate. The animals become part of the cast, but never in a sentimental or anthropomorphic way.

Lopez's accounts of polar bears are particularly worth reading, not least because these are animals the developed world has taken to its heart with a cloying sentimentality. Lopez gives them back their dignity. Early on he recounts how he and a friend, Bob, spot a polar bear gliding in the water 300 feet ahead of them. They follow him until he makes off across the ice. But now Lopez's description continues, folding in comments from other observers – how whalers referred to the polar bear as 'the farmer', because of his 'very agricultural appearance as he stalks leisurely over the furrowed fields of ice'; how a visitor in the late nineteenth century wrote about the bears moving 'as if the country had belonged to them always'.[11]

If you thought a polar bear was white, Lopez will make you think again. The bear's hair is colourless; it is the refraction of sunlight that makes us see it as we do – in much the same way that clouds appear white, he remarks. And, of course, it is not just 'white' but a whole subtle range of colours, depending on the age of the animal, the time of day and year – even whether it is held in a vigorously disinfected zoo or lives in the wild; and a host of other factors that only a skilled observer could notice. Lopez explains and expands with gems of facts that regularly make you want to pause from your reading, to relay to someone else what he has told you. Infrared photography, for example, revealed part of the secret of how polar bears regulate their body temperature. Photographs showed that the only bit of black that appeared on film was the bears' tracks, which remained warm for several minutes after they had moved on. Polar bears obviously shed excess heat through their feet.

Lopez cunningly uses quotations that add to his own distinctive voice, and which paraphrasing would dilute. He uses the report of the nineteenth-century explorer Lieutenant William Parry, for example, to convey the sound of the belukha whale-song. Parry's crew rowed as close as they could to the pods of whales, to hear what sounded to them like 'passing a wet finger around the edge, or rim, of a glass tumbler'.[12]

Annie Dillard's *Pilgrim at Tinker Creek*, which won the Pulitzer Prize in 1975, has often been compared to Thoreau's *Walden*. Both are based on the author's stay in a remote place, and both have a questing spirituality running through them. Dillard describes a landscape that is as lush as Lopez's arctic panorama is arid. The book begins with an alarming image, describing how she used to own a fighting tom, who would jump through an open window and land on her chest in the middle of the night. 'And some mornings I'd wake in daylight to find my body covered with paw prints in blood; I looked as though I'd been painted with roses.'[13] It is an unsettling start, and one that alerts the reader that this will not be a cosy nature book. We can expect violence as well as beauty.

Dillard wrote *Pilgrim at Tinker Creek* in 1972, when she was twenty-seven. In an Afterword written thirty-five years later she comments that it is a 'young writer's book in its excited eloquence and its metaphysical boldness'.[14] By using the first person she had tried to be in Emerson's 'ever-ludicrous phrase – a transparent eyeball'.

She seems characteristically honest about the structure of the book. Initially, she tells us, she had resisted the urge to tell her story through a year's seasons, because it seemed too conventional; but then she found that alternative structures injured the 'frail narrative', 'usually fatally'. But even within this traditional chronology the truth is manipulated: as one of our guest contributors, Sara Maitland, points out, she compresses three winters into one.

The second element of her structure is less conventional. She was fascinated by Neoplatonic Christianity, which describes two routes to God: the *via positiva* (in which God is seen as omnipotent and omniscient) and the *via negativa* (in which anything we might say of God is untrue, as we can know 'only creaturely attributes',[15] which she found more attractive). The first half of *Pilgrim at Tinker Creek* is the *via positiva*; a chapter called 'Flood' marks the demarcation line, and the second half continues with the *via negativa*.

Within this rather arcane structure, Dillard has woven the same extraordinary nuggets of information and sublime descriptions that make *Arctic Dreams* so compelling. At the start of her chapter on winter she tells us that starlings arrived in the USA on a passenger liner from Europe, and that one hundred of them were deliberately released in Central Park. The driving force behind their arrival was a rich New York drug manufacturer, whose hobby was to introduce into America all the birds mentioned in Shakespeare's writings.

Nor does she take herself too seriously. Her profundity is leavened with humour. When she describes collecting a Cynthia moth cocoon she says: 'My fingers were stiff and red with cold, and my nose ran. I had forgotten the Law of the Wild, which is, "Carry Kleenex".'

Towards the end of the book, when she is explaining that parasitic insects make up 10 per cent of all known animal species, she suggests that we are giving infants the wrong idea about their fellow creatures in the world. 'Teddy bears should come with tiny stuffed bear-lice; 10 per cent of all baby bibs and rattles sold should be adorned with colourful blowflies, maggots, and screw-worms.'[16] Linking babies to maggots, which normally accompany us at the end of life, is shocking, but also sardonic, poking fun at the sentimentalisation and commercialisation of childhood.

Harnessing an obsession

Most nature writing is born out of obsession – for a particular bird (as in Mark Cocker's *Crow Country* or J.A. Baker's *The Peregrine*), an animal (Philip Hoare's *Leviathan*), a place (Annie Dillard's *Tinker Creek*), a plant (Richard Mabey's *Weeds*) or an element (Roger Deakin's *Waterlog*). Vivid and surprising descriptions, telling details and absorbing stories make the reader see why the author is so mesmerised by their subject. *The Peregrine* has been described by Colin Thubron as a 'wonder of poetic exactitude', and Mark Cocker has been praised for creating a compelling work about a species that has generally had a very bad press. Part of the success of *Crow Country* is that he makes a virtue of his obsession and the affinity he feels for the birds; his book is as much autobiography as ornithology.

But nature writers have to learn how to be selective: how to be an ornithologist, say, who makes connections with the rest of the world, rather than a twitcher whose sole aim is to amass names and numbers in a notebook. This is why some of the most successful literary non-fiction books have a forward slash on the back cover showing the categories that define the work. Robert Macfarlane's *The Wild Places*, for instance, is called 'Nature Writing/Britain'. As he says at the start of his book:

I also decided that, as I travelled, I would draw up a map to set against the road atlas. A prose map that would seek to make some of the remaining wild places of the archipelago visible again, or that would record them before they vanished for good. This would be a map, I hoped, that would not connect up cities, towns, hotels and airports. Instead, it would link headlands, cliffs, beaches, mountain-tops, tors, forests, river-mouths and waterfalls.[17]

Much later in the book he describes with scientific precision how the human eye adapts to low levels of light, the effect of moonlight on a landscape, and what it means to be a night-walker in that eerie country. And then he takes us one step further, meditating on how the 'disenchantment of the night through artificial lighting' marks our increasing inability to imagine that we are 'part of something which is larger than our own capacity'.[18]

Nature writing in crisis?

Nature writers, possibly more than any other writers of non-fiction, are vulnerable to the charge that they are viewing the world through nostalgia-tinted spectacles. One theory about why some of the most celebrated nature writing in the world has emerged from America is that it still has wilderness, and a variety of landscape that Britain is too puny to imitate – on the European side of the Atlantic we lack vast untamed forests, immense glaciers and mountain ranges. Many Britons no longer work close to home, and many places that might once have been described as 'nature spots' have become commercialised.

Television documentaries about the natural world, on the other hand, have leapt in popularity. It is as if, since we no longer venture into nature, nature will arrive in our sitting rooms in glorious High Definition colour. We no longer have to imagine a whale emerging from the sea to eat a seal; we can see it in all its horrific drama. A hummingbird's frantic wings can be slowed down for us, or a flower's petals opening to the sun speeded up for our impatient eye. Minuscule cameras can shrink us to the size of a chick so that we too can wait with the hungry occupants of a nesting box to see a mother arrive with food. We can watch in 'real time', or whenever suits us.

It has been suggested that 'nature film' is a contradiction in terms – because of the special effects sometimes involved, or the fact that filming is so skewed towards holding the audience's attention that it cannot possibly hope to convey the natural pace of the wild. The difference is that between a children's birthday party centred around the muddy, messy experience of pond dipping, and one spent in the darkened comfort of a movie theatre, where the audience listens to Morgan Freeman's gravelly voice (in *March of the Penguins*) telling them how 'in the harshest place on earth love finds a way'.

How can nature writing compete with such visual pyrotechnics and Hollywood stars? Quite easily. As an exercise in the scope and diversity of writing about surroundings (in this case just sticking to waterscapes), compare Philip Hoare's description of swimming with whales in chapter XV of *Leviathan*, 'The Chase'; and the start of both Roger Deakin's gentle amble round the watery backroads of Britain and Charles Sprawson's paean to swimming and the meaning of water to different cultures in *Haunts of the Black Masseur, The Swimmer as Hero*. Each of these books has drama and humour; each is deeply personal. They connect the writer, reader and landscape in a profound and lasting way that television cannot hope to achieve after the final credits have rolled. Watching a nature documentary does not make many demands of the imagination; good nature writing does.

Notes

1. Daniel Swift, *Bomber County*, Hamish Hamilton, London, 2010, pp. 152–3.
2. *The Guardian*, 17 October, 2009.
3. Quoted in Midge Gillies, *The Barbed-Wire University*, Aurum Press, London, 2011, p. 265.
4. *Daily Telegraph*, 9 February 2009.
5. Annie Dillard, *Pilgrim at Tinker Creek*, Canterbury Press, Norwich, 2011, p. 108.
6. Richard Mabey, *Nature Cure*, Pimlico, London, 2006, p. 23.
7. Mabey, *Nature Cure*, p. 166.
8. Mabey, *Nature Cure*, p. 107.
9. *The Guardian*, 6 June 2004.
10. Robert Macfarlane, *The Guardian*, 6 December 2003.
11. Barry Lopez, *Arctic Dreams*, Picador, London, 1986, p. 79.
12. Lopez, *Arctic Dreams*, p. 348.

13. Dillard, *Pilgrim at Tinker Creek*, p. 3.
14. Dillard, *Pilgrim at Tinker Creek*, p. 283.
15. Dillard, *Pilgrim at Tinker Creek*, p. 279.
16. Dillard, *Pilgrim at Tinker Creek*, p. 236.
17. Robert Macfarlane, *The Wild Places*, Granta, London, 2010, p. 17.
18. Macfarlane, *The Wild Places*, p. 203.

7: Reflections on feminism

by Sally Cline

Feminism is a passion. Like food. I have been a feminist so long that I can't now imagine what it must feel like not to be one. Not to feel it in my bones. Not to have that internal guide as I make life choices. Not to feel rage and despair at the misogyny, the sexism, the job discrimination, the ongoing violence against women shown in the sexual abuse, battering, pornography, rape and worse that I hear about and see for myself every day.

In the 1960s, no one told women to shut up because we were rocking the boat, because we weren't even in the boat and indeed were never expected to climb inside, let alone rock it!

Margaret Atwood, in her non-fiction book *Second Words*, puts an interesting slant on the boat-rocking syndrome. She discusses the problem of those women still regarded as 'honorary men', who fail to understand that the phrase 'You think like a man' is less a form of admiration than an unconscious put-down. Atwood suggests there is still an incompatibility between the notion of 'woman' and the notion of 'good at something'. She points out that if women are 'good at something' some of them will not want to carry the stigma attached to the dismal category they have worked hard to escape from! They believe 'the only reason for rocking the boat is if you're still chained to the oars'.[1]

Of course, there are other and better ways to rock the boat, which fine writers like Atwood make us aware of.

There are strong, young voices like those of Kat Banyard and our guests Natasha Walter and Bidisha, who rock and shout and wave and rave with wit and passion and firmness of purpose. They believe, as their prose shows, that every woman who writes about what happens to her and to her sisters, women friends, daughters, mothers, grandmothers, makes it easier for the next woman to write and in writing rock the boat.

Why do we write and especially why do we write feminist non-fiction? Because we must? Hmm, that sounds a bit grand. Because nothing is quite as fine and dandy (at least on a good day)? Yes. Because it's risky? Of course. Because some of us are secretly subversive? I hope so.

Because we can lie outrageously yet search for the truth? That is where writing literary non-fiction comes in. If we translate the phrase 'outrageous lies' into the phrase 'creative imaginative prose' then that statement lies at the heart of literary non-fiction.

I search my library for some precious examples of feminist writing that transcend anger and passion or contemplation and scholarship in order to bring readers originality, imagination and a lasting universal theme with truth at its centre.

I take down from the shelves some wonderful classics. *Against Our Will*, Susan Brownmiller's classic study of rape (1975). Then *The Female Eunuch*, Germaine Greer's defining manifesto for the Feminist movement from 1960. Momentarily I am caught by Betty Friedan's *The Feminine Mystique* (1963), the unexpected call to arms that started off the Second Wave of Feminism. I linger over the shelf devoted to Adrienne Rich. Her poems, her essays – many collected in *On Lies, Secrets and Silence: Selected Prose 1966–1978* – and her controversial pamphlet *Compulsory Heterosexuality and Lesbian Existence* (1980). Then I spot my most loved, most dog-eared Rich: *Of Woman Born*, an unforgettable insight into mothering as a practice and experience and mother-hood as an institution. Read it when you have small children; it will almost certainly make you view the experience differently.[2]

On another shelf, both Maya Angelou's moving autobiography *I Know Why The Caged Bird Sings* and Audre Lorde's *The Cancer Journals* move between autobiography, memoir, journal, near-fiction, solid fact and exposition.[3]

It is hard to know what to select for this chapter. Can I *not* write about Simone de Beauvoir's *The Second Sex* (1949)? Or, what about the late Andrea Dworkin's amazing bombshell *Intercourse*, which examines heterosexual practice as a form of possession and control? To be up to date, should I think about Caitlin Moran's *How To be a Woman*? I dither, turning over a biography I know to be written in riveting dynamic language: *Her Husband: Ted Hughes and Sylvia Plath, a Marriage*, by Diane Middlebrook.[4]

Kate Millett had already achieved an unexpected success with her explosive *Sexual Politics*, a world bestseller, when out of the chaos and fallout of that success she wrote her most unusual non-fiction book, *Flying*.[5] I hold both books in my hand, feeling their separate excitements.

It is especially hard for me not to write about Adrienne Rich's *Of Woman Born* or *Flying* by Kate Millett, for they both exemplify many of those blurred-edged graces that can occur in the bravest literary non-fiction.

When I decide not to write about them, I reread them again instead (cross-legged on the study floor for many hours) and so could you. Ultimately I decide to focus on five exceptional authors: Margaret Atwood, Dale Spender, Fauziya Kassindja, Susan Faludi and Kat Banyard.

Margaret Atwood's non-fiction books, as well as her novels, have been widely acclaimed for their feminist, mythological and dystopian themes. Her work is often regarded as a barometer of feminist thought, but Carmen Callil, who brought Canadian Atwood to UK attention with the Virago imprint, feels that Atwood's work ranges more deeply and more widely than that. Callil says that 'like George Eliot, she connects women's lives to injustice and to politics generally'.[6]

This can clearly be seen in her non-fiction book *Moving Targets: Writing With Intent* and particularly in the chapter 'Laughter vs. Death', which was sparked off by the research she did for her suspense novel *Bodily Harm*.[7] The novel's journalist heroine Rennie has just had a mastectomy and Atwood filters Rennie's inner torment through a web of violence and pornographic actions and images in a world of brutal power and sexual politics. In the non-fiction 'Laughter vs. Death', Atwood overtly offers her own outraged reflections on the pornography industry as she explores its social consequences. In both the fiction and non-fiction, while Atwood questions who has power over the female body, she keeps her eye on the issues that lie around and outside that question. She argues that, although freedom of expression is vital in our society, it must have a limit because unbridled pornography functions to destroy men as well as women.

Atwood's non-fiction, such as *Moving Targets: Writing With Intent* and *Second Words*,[8] is filled with the same savage humour, caustic wit, original style and razor-like intellect as the novels, and similarly depicts women's deep anxieties, fears, passions and even desire for revenge. In 'Writing the Male Character', a chapter in *Second Words*, Atwood gives a memorably dark description of the difference between male and female fears. Pursuing the question of why each sex feels threatened by the other, she asked a male friend: '"Why do men feel threatened by women?" . . . "They're afraid women will laugh at them" he said. "Undercut their world view."' Then Atwood asked some women students why do women feel threatened by men? '"They're afraid of being killed", they said.'[9]

Atwood has always been concerned about gender roles in society. But she never serves this idea up straight. It is her ability to cleverly manipulate cultural images that gives her non-fiction work its original slant. She improvises within literary and cultural constraints. It is as if she is recycling and recombining a variety of cultural norms and ideas so that she can stretch their boundaries.[10] She uses her prose to push the bounds of the roles of women.

In *The Handmaid's Tale* we see a society constructed by men where women's lives are defined by their position and status.[11] In Gilead, a dystopian theocracy, women are not permitted to read, hold jobs, own property, or in some cases have children or husbands. Through them Atwood deals with the way sex influences society and how we distribute power as a consequence.

Her fiction heavily criticises any reactionary society, and does not merely condemn the patriarchal religious right. She is never simply a crusader for radical feminist action. Her interest is in warning readers of the dangers of taking any belief too far.

Atwood's fiction and non-fiction constantly inform and reinforce each other. The open seriousness of her non-fiction themes becomes a half-hidden depth in the novels, while the beautiful imagery of the fiction winds itself between disciplined passages of non-fiction prose.

One of the great classics of the women's movement, Dale Spender's *Man Made Language,* opened our eyes to the myriad ways in which the rules and uses of language promote a male, and therefore a partial, view of the world.[12] Once my eyes had been opened I found it impossible to see the world as I had seen it before. Spender sprinkles her work with startling images not dissimilar to the violent yet addictive pictures in television series such as *Waking the Dead* or *The Body Farm*. Once you have absorbed those images it is hard to erase them from the mind's eye. Similarly with Spender's cut-and-thrust words and images.

Spender's radical feminist analysis of language, which is sharp and in places unexpectedly funny, has been an extraordinarily influential book articulating a theory of male control over the English language and the way that women have been systematically silenced through the forms of language, the conventions of male and female speech, the exclusion of women from print culture and the patriarchal structures at the heart of the gatekeeping process.

Spender's passionate account of the male bias implicit in language alerted readers and writers to a new way of looking at language, but subsequently had its detractors. This has been useful. For Spender started a dialogue which has since been replicated and developed by such fine thinkers as Deborah Tannen but so far has not been replaced.[13] This has allowed *Man Made Language* to become a landmark text of modern feminist thought.

One review, unconsciously highly amusing, which makes all Spender's points for her, is from a certain Johan D. Tangelder, who much admires her tract 'the Power of Language'. Tangelder says: 'Language, claims Dale Spender . . . is not neutral; it is itself a shaper of ideas. He argues that . . . ', etc.[14]

Oh dear, Mr Tangelder (I hope not Professor Tangelder), what a trap to fall into. Because you rate Dale Spender's book as good you assume Spender is a male!

Man Made Language has been especially important to female writers and readers because it makes the point that, as men have been associated with the public sphere (including published writing) while women are still associated with the private sphere, those women who take up the pen at least have the potential to cross over classification boundaries and enter the public sphere.

There are differences between polemicists or social-political authors and literary writers that involve ideas of literary excellence. The goal of a political movement or of social propaganda is to encourage people to act. To make changes that they hope will improve people's lives. The goal of fine writing, however, is to use words to create a world that may be realistic, but comes from and is fuelled by the imagination. Polemicists are change-makers. Writers are witnesses.

So what is it that allows Spender's work of non-fiction, a polemical book about bias in language, that is born from a political movement, to transcend both the sociological classification into which it might have fallen and the academic undergrowth into which it could have been confined?

It is partly its originality, the fact that it offered a new way of perceiving an old landscape; partly its powerful content, written in a language that is both polished and accessible; and partly the fact that its theme lasts. It just won't go away! The result is that Spender's book springs as literature from the heart of feminist theory, and therefore becomes important to readers from many groups, not merely from one.

Fauziya Kassindja's *Do They Hear You When You Cry* is on first reading a straightforward feminist memoir, or rather a horror story, about a young African woman who flees to the United States to escape female genital mutilation and who ends up imprisoned for over a year as an illegal immigrant.[15]

However, Fauziya's story is much more than that. It is a tale of faith, as the young African woman is a devout Muslim who says repeatedly that only her belief in God helped her survive desperate and demeaning treatment. It is also a tale of sisterhood across countries and continents, as Fauziya is befriended by a young law student, Layli Miller Bashir, who becomes her advocate and after many months secures her release and vindication. It is also a universally important tale of the violation of human rights. And it reads like a fast-paced novel. Readers are gripped at once.

At 17 Fauziya had lived an idyllic childhood in Kpalime, Togo, with two brothers, four older sisters and a mother who adored her, and an exceptional father who flouted tradition by educating his daughters. Though it was traditional for all young women of their father's tribe to undergo female genital mutilation before marriage, he protected Fauziya's sisters from a practice he detested until each of them was safely married. Then in January 1993 her father suddenly died. Away at school in Ghana, she was immediately summoned home and put under the fierce guardianship of her uncle, an orthodox Muslim who at once exiled her mother to Nigeria, and contracted 17-year-old Fauziya to a marriage with a man of 45 who already had three wives. Fauziya's proposed husband insisted all his wives went through kakia, the rite of passage blandly called female circumcision but which is a terrible mutilation of girls' genitals. It was traditionally performed by village women who used old knives, razor blades and pieces of broken glass under unsanitary conditions and with no anaesthesia. Fauziya panicked. She knew the risk of infection was high. She knew her mother's sister had died from complications following this barbaric practice. She knew several of her women friends had died in pain and isolation.

Fauziya decided she must escape. Her widowed mother gave her money. Her elder sister helped her. She crossed the border to Ghana and flew to Germany. Lonely, unable to speak the language, she decided her only hope was to get to the USA. Foolishly she flew on a false passport, believing that once she entered America she could seek and obtain asylum from kindly US authorities. How wrong she was. After landing at Newark in December 1994, she was immediately arrested. Cultural modesty forbade her from telling Immigration and Naturalization Service (INS) officials (who run a court system separate from America's main court system) about the threat of genital mutilation. She was given a choice by the INS of being deported immediately or going to prison until she could appear before an immigration judge. She was told her hearing would take place in four days. Only 17 and very naïve, she believed them.

Fauziya waited in prison for that first hearing for over eight months. She was strip-searched, shackled in chains from head to foot, put in solitary confinement for over two weeks after being misdiagnosed with tuberculosis, then housed in a maximum-security prison with violent criminals. The prison refused her numerous pleas for medical care for severe asthma and what would later turn out to be a peptic ulcer. She was forced to remain in that prison for 18 months. Even when she broke down and begged to be allowed to return to Togo her request was ignored.

It was during her incarceration that she met Layli Miller Bashir, a dedicated law student at the American University in Washington. The two women formed firm bonds at once.

After a long struggle, Bashir enlisted the help of the American University's International Human Rights Clinic, along with several FGM (Female Genital Mutilation) activists, and initiated a high-profile fight to free Fauziya and finally grant her asylum on 13 June 1996. Fauziya Kassindja and her legal team had won a landmark case that would set the standard for anyone seeking asylum in the USA on the grounds of gender-based persecution.

The book is both feminist and international and it has universal implications for racism and justice as well as for feminism. In the research done by

Bashir and Kassindja they cite a 1995 study that reveals that over 97 per cent of detained immigrants in the US are people of colour, even though five of the top twenty countries of origin for illegal immigrants are Caucasian. Sixteen years on, the figures have not substantially improved.

And if anyone imagines that things are any different in the UK, for instance, they are mistaken. Every one of the abuses and injustices of the American asylum systems is reproduced in Britain.

Nonetheless, Fauziya said that her book was a chronicle of triumph rather than of pain and readers will agree. Despite the horrors, what stays with us is the resilience of her hope and the excellence of her prose.

Susan Faludi, a reporter on *The Wall Street Journal* and already a Pulitzer Prize winner, was thirty-two when she wrote *Backlash*, the international bestseller which exposed the myths on which the aggressive resistance to feminism in the 1990s was based.

Faludi deals with two contradictory myths. One is the apparent growing threat of 'militant feminism'. The other is the myth that feminism has failed. Backlashers want to have it both ways. They accuse the women's movement of succeeding, i.e. going too far and thus wrecking relationships with good, friendly and reasonable men. At the same time, backlashers accuse feminists of failing so badly that the movement can only be seen as a well-meaning but foolish experiment.

Lucidly, Faludi exposes the way these strategies divide women at a point in history when they need unity in their struggle for independence and equality. She dissects in forensic detail the mechanisms by which negative stereotypes are levelled at women with careers. Under her surgical blade goes biased and insidious reporting of issues concerning women: dangers of plastic surgery, the foolishness of new (i.e. repackaged old) restrictive clothing, footwear and even tight corsets reminiscent of Scarlett O'Hara. Faludi cuttingly debunks myths of an infertility epidemic, barren wombs and man shortages.

In 2006, her book was republished as a fifteenth-anniversary edition in which the author brought backlash consciousness up to date. Sadly, it seemed that both American and British media sold the same backlash messages as fifteen years earlier. Today, a further six years on, they have hardly changed at all. In the USA, women's career ambitions are regarded as dangerous to 'the family'; the glass ceiling is still there for most women, and fundamental reproductive rights are again under vicious attack.

When Faludi's book caused its initial uproar, it focused on American women. Then she revised it to look at Britain, Australia, New Zealand and other countries where she saw the same right-wing anger, and the same small gains women had made.

The book is meticulously documented and vividly written. You don't win Pulitzers for poor writing. As Elaine Showalter said, it was the right book at the right time. She called it *The Bonfire of the Vanities* of the backlash business.[16] We are in a different time but it remains the right book.

Kat Banyard, described today (2011) as the UK's most influential young feminist, founder and director of UK Feminista, an organisation supporting grassroots feminist activism, is not yet thirty. In her book *The Equality Illusion,* she is still struggling to bring to public attention the same break-your-heart issues, the same glaring wrongs upon which Faludi first focused her searing yet elegant prose in 1992.[17] Her passionate argument is that feminism is one of today's most relevant and crucial social justice campaigns.

The prose style, seemingly artless and casual, is cleverly wrought, each lean athletic phrase meticulously thought out. The narrative, hard like Hemingway's, avoids adjectives and adverbs, uses vigorous English that is cut and re-cut, and often uses cinematic techniques of cutting swiftly from one scene to another. She strengthens verbs to make them count. She moves from dialogue to action and then to silence – an intriguing literary combination.

The content challenges how readers think about empowerment and about choice, both ideas that have been taken over by the beauty and sex industries.

Banyard's interviews with youthful sex workers about exploitation are as forceful as those with young migrant women. She speaks to the young about being young. What is the impact on their teenage lives of ideas of female submission which have filtered from pornography and prostitution almost invisibly into the mainstream – into the magazines they read and the television adverts they see?

She interviews young people about sexual harassment and aggression. She discovers that it is now routine for boys to make sexist remarks to girls and to grope their breasts, while teachers mouth outworn phrases such as 'boys will be boys'. At home mothers, often not very old themselves, struggle with the out-of-control behaviour of their young sons, afraid to reprimand them, either from fear of being unloving, or simply from fear.

Banyard points out how such behaviour patterns give both sexes poor expectations about life, with destructive consequences, especially for women. She argues against all outdated notions that biology is at the heart of gender inequality. For her, the equality agenda has been manipulated by political and corporate interests. Though many would say that sexist stereotyping is a symptom rather than a cause of inequality, she sees it as a causal foundation, basing her case on academic research and on her experience in the field as Campaign Director for the Fawcett Society.

Stylistically she makes many of her points by using the Iceberg Theory of Language.[18] Just as 91 per cent (or nine-tenths of the volume) of an iceberg is under water, so the art of writing is knowing what you can leave submerged so that the readers will fill it in. The facts float above water, the symbolism and the structure remain out of sight.

Her book has been criticised for not offering solutions to the problems it poses. But literature doesn't do that. It is not a problem-solving exercise. It is a means of looking at the world anew through a viewfinder of good prose.

In the way Banyard looks at the world, in the way her writing makes sharp darts in our consciousness, the book is fresh. Alarmingly fresh. 'Read it now' is my response, although there is no 'use by' date. I think it will stand that clichéd test of time and be a book our children and their children will read. I hope it will do so because it is an example of powerful literary non-fiction and not because there is still a need for the action it calls for.

Notes

1. Margaret Atwood, *Second Words: Selected Critical Prose*, House of Anansi, Toronto, 1982, p. 193.
2. Adrienne Rich, *On Lies, Secrets and Silence: Selected Prose 1966–1978* (W.W. Norton, New York, 1995); *Of Woman Born* (W.W. Norton, New York, 1976, 1986).
3. Maya Angelou, *I Know Why The Caged Bird Sings*, Virago, London, 1984. Audre Lorde, *The Cancer Journals*, Aunt Lute Books, San Francisco, 2007.

4. Andrea Dworkin, *Intercourse*, Basic Books, New York, 2006. Caitlin Moran, *How To be a Woman*, Ebury Press, London, 2011. Diane Middlebrook, *Her Husband: Ted Hughes and Sylvia Plath, a Marriage*, Little, Brown, London, 2004.
5. Kate Millett, *Sexual Politics*, Virago, London, 1977 (originally published 1970); *Flying*, Knopf, New York, 1974.
6. Quoted by Robert Potts, 'Light in the Wilderness', *The Guardian*, 26 April 2003.
7. Margaret Atwood, *Moving Targets: Writing with Intent, 1983–2005*, House of Anansi, Toronto, 2004; Carroll & Graf, New York, 2005; *Bodily Harm*, Jonathan Cape, London, 1982.
8. Also: Margaret Atwood, *Curious Pursuits: Occasional Writing 1970–2005*, Virago, London, 2005.
9. Atwood, *Second Words*, p. 413.
10. Stephen Greenblatt talks about how good authors use cultural constraints in his essay 'On Culture', *Critical Terms for Literary Study*, ed. Frank Lentricchia and Thomas McLaughlin, University of Chicago Press, Chicago, 1995, pp. 225–32.
11. Margaret Atwood, *The Handmaid's Tale*, Anchor Books, New York, 1998 (first published 1985).
12. Dale Spender, *Man Made Language*, Routledge & Kegan Paul, London, 1980.
13. Deborah Tannen, *You Just Don't Understand: Women and Men Talking*, Virago, London, 1991. Another hugely influential book whose source stretched back as far as Spender is John Gray's *Men are from Mars, Women are from Venus*, HarperCollins, New York, 1992.
14. Johan D. Tangelder, 'Reformed Reflections: The Power of Language', www.reformed reflections.ca/faith-and-life/power-of-language.html, accessed 9 September 2011.
15. Fauziya Kassindja, with Layli Miller Bashir, *Do They Hear You When You Cry*, Delacorte Press, New York, 1998.
16. Elaine Showalter, quoted on jacket cover of Faludi, *Backlash*, 1991 and 1992 editions.
17. Susan Faludi, *Backlash. The Undeclared War Against Women*, Chatto & Windus, London, 1991, 1992; Vintage, London, 1993. (In some editions the subtitle is *The Undeclared War Against American Women*.) Kat Banyard, *The Equality Illusion: The Truth about Women and Men*, Faber and Faber, London, 2010.
18. Also called the Theory of Omission.

8: Reflections on history

by Midge Gillies

I sometimes think the reason I enjoy reading about the past is similar to the reason I enjoy ghost stories: I love reaching out and connecting with lost lives and missing worlds.

History, like a good ghost story, holds the power to transport. Anyone who has written a biography or researched a past period will recognise how haunting the experience can be. I can sympathise with the biographer who dated a cheque in the 1700s, because that was the century he was inhabiting at the time. When I was researching the life of the Edwardian music hall performer Marie Lloyd, I found that my handwriting as I took notes was getting smaller and smaller. I finally realised the reason why: I had been reading about the Great War, and felt the need to conserve paper because of the shortage. During this period of intense research I would also dream that Marie Lloyd was standing by the side of my bed − an apparition that I found thrilling, but which unnerved my husband.

L.P. Hartley famously began his novel *The Go-Between* with the line 'The past is a foreign country: they do things differently there.' I don't think we were different people in the past, but I am fascinated by the forces that made us act differently. If I had been in domestic service at the start of the twentieth century, would I have been an ardent suffragette? If not, why not? If I had lived in 1930s Germany, would I have spoken out against the Nazis − or kept my head down? How would I have behaved if I had been a screenwriter living in Hollywood in the McCarthy period?

The past is not immutable, and it is different for different people. I grew up in a family where history was always interpreted through a Scottish lens. This was particularly interesting when I studied the Tudors and Stuarts at a traditional English girls' school. In history lessons I delighted in reversing the usual order, calling King James 'James VI of Scotland and I of England'. At school we were taught what a nuisance Elizabeth I's cousin Mary Queen of Scots was;

at home she was a brave and honest heroine. I always felt rather sorry for the lone Catholic in our class, who was expected to speak up for the whole of the Catholic world when it came to the Reformation and explaining transubstantiation.

When I was growing up, *1066 And All That* was about as funny as history got – and even then you had to understand a fair bit about the subject to appreciate the jokes. Otherwise, any humour in serious books about the past was seen as devaluing the work. Thankfully, that is no longer the case. Celebrating quirkiness, if not actually aiming for laughs, can be a useful way of varying the texture of narrative history. Our ancestors, after all, had a sense of humour too. Although *1066 And All That* has long since fallen from popularity, the Horrible History series – ostensibly aimed at children, and taking in everyone from the Rotten Romans to the Terrible Tudors and the Blitzed Brits – has won a cult following among adults. It is not just the alliteration that has proved a winner, but the humour, gore and surprising facts that make the series irresistible.

Of course, the Horrible History series is not literary non-fiction, but its formula brings the past to life in a vivid and whimsical way. Using humour is a risky business, because if the reader does not 'get' the joke the author risks alienating them. But it can be a tool to change the pace, and, if an author can make their reader laugh, that reader is more likely to be on their side.

Although I read it probably twenty years ago, there is a section in Diana Souhami's *Gertrude and Alice*, about the relationship between Gertrude Stein and her companion Alice B. Toklas, that still makes me laugh out loud. In it Souhami quotes in full a letter Stein received from a publisher when he returned her manuscript of *Portraits*. The letter mimics perfectly Stein's unusual style in a witty, if cruel, rejection:

19 April 1912

Dear Madam

I am only one, only one, only one. Only one being, one at the same time. Not two, not three, only one. Only one life to live, only sixty minutes in one hour. Only one pair of eyes. Only one brain. Only one being. Being only one, having only one pair of eyes, having only one time, having only one life, I cannot read your MS three or four times. Not even one time. Only one look, only one look is enough. Hardly one copy would sell here.

Hardly one. Hardly one.

Many thanks. I am returning the MS by registered post. Only one MS by one post.

Sincerely yours

A.C. Fifield[1]

As the pages of references and bibliography show, Souhami – one of our guest contributors – had a mountain of sources she could have quoted from. This letter earns its place for several reasons: it gives a sense of the publishing world at that time and how Stein's unique style was viewed, but it also adds humour and varies the pace. This skill – to judge what is best to quote – is learned by experimentation, and by reading other books to identify what you think is successful.

Stephen King would not claim to be a writer of literary non-fiction (or even perhaps of literary fiction). But his 'memoir of the craft', *On Writing*, is wonderfully honest about the 'job' of writing, and he is a strong advocate of reading as a route to good writing. He says that, despite being a slow reader, he usually gets through seventy or eighty books a year, and believes that even reading bad prose can be helpful as a way of learning what not to do.

King's no-nonsense advice is superb, especially for anyone who has yet to realise that writing needs to be approached like any other work,

> *like laying pipe or driving long-haul trucks. Your job is to make sure the muse knows where you're going to be every day from nine till noon or seven till three. If he does know, I assure you that sooner or later he'll start showing up, chomping his cigar and making his magic.*

Apart from the fact that my muse is female and a non-smoker, I agree with him wholeheartedly.

Borrowing from fiction

Writing about the past, whether in the form of biography or narrative history, requires mastery of the facts – but also the confidence not to swamp the reader with each and every one of those hard-won facts. Literary non-fiction should have all the elements of good fiction: intriguing characters, variety of pace and vivid descriptions. It should make you think about the human condition, about the motives behind what people did, and whether they were driven by emotions or by outside influences such as national events or the mores of their day.

History has its own in-built drama. Traditionally, that drama circled around battles and the births and deaths of kings and queens; in recent years it has moved towards looking at how worldwide events impinged on ordinary lives. Edmund de Waal's *The Hare with Amber Eyes* is a good example of how the actions of a dictator affected a family. Although de Waal's ancestors, the Ephrussis, were hardly ordinary (they were immensely wealthy and cultured, and Proust based Charles Swann in *Remembrance of Things Past* on one of them), they were caught up in two World Wars, and *The Hare with Amber Eyes* follows their story through Paris, Vienna, Tokyo and London. De Waal describes how, in March 1938, the Nazis break in on the Jewish family:

> And it is on that first night that the sounds of the street become shouting in the Ephrussi courtyard, echoing around the walls and off the roof. Then there are feet pounding up the stairs, the thirty-three shallow steps to the apartment on the second floor.
>
> There are fists on the door, someone leaning on the bell, and there are eight or ten, a knot of them in some sort of uniform – some with swastika armbands, some familiar. Some are still boys. It is one o'clock in the morning and no one is asleep, everyone is dressed. Viktor and Emmy and Rudolf are pushed into the library.[2]

Antonia Fraser's *The Gunpowder Plot: Terror and Faith in 1605*, by comparison, focuses on a single, well-known event, rather than surveying several generations of a family, as de Waal does. It is a 'history book' that reads like the best gripping fiction. One reviewer compared it to a John le Carré novel, and it won the 1996 Crime Writers' Gold Award for Non-Fiction. Of course, Fraser had an exciting event at the core of her book, but she still had to unravel the political and religious complexities that led up to the plot and the motives that drove the protagonists. This book also contains one of the most imaginative and chilling uses of a visual image I have come across in a work of non-fiction. Among the contemporary drawings of the conspirators is a reproduction of Guido Fawkes' signature, before and after torture. The first hand is strong and bold, the second a shaky, truncated scrawl. It is an effective and subtle way of depicting how his body and spirit were broken by the rack, and a reminder that sources are not limited to diaries, letters and dusty documents.

A book like *The Hare with Amber Eyes*, which weaves across continents and generations, has a cinematic sweep, but there is also pleasure to be found in the smaller-scale nuggets of information that pepper books about the past. I was more shocked to read in Deirdre Bair's biography of Simone de Beauvoir that French women only won the vote in 1944 than by anything she wrote about Beauvoir or Sartre. When I read in Juliet Gardiner's history of the 1930s that the term 'Jerry-built'[3] came from 'Jericho' (the walls of which came tumbling down in the Bible) rather than, as I had always imagined, from a Nazi bombing campaign, it gave me an insight into the pre-war years, and also allowed me to reclaim a word I thought I knew.

Sometimes the smallest details are the most telling. Margaret Forster's family memoir, *Hidden Lives,* tells the story of three generations of women: her grandmother, Margaret Ann, who was a domestic servant; her mother, Lily, who gave up her office job to raise a family; and Margaret Forster herself, who escaped to study at Oxford University. A twenty-first-century reader may need reminding that the lack of modern inventions made keeping a home an onerous and never-ending task in the past; in the absence of a fridge, for instance, shopping had to be done every day. But Forster points out subtler changes that may not have occurred to the reader. Thus she describes how housework always seemed to be carried out in semi-darkness, because not much natural light made its way through the net curtains, and the gas lamps were not lit until late afternoon.

I find that the most satisfying details fall into two categories: the kind that confirms or amplifies something you already know, or thought you knew; and the new fact that is so interesting you instantly want to pass it on to someone else. The Cambridge University classicist Mary Beard is particularly skilled at both. She is well aware that our impressions of the Ancient Roman empire are distorted by myths, but, rather than dismiss them out of hand, she makes a virtue of explaining their origins and the extent to which they may contain elements of truth. In her book about Pompeii she points out that the eruption did not wipe out the entire population in a day, and the citizens were not all sex-obsessed sybarites; disappointingly, there was probably just one brothel. But she is not above tackling the subjects everyone yearns to know about. She tells us that, while countless movies and TV programmes make it seem as if dormice were the mainstay of a well-to-do Pompeiian's diet, the wretched creatures were only a rare delicacy.

She cites a Roman cookery book which contains a recipe for stuffed dormice as the source. But she concludes that 'these poor little creatures played a smaller role in Roman cookery than they do in modern fantasies about the luxury and excess of Roman eating habits, which are one of the most celebrated and mythologised of all aspects of Roman life'.[4] Then, deliciously, she explains how the animals were kept in special pottery jars made with grooves for them to exercise in (just like a pet hamster using a wheel today) and equipped with basins for storing their food: acorns, walnuts or chestnuts.

Narrative history has to juggle with this foreground and background, making sure the reader never loses sight of the principal characters, while painting a picture of the historical context that influences them. Thus, Beard gives the dormice their moment before returning to the main story about Pompeii.

Judith Thurman in her *A Life of Colette* is equally skilled at maintaining this balance between fascinating minutiae and the overarching story she is telling. In this example (again involving a rodent) she describes the decadence of *fin de siècle* Paris: 'The ranks of Gomorrah swell with the wives of bankers and politicians, as well as with the cabaret singers and laundresses of Montmartre.'[5] She then goes on to a further example of this decadence: the writer Rachilde, who owned two sewer rats called Kyrie and Eleison and who presided over her 'Tuesdays' at the *Mercure de France* with them perched on her shoulders. A little more detail and Rachilde might have been in danger of edging too far into the foreground, when she belonged firmly in the background. But Thurman immediately returns Colette to centre stage: 'On every storm-tossed vessel filled with retching bodies there is usually one passenger, freakishly sound, who strolls the pitching deck on steady feet while insolently eating a ham sandwich. Colette was that sort of freak at the *fin de siècle*.'

Rachilde flits through the biography, only ever illuminating Colette's life rather than distracting us from it.

Storytelling

In most history it is people – whether high-born or lowly – who drive the story forward: Henry VIII searching for a wife who can give him a male heir or Detective Inspector Jonathan Whicher trying to save his career by finding the murderer at Road Hill House. For a while there was a vogue for history to follow the story of an object. Mark Kurlansky is perhaps the best-known proponent of this idea, having written social histories of both Cod and Salt.

History provides the opportunity for great storytelling, even when the story is not as obvious as the Gunpowder Plot or the Second World War. One of my favourite 'history' books is *The Surgeon of Crowthorne* (or *The Professor and the Madman*, to give it its US title) by one of our guest contributors, Simon Winchester. This story of the founding of the *Oxford English Dictionary* is remarkable on several different levels.

First there is the dictionary itself. This was a monumental work that took fifty years to complete, and the assistance of thousands of volunteers who read many thousands of books and made word-lists of all that they read. They were asked to keep an eye out for certain words, and then to send in on a slip of paper details of the word cited: date, author, title of book, volume and page number, and a sentence illustrating the use of the word. This technique is still used today.

But *The Surgeon of Crowthorne* is also about two remarkable men: its editor, John Murray, and John Minor, one of its most prolific contributors. Minor refused ever to visit Oxford, where the book was being assembled. His interest piqued, Murray decided to visit him – only to discover that he was working from a cell in Broadmoor Asylum, where he was being held for murdering a brewery worker in London. Winchester traces the story behind both men.

Murray was self-taught, the eldest son of a tailor from a market town on the Scottish Borders who began his career as a schoolmaster before moving to London, where his interest in philology put him in touch with some of the leading scholars of his day. Minor was born in Ceylon (modern-day Sri Lanka), like Murray to religious parents. He studied medicine at Yale University and served as a surgeon in the Union Army during the American Civil War. It may have been his experiences among the injured that precipitated his slide into insanity.

For me, the book is so satisfying because of its author's careful blending of the themes of madness, learning and friendship, and contemporary attitudes to all three. The initial fascination is with the extraordinary story that Winchester has uncovered, but the book becomes so much more than this because of these important underlying themes. It is gripping, absorbing and finely balanced, because neither of the two main characters (three, if you include the dictionary itself) overpowers the other.

While *The Surgeon of Crowthorne* exhumes an unknown story from the past, Kate Summerscale's *The Suspicions of Mr Whicher* focuses on the murder at Road Hill House in 1860, which many readers familiar with the Victorian world will have come across before. It is the way she tells the story rather than any new discovery that makes the book so successful.

Her style is as gripping as Wilkie Collins's in *The Moonstone*, a novel heavily influenced by the murder itself. But *The Suspicions of Mr Whicher* is more than simply a highly accomplished page-turner. It explores how the case fuelled 'detective-fever' in a nation still coming to terms with the existence of such a profession, and how it played a key part in the development of a new genre, detective fiction. The author looks at the murder, too, from the perspective of the Victorian family, and how the scandal shook its idea of cosy domesticity.

The multilayered approach
Some of the most successful works of literary non-fiction in recent years have been books that approached a famous subject from a new angle, or through new eyes. Alison Light's interpretation of Virginia Woolf's life and work through

the stories of her servants, for example, is a brilliant new 'take' on a writer who has been analysed from endless different perspectives. *Mrs Woolf and the Servants* offers an insight into what the subtitle describes as 'the hidden heart of domestic service', while at the same time comparing Woolf's writing about class to her own personal treatment of her staff. The fact that Light's own grandmother was a live-in servant gives the book an added piquancy. Woolf's life forms the backbone of the book, but Light occasionally steps out of the strict confines of non-fiction to fictionalise parts of the story (which appear in italics).

Clare Tomalin did something similar in *The Invisible Woman*, about Charles Dickens's mistress, the actress Nelly Ternan. Tomalin did some brilliant detective work to drag Nelly out of the shadows, while at the same time giving the reader a fascinating glimpse both into the world of Victorian theatre and into Dickens's relationship with women and how it might have informed the female characters he created in his novels.

While Nelly Ternan and Virginia Woolf's servants surfaced because of their relationship to famous writers, other historians have reclaimed the non-famous by mining letters, diaries and oral records (from their own interviews or sound archives) of ordinary people. In Britain, the Mass Observation Archive (particularly the diaries) have been used by a huge array of writers – of both non-fiction and fiction – to paint a picture of post-war Britain. Mass Observation was started in 1937 by three young men who wanted to create an 'anthropology of ourselves'. A team of diarists recorded their lives in the sort of detail that historians long for. In *Waiting for Hitler* I used the diaries of two young sisters who ran a petrol station near the coast in rural Norfolk to convey what it was like to live in an area that was braced for Nazi invasion in 1940. Their diaries were funny and lively, and I felt as though I knew both women and the village where they lived intimately.

David Kynaston, who has written the Foreword to this book, also drew on the Mass Observation Archive for his masterly social history of the six years after the Second World War, *Austerity Britain*. His book is alive with a whole chorus of voices from that period, excavated from a variety of different sources, and underpinned by a deep understanding of the political forces that shaped those years and the ones that followed. *Austerity Britain* marks the start of a sequence of books called *Tales of a New Jerusalem*, which will examine Britain between 1945 and 1979. Kynaston explains his approach in the preface to *Austerity Britain*:

> *It is a history that does not pursue the chimera of being*
> *'definitive'; it does try to offer an intimate, multilayered,*
> *multivoiced, unsentimental portrait of a society that evolved in*
> *such a way during these 34 years as to make it possible for the*
> *certainties of '1945' to become the counter-certainties of '1979'.*[6]

Austerity Britain is one of the key sources cited in Virginia Nicholson's wonderful social history *Millions Like Us, Women's Lives in War and Peace 1939–1949*. Like Kynaston, she has succeeded in building a multilayered picture of a particular period in time. She begins with the new bronze statue in London's Whitehall, dedicated in 2005 by the Queen to the women who served in the Second World War. Nicholson points out that the monument is faceless – a collection of clothes and belongings representing the women, rather than themselves. She sets out to discover who they were, what their lives were like, and how their wartime experiences changed their lives afterwards. She arranges her chapters chronologically, and uses the personal stories of a 'fifty-strong cast of characters in the spotlight against a backdrop of important social, political and international events'. These women spanned all social classes and age groups and came from all around Britain. Their stories emerge from memoirs, diaries such as Mass Observation's, and her own interviews.

Nicholson is clear about her strategy: 'My approach to historical research is, as far as possible, to merge it with biography, and the telling of stories. I believe that the personal and idiosyncratic reveal more about the past than the generic and comprehensive.'[7]

Her style is intimate, and she refers to each member of her cast by their first name. For example, Phyllis Beck is 'Pip', who, 'impressionable, naive, poetry-loving and dazzlingly pretty, is growing up in the little market town of Buckingham'.[8]

Many of Nicholson's sources are women she has interviewed herself, including her ninety-four-year-old mother.

Oral history, although not always wholly reliable, brings the past searingly to life. Max Arthur did this to stunning effect in *Forgotten Voices of the Great War* and its sequel *Forgotten Voices of the Second World War*, for both of which he used the Imperial War Museum's Sound Archives. His skill is to select the most vibrant and moving testimonies, and then stand back and allow his cast to speak for themselves. The author remains in the background, offering a few paragraphs on historical context and acting – as he says himself – as a 'catalyst'.[9]

Max Arthur's was a fresh approach to social history in Britain, at least since the legendary interviewer Tony Parker. But Studs Terkel had been doing something similar in the USA for decades, where he won a Pulitzer Prize in 1985 for *The Good War: An Oral History of World War II*. Terkel, who died in 2008 at the age of ninety-six, spent most of his adult life interviewing a huge range of Americans, both rich and poor, famous and unknown, and is often credited with making oral history a legitimate form of literature.

Perhaps the growing interest in recording the testimony of those who witnessed history comes from a desire to see the past through the eyes of ordinary people. Oral history does not hold all the answers: there will always be questions about its veracity, and the literary challenge of how to include such testimony into a smooth narrative. But, for me, interviewing someone who has had first-hand experience of the period I am writing about is a living link with the past – an important addition to the military records, census returns and birth, marriage and death certificates that have to be sifted through. Asking 'What was it really like?' holds the same thrill as embarking on a good ghost story.

Notes

1. Diana Souhami, *Gertrude and Alice,* Rivers Oram Press/Pandora List, London, 1992, p. 103.
2. Edmund de Waal, *The Hare with Amber Eyes: A Hidden Inheritance,* Chatto & Windus, London, 2010, pp. 239–40.
3. Juliet Gardiner, *The Thirties: An Intimate History,* Harper Press, London, 2010, p. 306.
4. Mary Beard, *Pompeii: The Life of a Roman Town,* Profile Books, 2009, p. 217.
5. Judith Thurman, *Secrets of the Flesh: A Life of Colette,* Bloomsbury, London, 1990, p. 83.
6. David Kynaston, *Austerity Britain, 1945–51,* Bloomsbury, London, 2007, p. vii.
7. Virginia Nicholson, *Millions Like Us: Women's Lives in War and Peace 1939–1949,* Viking, London, 2011, p. xvii.
8. Nicholson, *Millions Like Us,* p. 5.
9. Max Arthur, *Forgotten Voices of the Second World War,* Ebury Press, London, 2005, p. x.

9: Reflections on sexuality, friendship and death

by Sally Cline

Some non-fiction has the power to entice us with the truth but may lack the art to help readers to transcend it. It may be too firmly rooted in facts, without sufficient imagination, or it may lack felicity of expression.

When this lack of art occurs in writings about sexuality, friendship or death (three key subjects) readers may be willing to sacrifice beautiful language, but writers trying to transcend mere factual material must avoid a few obvious pitfalls.

Sexuality

The traps

'Sex sells' is a publishing maxim, and indeed much of it does. But for a book about sexuality to be literary as well as a bestseller it must first shun crudeness, pornographic writing and ridiculous phrases. If you scan the library shelves for books on sexuality you will find there are an awful lot of foolish phrases, overblown vocabulary and − bluntly − bad sex writing.

There is so much bad sex writing that in the UK there is even a Bad Sex Award, to immortalise the most crass or cringeworthy prose. Initially, the award, established in 1993, concentrated on fiction, but more recently it has turned a spotlight on poor writing about sex in non-fiction as well. In both genres the judges at the *Literary Review*, Britain's principal literary monthly, find no shortage of bad sex material. They must adjudicate between the foolish and fatuous, the violent and vacuous, the repellent and rude. Living winners of the award have produced such killer sentences as: 'Like a lepidopterist mounting a tough-skinned insect with a too blunt pin he screwed himself into her.'[1]

One bad sex writer even won it posthumously in 2007 with a description of oral sex in which the male member is likened to 'a coil of excrement'.[2]

The judges could not resist such tasteless lines.

Sadly, bad sex descriptions can be found in all branches of literary non-fiction: biographies, histories, travel, sometimes even food writing. Even the incomparable and funny Julie Powell, author of the Julie/Julia Project, slips down the bad sex slope when she arrives at Julia Child's 357th recipe (of the 524 she is working her way through and writing about in 365 days):

> Now, this is going to be a stretch for some people, but I believe that calves' liver is the single sexiest food that there is . . . I've spent most of my life hating and despising liver . . . to eat it you must submit to it – just like you must submit to a really stratospheric fuck. Remember when you were nineteen and you went at it like it was a sporting event? . . . With liver you've got to will yourself to slow down. You've got to give yourself over to everything that's a little repulsive . . . when you eat it, slowly, you never can get away from the feral fleshiness of it.[3]

Several fine non-fiction writers have fallen down badly when they added sex to their occasional or debut fiction: Melvin Bragg, Giles Coren, A.A. Gill and Tom Wolfe, for instance.

When in 2010 the Bad Sex committee decided to allow in non-fiction, Tony Blair's toe-curling reminiscences of a night of passion with his wife Cherie were nominated as the first non-fiction contender. In his political memoir *A Journey,* he wrote: 'On the night of 12 May 1994 I needed that love Cherie gave me, selfishly. I devoured it to give me strength. I was an animal following my instinct.'[4]

I shall leave it there, though he did not.

Bad sex authors have one other thing in common as well as their dreadful prose: their gender.

Of the eighteen winners so far, seventeen have been men. The only woman to write as badly about sex has been Rachel Johnson.[5] Mark Kennedy in *The Guardian*, commenting on the rarity of a female winner, pointed to the fact that, when Johnson was appointed editor of *The Lady* magazine, the formidable magazine owner Julia Budworth said of her: 'You can never get her away from penises. I think it comes from growing up with all those boys.'[6]

OK guys (and one gal), you now know what to avoid: everything about sex or the body that is stereotypical, everything about the body or sex that is clichéd. If you see a cliché hovering, dodge and duck. If you must sink under bad vocabulary then at least let it be your own bad vocabulary.

A trap

Another challenge of writing non-fiction books that include sexuality can come from your publisher. This happens when you find that a book you have written, which is partially about sexuality, is being promoted in a way you hadn't planned and have little control over. Take my experience in writing a study of celibacy. Its theme was celibacy as a positive experience. Celibacy as a choice. Celibacy as a way to self-determination and self-esteem.[7]

Younger and more naïve than I am today, I genuinely thought that my very nice British publisher would share my goal of wishing to offer information and insights for feminist, religious and historical scholarship.

Well, I expect he did. But he also wanted both of us to make a few pennies and if possible get on someone's bestseller list. So both my original title of *Women and Celibacy* and my runner-up suggestion of *Celibacy and Women* were immediately rejected.

> BRITISH PUBLISHER: We must get SEX into the title. Surely you can see that?
>
> AUTHOR (*patiently*): I think the introduction of the word 'sex' in the title might change the theme of the book.
>
> BRITISH PUBLISHER (*pleased*): Great. Quite so. Good girl. So glad we agree. Now, how about the title *Sex, Women and Celibacy*?

After a few days of wrangling (my version) or discussion (his), we agreed the word 'celibacy' should at least have second place, and 'passion' might be a more discreet word for sex. The British title went into print as *Women, Celibacy and Passion*.

A few weeks later a long-distance conversation took place between me and my American publisher.

> AMERICAN PUBLISHER (*stridently*): Hi! Nice to have you on board! Curious title though. We have of course put the word 'celibacy' third, and 'passion' in the middle. Your first word, 'women', that can stay. Women are suddenly selling disproportionately so at present women are OK. Any queries?
>
> AUTHOR (*meekly*): None, thank you. Happy to be on board.

Did I really say 'Happy to be on board?' Sadly I did.

In commercial terms, of course, the publishers were right. I watched the book's progress every day with amazement. The sexual slant lasted so long that even today you can see it listed on eBay as 'no sex sexuality' and find it online in 'health and good relationship' forums, along with advice about spanking and books that include *Hot Monogamy: Essential Steps to More Passionate Intimate Lovemaking*.[8]

A triumph

Psychotherapist and writer Adam Phillips avoids all the hazards of writing about sexuality. His non-fiction, which extends through a range of subjects including kissing, tickling, flirtation, terrors and boredom, is filled with elegant storytelling. He is thoughtful, witty and curious about almost everything and open to every question. In a book about monogamy, he shows insights into sexual behaviour and attitudes and finds the words – in this case through 121 aphorisms – to voice what many writers have tried and failed to express.

Adam Phillips asks the difficult questions. Why do we believe in monogamy and why do we find it so difficult to think about? He suggests that all the present controversies about the family are in fact covert discussions about monogamy. Often the apparent goal of monogamy is a cover for the challenges of coupledom. As he says, 'A couple is a conspiracy in search of a crime. Sex is the closest they can get' (aphorism 21).[9]

Phillips has a wonderful way with words which enables readers to see an old situation through fresh lenses. Here is a good example: 'Infidelity is such a problem because we take monogamy for granted; we treat it as the norm. Perhaps we should take infidelity for granted, assume it with unharassed ease. Then we would be able to think about monogamy' (aphorism 2). Part of the problem, he points out, is that, although not everyone believes in monogamy, everyone behaves as though they do.

Phillips suggests that infidelity is as much about the drama of truth-telling as it is about the drama of sexuality. I am not sure about that, but I like the opening out of debate into a thought-provoking question. This makes for good writing about sexuality. It is the good writer's curiosity about the subtleties of human behaviour; the literary anthropologist's smart scavenging into the essential strangeness of everyone we meet.

On lying in relation to infidelity, Phillips says that the wish to be found out, in effect the poor lie, reveals our fear about what we can do with words. Lying, he believes, is not so much keeping our options open but discovering what they are. His trenchant summary is: 'Fear of infidelity is fear of language' (aphorism 4).

If you can write that, you are writing literary non-fiction about sexuality.

Friendship

One challenge in writing books about friendship, in both commercial and literary terms, is to avoid dullness. Friendship must be seen to be – as indeed it can be – supportive, empowering, life-enhancing.

Friendships abound in literature. The best of them, the best written, stay with us as readers for life. If you were Hemingway's Jake, would you not be glad of Bill? If you were Celia escaping to the Forest of Arden, would you not want Rosalind as your companion? If I was Chloe, I would be grateful Olivia was in my neighbourhood.

If you were writing a book about different types of marriages, where would you place the romantic-friendship kind, the one where companionship is more important than sex? I might place it high on my list. I would look closely at the lifelong, often mysterious companionship between the lesbian writer Jane Bowles and her bisexual musician-novelist husband Paul Bowles. They lived together, they lived apart, they loved each other and were devoted to each other's interests, health, welfare and passions; they respected and exemplified their unbreakable bond, their friendship.[10]

A fine example of a literary non-fiction book in which friendship stands for more than itself is Ann Patchett's memoir *Truth and Beauty*. On the surface this is an intense and exquisitely written study of novelist Ann Patchett's friendship with her fellow writer and best friend Lucy Grealy, who lost part of her jaw to childhood cancer and spent a life enduring radiation, chemotherapy and endless reconstructive surgeries, always supported by Patchett.

In addition to the powerful portrait of unstinting loyalty, the book also poses universal and testing questions such as: What happens when the person who is your family is not someone bound to you by blood? What takes place and what does it mean when the person you promise to love and honour is not your lover, husband, wife or partner but your closest friend? This is a book that explores the world of women's friendships, and examines the ties of loyalty and faith that bind people together.

The book also unleashes some complex questions relating both to craft and to ethics. Lucy Grealy wrote her own very successful memoir, *Autobiography of a Face*, but never managed to equal it, while Ann wrote to greater and greater literary acclaim.

Ann Patchett's *Truth and Beauty* was a first in that it was a book of literary non-fiction by a well-published novelist. It was also a first in that it was neither a biography of Lucy's life nor an autobiography of her own, but a non-fiction portrait of a twenty-year time period and an unwavering commitment to a friend which lasted until Lucy suddenly died from an accidental overdose of heroin, aged only thirty-nine.

The book, compiled through a mixture of dialogue, memories and snippets of Lucy's letters to Ann, is a description of the portions of their life they shared – long cold winters in the Midwest, book parties and celebrations in New York and surgical wards everywhere.

Despite Patchett's claim that her book was only about the part of Lucy's life they shared together, after it was published to phenomenal success, the Grealy family dissented. Lucy's elder sister Suellen said and wrote publicly (with the support of Sarah, Lucy's non-identical twin) that they thought they had been left out, that their inclusion in their sister's doomed life had not been validated, that their parents' part had been inaccurately presented. In fact, neither the sisters nor the parents had taken much, if any, part in the shared life of Lucy and Ann. Nevertheless, Suellen went so far as to claim that Patchett had been a grief thief.[11]

This bears heavily on two issues: that of ownership of material and that of the magic of print. Who owns another person's story? What rights do authors have over personal material belonging to someone else? Patchett took all the correct steps in obtaining the sisters' permission to use portions of Lucy's letters to her, as well as other materials. The sisters signed willingly. Patchett even offered them a sum of money in exchange for the permissions, which Sarah and their brother Nicholas accepted, feeling that it was right and fair to take a contribution to the care of their sick mother.

Despite this meticulously handled procedure, when *Truth and Beauty* was published, the sisters felt they had been betrayed. Even though Suellen admitted in her article that 'Ann was a far better "sister" to Lucy than I could ever have been', she could not contain her anger. The problem for her and the rest of Lucy's family was that suddenly they found themselves in the unfamiliar and frightening territory of book publications, press releases, newspaper reviews, film rights. The so-called 'magic-of-print' syndrome was working. This is a strange process in which what is on the printed page is believed and the real-life participants in events often feel ignored and disinherited.

Suellen had admired Ann Patchett and openly acknowledges that she had originally 'defended her need to write as an artist'. But then she adds sadly: 'I hoped she would finish it [the book] off, for herself, and put it under her bed.'

Suellen Grealy, unlike her sister Lucy and Lucy's friend Ann, was not a professional writer. Well-published professionals rarely write for under-the-duvet and never write for under-the-bed! They write for a public, even as they try to give as honest a portrayal of people and situations as they can. But Lucy's family, especially Suellen, treasured their own memories; and Suellen's distress was that she must now share those precious memories of her sister with thousands of total strangers who didn't know Lucy at all, but 'who think they understand Lucy through Ann Patchett's personal vantage point'.

As a writer I am driven to ask: From what other vantage point could Patchett have written? But I am also aware from my own experience in the magic-of-print field that writing can be hazardous to other people. Even when someone gives you oral and written permission to use incidents or materials from their life, when they see them in print they can be horrified and furious. Somehow the printed version looks different from the real-life experience they have had. Subjects of non-fiction studies, if they are not plants or oceans, are real people who can feel hurt or harmed. Every non-fiction writer must be aware of that.

Writers, however, seek to establish a relationship of feeling, of meaning, of sharing, with readers. Writers want the company of readers. And of course a writer rearranges life (it could be her life or it could be your life); a writer devises beginnings and endings where perhaps there were only driftwood and chance encounters; a writer needs to shape events and craft lives. That shape may not be the one that any one else feels is correct.

When the book is a study of a friendship, even friendships may be in peril.

Death

An obsession with death lies at the heart of human experience. Historically religion used to provide explanations for the afterlife as well as for life. Then in the late nineteenth and early twentieth centuries new notions from evolution, Communism, psychiatry and other sources put pressure on this traditional framework. There were suggestions from science and psychology that our fate was in human hands. How did God and death fit into the plan?

Recently the philosopher John Gray has written an enthralling yet frightening piece on how societies have faced their new solitary place in the universe. In order to scrutinise our delusional quest for immortality, Gray picks out two theories as key examples. One was the belief held by some Edwardian intellectuals that a form of life after death could be accessed by automatic writing and by mediums. The other was more than a belief – it was practically a certainty that in the new USSR a science-based Communism could remake humankind, free it from death and reshape the planet.

Gray's book brings together fascinating stories of spiritualists, embalmers, mass-killers, zany inventors and philosophers, through an analysis of scientific and psychological theories. What he shows is that death frightens us all, and it forces us to ask that most fundamental question about what it means to be human.[12] The book raises the indisputable point that death is an unsettling subject. Its approach makes some of us angry, others frustrated, many fright-ened. Fear is a quick answer to something we cannot control, cannot know, and often cannot deal with.

In the past, certainly the recent past, death and dying were subjects no one wanted to deal with. It is sad but true that even today when someone dies, leaving a grief-stricken partner or child, people who know them well hurry along on the other side of the street, scared to talk, because they don't know what to say. The truth is that saying anything, merely acknowledging that someone we know has died, is better than ignoring the death and the bereaved.

Part of the problem has been that, until recently, if death was not much spoken of, it was also not much written about. There were not enough books – ordinary books, funny books, angry books, compassionate books, loving and warm and sane books – on the shelves to help us all deal with this challenge.

Literary non-fiction writers were rarely encouraged to offer mortality as a topic. I know this because for years I wanted to write a book about death. How do people think about it? How do they cope with it? Can literature help? Over and over I asked my publisher if I could write a documentary study about death. For years the answer was no. No, it was insane. No, it wasn't commercial. It wasn't literary. Nobody would read it. No! Please could I find another subject.

No, I said firmly. I would not. Sometimes writers have to be persistent. Finally they gave in.

During the long years of persuasion, I had plenty of time to work out a plan – what to tackle, what to avoid. There are so many traps attached to writ-ing a literary book about death that I needed to take precautions.

I wanted to look at the image and language of cancer. I wanted to explore how women diagnosed with Alzheimer's as young as forty dealt with the progress of their disease. I wanted to understand the frustrations and lone-liness and sheer hard work taken on by middle-aged daughters caring for elderly parents on the brink of death. I wanted to explore how it felt to be the remaining partner – or, as somebody called it, 'the left-over life'. I wanted to ask whether the job of a funeral director impinges on or even takes over their ordinary family existence. I wanted to talk to the bereaved parents whose children had committed suicide. The boys of fourteen who had hanged themselves in the garage. The girls of twelve who had stuffed down hundreds of pills. The child who ran to a railway track and didn't stop. As a mother myself I could not contemplate what this must feel like, but I knew I could not leave it out.

Talking to people in extreme situations demands moral courage. On both sides. The ideal in interviewing and in writing is to be brave and if necessary bold, but not cruel or cold. It is also vital to avoid being over-sentimental or cloying. Compassion but not sugar. Curt held-back prose works best.

Books about death must avoid the crass, the weepie tone, the telling of easy lies if it is a memoir, or offering yards of dull statistics if it is a factual study. The latter was the hurdle I particularly needed to jump over. I managed it by giving each series of facts a human face. All 200 interviewees were from real life in several countries, but all were painted with a fiction writer's brush.

Invisibility around a subject like death has always been a challenge to writers.

Today a new impediment to writing books on death can be the celebrity on your shoulder. Serious writers may now be given a warning by agents and publishers. If a book about mortality is to succeed in today's market it may have a better chance if it is written by a celebrity or a celebrity's ghost. This is true also for books about fatal or chronic illnesses. Recently an established writer I know was told by four different agents that her expert memoir about the painful yet romantic relationship of her mother and father once they had both contracted Alzheimer's would be snapped up by a publisher 'if only she was a celebrity not a mere writer'.

I am glad to report, however, that books with death at their centre have recently had a major growth spurt. Today grief and bereavement shelves are bursting in bookstores on both sides of the Atlantic. I have come across several exceptional examples whose writers have leapt over all the literary obstacles with what appears to be ease, but must have been very hard work.

One book that has the force of life itself in its impudent and provocative rendering of dying is Anatole Broyard's meditation on mortality, *Intoxicated By My Illness*.

Broyard had already written about his father's death from cancer when he was a young man. His wife Alexandra said that the experience 'gave shading

and resonance to the rest of Anatole's life'.[13] When he was suddenly diagnosed with prostate cancer himself, his curiosity about the subject, far from
diminishing, actually expanded. He was determined to challenge his illness,
report on it, analyse it, and be seen to be forcefully alive until the last moment.
He did it with purpose and with pen. He made a point that could be very
useful to other writers – that in order to make illness bearable we need to
bring it under control by turning it into a narrative. We need to die with literary
style. And he did so because of the force, clarity, wit and urgency of his
writing.[14]

A finely wrought book called *The Darker Proof* is, in Emma Tennant's
words, 'proof indeed that a new literature, halfway between reportage and
fiction, is . . . being born'.[15] The book's subject is the initial Aids crisis. The co-
writers are Adam Mars-Jones and Edmund White, whose essays/stories are
factual and grim, but unsentimental and hauntingly written.[16]

In 'An Executor', for example, Mars-Jones delineates a real-life death scene.
Charles is dying of Aids. Gareth has been installed in Charles's house to run
errands, take phone calls, monitor visitors, clear out the fridge, bury the cat's
waste, remove Charles's waste – help the dying man leave what remains of
his life. Towards the end Charles is taken into hospital. Gareth visits to find
Charles' Catholic mother by the bed. Charles, resisting an oxygen mask,
resisting reconciliation with his mother, begins to Cheyne Stoke. What's that?
asks the mother. 'It is a particular sort of breathing,' Gareth tells her. 'It means
there's not far to go.' Charles's mother offers to run for a nurse but it is Gareth
who escapes to the doctors' room, empty except for one of the nurses. She
has a cigarette in her mouth and is looking at a list of patients on a
whiteboard: 'There was a sponge in her hand, and Gareth couldn't help
thinking that she was just about to wipe someone's name out . . . Then the
appalling idea came to him that she had already rubbed a name out, and that
the name was Charles's.' They return to the room, where Charles's mother is
still standing on the same spot, while Charles has moved from one state to
something else. The nurse closes his eyes – a practised gesture.

'It's over. He's gone. He's dead.'

There remains only the funeral. The mother, the father, the brother invite
Gareth to attend. The father shakes his hand warmly, the brother Arthur's

'handshake a few seconds later was even warmer and firmer, and contained an extra squeeze that represented apology'.

But then he adds the request that made it necessary. 'I wonder if I can ask you, my parents and I have been thinking, not to mention the cause of death?'

The brevity of the death scene, the spare sentences, the unflinching honesty of the language, make this story a model of how to deal with death in prose. Nothing is overblown, there is not a hint of sentimentality, there is hard black humour, but there is also compassion. Every brutal fact not only stands for itself but also embodies the fear and guilt of the onlookers and the defiant bravery of the victims.[17]

Brevity, honesty, dignity and a style that speaks for more than its subject are all important in writing about death, as they are in writing about friendship and sexuality. All three subjects lie at the core of our experience.

Notes

1. Rowan Somerville, *The Shape of Her*, W & N, London, 2010. Winner of 2010 Bad Sex Award.
2. Norman Mailer, *The Castle in the Forest*, Random House, New York, 2007.
3. Julie Powell, *Julie/Julia Project: Bon Appetit Blog*; e Pub Bud Books, Day 237, Recipe 357; *Julie and Julia: 365 Days, 524 Recipes, 1 Tiny Apartment Kitchen*, Little, Brown, New York, 2005.
4. Quoted by Frances Perraudin, Time NewsFeed, 15 October 2010. *Tony Blair, A Journey*, Hutchinson, London, 2010; Knopf, USA, 2010.
5. Rachel Johnson, *Shire Hell*, Penguin, 2008. Winner of 2008 Bad Sex Award.
6. Mark Kennedy, *The Guardian*, 30 November 2010.
7. Sally Cline, *Women, Passion and Celibacy*, Carol Southern Books, New York, 1993. Originally published as *Women, Celibacy and Passion*, André Deutsch, London, 1993.
8. Patricia Love, *Hot Monogamy: Essential Steps to More Passionate Intimate Lovemaking*, Plume, New York, 1995.
9. Adam Phillips, *Monogamy*, Faber and Faber, London, 1996.
10. Ernest Hemingway, *The Sun Also Rises*, Scribner, New York, 2003; William Shakespeare, *As You Like It*; Virginia Woolf, *A Room of One's Own*, Penguin Modern Classics, 2002; Hallam Tennyson Tennyson, *Alfred Lord Tennyson: A Memoir by his Son, Vol. 1*, Macmillan, London, 1897; Millicent Dillon, *A Little Original Sin. The Life and Work of Jane Bowles*, University of California Press, USA, 1998 (first published

1981); Millicent Dillon, *You are not I. A Portrait of Paul Bowles*, University of California Press, USA, 2000.

11. Suellen Grealy, *The Guardian*, 7 August 2004.

12. John Gray, *The Immortalization Commission. Science and the Strange Quest to Cheat Death*, Allen Lane, London, 2011.

13. Anatole Broyard, *Intoxicated By My Illness*, Clarkson Potter, New York, 1992; foreword by Oliver Sacks, p. xi.

14. There is similar work to Broyard's by the late Susan Sontag in *Illness as Metaphor and Aids and its Metaphors*; and *Regarding the Pain of Others*. Susan Sontag, *Illness as Metaphor and Aids and its Metaphors*, Picador, 2001; *Regarding the Pain of Others*, Picador, New York, 2004.

15. Review by Emma Tennant (quoted on the book jacket), Adam Mars-Jones and Edmund White, *The Darker Proof*, Faber and Faber, London, second revised edition, 1988.

16. Despite our caveat in the exclusions section of 'What is literary non-fiction?' I have included this as it may be useful to readers of Section 3.

17. Mars-Jones and White, *The Darker Proof*, pp. 36, 45.

10: Reflections on the mysteries of mind and body

by Sally Cline

When neurologists, medics or psychologists encounter strange syndromes in their patients, many of them write case studies to examine them. Some of these books are absorbing yet do not achieve the status of literary non-fiction. Some remain too closely linked to their technical genres; others are too rigidly factual. Facts, which themselves are unstable entities, are important, but, as Virginia Woolf wrote, a writer's vision can be hampered by facts.[1] Some non-fiction writers with a scientific background may be insufficiently imaginative or too conservative. Few choose to employ even the most relevant fictional or other literary tools that might add a new dimension to their non-fiction writing.

Some anthropologists, psychologists, scientists and medical writers, however, do achieve this fine balance and also manage to step outside their generic frame to write books of high literary merit.

Five writers who come to mind are Oliver Sacks, Rebecca Skloot, Lewis Wolpert, Kay Redfield Jamison and Siri Hustvedt.

Oliver Sacks, esteemed as a physician, and Professor of Neurology and Psychiatry at Columbia University, also holds a second post unusual for a scientist. It is that of being the first and only Columbia University Artist. This is not surprising, for the man who has become the world's best-known neurologist is also the bestselling author of eleven neurological adventure books. These case studies of broken minds by the man who describes himself as having become 'both a physician and a storyteller' offer us brilliant insights into the still unexplored territory of the brain.

Though Sacks grew up in a household full of doctors (his father and elder brothers were general practitioners and his mother a surgeon) where dinner-table talk was about medicine, it was never reduced to being about mere 'cases'. He says: 'In my parents' conversation, cases became biographies, stories of people's lives as they responded to illness or injury, stress or misfortune.'[2] It is this, perhaps, that inspired Sacks to treat his patients as a biographer would treat her subjects. It also enabled him to reveal landscapes inhabited by people with fragile minds and unquiet bodies as a novelist would reveal the shattered lives of her characters.

Sacks's case studies in *Awakenings* are so compulsively readable and so humane that the book, which hovers somewhere between a moral essay, a memoir and a romance, not only won the Hawthornden Prize in 1973 but also inspired a TV documentary, several radio and stage plays, and a major feature film. It is the extraordinary account of twenty patients, survivors of the great sleeping-sickness epidemic that swept much of the Western world in the 1920s, who forty years later experienced an explosive awakening through a new drug administered by Dr Sacks.[3] This miracle is moving enough; what happens after it (which I won't describe, in case some readers have not yet read *Awakenings*) is even more so.

In *The Man Who Mistook His Wife for a Hat*, the cast (and I use that word deliberately) are as strange as any in fiction. There is the man who leans like the Tower of Pisa and needs a spirit level built into his spectacles to keep himself upright. There is the woman who keeps flopping down because she has lost all sense of her own body. There is the musician, the man in the title, who has visual agnosia and cannot recognise everyday objects or familiar people: hence he genuinely did mistake his wife for a hat.[4]

All Oliver Sacks's books contain the same passion, the same generous imagination and the same literary talent to show readers the awesome powers of our minds and what happens when we lose our hold on them.

Like the most stimulating fiction, his books ask the question: What is identity and what happens when we lose it?

At the beginning of *The Man Who Mistook His Wife for a Hat*, Sacks uses two epigraphs. The first states: 'To talk of diseases is a sort of Arabian Nights entertainment' (William Osler). The second suggests: 'The physician is concerned (unlike the naturalist) . . . with a single organism, the human subject, striving to preserve its identity in adverse circumstances'[5] (Ivy McKenzie).

Sacks confesses that the doubleness of the epigraphs, the contrast between the physician and the story-spinner as well as that between physician and naturalist, and the scientist and the humanist, all correspond to a certain doubleness in himself.

'I feel myself a naturalist and a physician both; and that I am equally interested in diseases and people.' He concludes that he is 'equally, if inadequately, a theorist and dramatist . . . equally drawn to the scientific and the romantic, and continually see[s] both in the human condition'.[6]

Sacks believes that animals get diseases but only humans fall radically into sickness.

It is those humans who become the characters in Sacks's stories and the stories have a similar narrative arc to the historical pattern of disease.[7] The ancient medical idea is that disease has a course, which starts from contraction of disease and moves towards a crisis; then there is a relapse, before there is another resolving crisis. Similarly, in fiction, there is the stasis or quiet beginning; then an obstacle, followed by crisis, followed by change, until finally there is a decisive resolution.

He says: 'To restore the human subject . . . the suffering, afflicted, fighting, human subject – we must deepen a case history to a narrative or tale: only then do we have a "who" as well as a "what". A real person.'[7]

This is the stuff of literature as well as of science.

Rebecca Skloot (already referred to in Chapter 3) is the American award-winning science writer whose book *The Immortal Life of Henrietta Lacks* became a *New York Times* bestseller within weeks of its publication. Skloot, who as well as a scientific expert is also a Lecturer in Creative Non-Fiction at the University of Memphis, has written a heartbreaking account of the injustice and racism suffered by a poor black tobacco farmer whose cancer cells were taken without her knowledge or that of her family to become the basis of a multimillion-dollar industry, as well as one of the most significant tools in modern medicine.

The farmer's birth name was Henrietta Lacks, although the ignorant and the careless often called her Helen Lane or Helen Larson, but scientists who use the cancer cells cut from her cervix just months before she died usually call those human cells HeLa cells and leave the person nameless.

Rebecca Skloot has given the woman back her name, and has traced her tale and that of her disinherited, disenfranchised family. Through their story, as gripping as any mystery, she has raised vital issues relating to ethics, class, science and race.

Skloot starts her book as a novelist or a biographer might:

> There's a photo on the wall of a woman I've never met, its left corner torn and patched together with tape. She looks straight into the camera and smiles, hands on hips, dress suit neatly pressed, lips painted deep red. It's the late 1940s and she hasn't yet reached the age of thirty. Her light brown skin is smooth, her eyes still young and playful, oblivious to the tumor growing inside her – a tumor that would leave her five children motherless and change the future of medicine.[8]

With these words we have our protagonist and a clear hint of the tragedy in which she is about to be involved.

Skloot could have dropped her powerful and necessary research into any one of a dozen scientific journals and been read only by a handful of academic experts. She chose instead to make her work highly accessible, so that her exploration could reach dozens, hundreds, thousands of readers.

Skloot's clarity draws us in at the outset by simple homely explanations, such as the fact that under a microscope a cell looks a lot like a fried egg. 'It has a white (the cytoplasm) that's full of water and proteins to keep it fed, and a yolk (the nucleus) that holds all the genetic information that makes you you.' The cytoplasm, she adds, 'buzzes like a New York street. It's crammed full of molecules and vessels endlessly shuttling enzymes and sugars from one part of the cell to another, pumping water, nutrients, and oxygen in and out of the cell.' Who wouldn't feel a new world opening up after such an explanation?

And when she tells us that 'the nucleus is the brains of the operation; inside every nucleus within each cell in your body, there's an identical copy of your entire genome', a non-scientific reader will feel that the fundamental material is within her grasp and she can move on to the considerably more complex issues the book will deal with.[9]

Although the book is clear and accessible, it is also highly literary, for Skloot has a marvellous tale to tell, full of intrigue, and she knows how to tell it.

She first heard Henrietta Lacks's name in 1988, when she was sixteen (thirty-seven years after Henrietta's death), sitting in a community college biology class taught by Donald Defler, a gnomish bald-headed instructor.

Defler explained that the process of cell division (mitosis) makes it possible for embryos to grow into babies, but, if one enzyme misfires, if there is just one wrong protein activation, you have cancer! Mitosis goes haywire. Defler said, 'We learned that by studying cancer cells in culture.' Then Skloot watched him write two words in enormous print on the blackboard. The two words were HENRIETTA LACKS. Laconically he added, almost as an afterthought: 'She was a black woman.'[10]

Defler then explained to his class that, just before Henrietta died in 1951 from a vicious cervical cancer, a surgeon took samples of her tumour and put them in a Petri dish. Up till then no one had managed to keep human cells alive in culture, but Henrietta's cells were remarkable. They reproduced an entire generation every twenty-four hours, and they never stopped.

'They became the first immortal human cells ever grown in a laboratory,' writes Skloot.

When she learned that Henrietta's cells had now been living outside her body far longer than they had ever lived inside it, she was desperate to know who this woman was. Had her family been paid for her cells? What did they know of this process, which had turned Henrietta's cells into a research programme that made the understanding of cancer-causing genes possible, that helped develop drugs for treating herpes, haemophilia, influenza, leukaemia and Parkinson's disease?[11]

No one, it seemed, knew anything about Henrietta. Or her family. Or about any compensation for her low-income household. Or the ethics of the procedures. This despite the fact that the HeLa cells were one of the most critically important things that had happened to medicine in the previous one hundred years.

Thus began Rebecca Skloot's quest for an unknown black woman's identity and for the truth surrounding these policies, which shook the scientific world.

Skloot balances the drama of scientific discovery with ethical questions about who owns the materials of our bodies, and how powerless people can be deprived even of their identity. Her book is as gripping as a fine detective yarn combined with a quest biography. It has the wisdom of science and the wit and fire of literature.

Embryologist **Lewis Wolpert**, Emeritus Professor in Cell and Developmental Biology at University College London, is a broadcaster and distinguished author whose non-fiction prose reads like fiction or a creative memoir. He shares his passionate enquiry into depression, his most famous subject, with the American memoirist **Kay Redfield Jamison** whose book *Touched with Fire*, Wolpert said, had particularly influenced him.[12]

Like Oliver Sacks, Jamison holds two contrasting positions: one as Professor of Psychiatry at Johns Hopkins University, the other as Honorary Professor of English at St Andrews University. In her discussions of 'madness' (she always uses that term), Jamison's involvement in literature as well as science leads her to include portraits of writers such as Dante, Blake, Byron, Lowell, Sexton and Fitzgerald, who were all plunged into desperate mental states.

As well as being expert theorists and practitioners in depressive illnesses, these two writer-scientists are also sufferers, Wolpert of severe clinical depression and Jamison of lifelong manic depression. They both employ the memoir form to elaborate and analyse their own and other people's depressive conditions.

Wolpert begins his memoir of intense grief and suffering with three powerful sentences: 'It was the worst experience of my life. More terrible even than watching my wife die of cancer. I am ashamed to admit that my depression felt worse than her death but it is true.'[13]

Wolpert describes his pre-depressed self as a person who believed in the Sock School of Psychiatry: 'just pull them up when feeling low'.[14] But, as he was to find out, to his great cost, such an attitude does not work with serious depression. He describes a battery of dreadful fears and anxieties. He became totally self-involved and totally negative. He thought about suicide most of the time. Huddled in his bed for many hours each day, he was unable to work or write, ride his bike or even leave the house. He was afraid to go out alone.

He began to experience frightening physical symptoms: his skin felt on fire, he had uncontrollable twitches, insomnia most nights, and terror that he would be unable to urinate. He was frightened that he would never work again, or even partially recover, and that he would go mad.

He felt that, as he said, 'Depressives are victims in the sense that they have a frightening and disabling illness.' But he became aware that those around him were suffering too.

At that time there was such a stigma around mental illness that his wife, the writer Jill Neville, embarrassed by his depression, told their friends and colleagues that he was exhausted from a minor heart condition.

After living month after achingly hard month with her husband's disease which had taken him over, while seriously ill with breast cancer herself (she died in 1997, two years before the book was published), Jill Neville did encourage Wolpert to write about it as powerfully as he was able. Defying the stigma and silence around the disease, Wolpert finally determined to do so.

His purpose was fourfold: to help those like Jill, living or working with a sufferer, to understand depression, since, as he acknowledged, 'depressives are not easy to be with'; to help victims understand themselves; to remove the stigma; and last – but for Wolpert most significantly – to try to understand the nature of 'this dreadful affliction' in scientific terms.[15]

Nonetheless, the project of writing about a searing experience is a literary endeavour as much as or more than a scientific one, and Wolpert's book is both. His language is as direct, rhythmic and euphonious as his expertise is vigorous and clear. And in the end his passion and compassion take precedence over his detached scientific account and analysis of the disease. The factual side of his enquiry does not submerge the literary quality of his anatomy of depressive illness.

Partly this is due to the fact that he balances his historical and clinical understanding of the theories of depression with the vivid personal cases of the American Pulitzer Prize-winning poet Theodore Roethke, the British novelist Virginia Woolf, the American poet Robert Lowell and the English art critic and painter John Ruskin. Partly it is due to the way Wolpert takes a wide-ranging approach. He writes about discoveries and healing treatments in the East as well as the West and describes Japanese psychotherapies based on Buddhism. He also uses paintings and engravings from world-renowned artists to help him reflect upon and understand the 'malignant sadness' in his book of that title.

The success of his book in literary terms is that in part it was a personal quest, like Robert Burton's *The Anatomy of Melancholy*, to try to understand the nature of depression, as well as show how it can be prevented or treated. He takes from Burton one excellent piece of advice for sufferers: 'Be not idle.'[16] This truly is worth passing on to those afflicted with the disease.

Kay Redfield Jamison's *An Unquiet Mind: A Memoir of Moods and Madness* has a similar candour, courage, humour and humanity. Jamison examines manic depression with its exhilarating highs and devastating lows from two perspectives: that of the professional trying to heal her many patients at the mercy of the disease, and that of the patient trying to heal herself while subject to the same shame, the same terrors, the same cruel allure.

Her book is a landmark in the history of writing about manic-depressive illness. Jamison, already a foremost authority on the disease, decided to explode any notion that she was a detached observer. Far from it. Her own work and life were being torn apart by the horrors of the disease and she determined to write about it openly.

She describes how as early as her medical student years she could be found at two in the morning running crazily around the UCLA hospital parking lot, 'trying to use up a boundless, restless, manic energy'. She says of those times, 'I was running fast, but slowly going mad.'[17]

By the time she was twenty-eight, she was, she says, 'well on my way to madness'.[18] Within three months she was manic beyond recognition. Having been from childhood relentlessly caught up in cycles of frightening depression and mercurial mania, she now became by necessity and inclination a student of moods, then a healer of those same disorders that have killed thousands, and on several occasions almost killed her.

The quality of her prose becomes clear early on in the book, where she discusses different belief systems about the illnesses that make monsters of us.

> *The Chinese believe that before you can conquer a beast you first must make it beautiful. In some strange way, I have tried to do that with manic-depressive illness. It has been a fascinating, albeit deadly, enemy and companion. I have found it to be seductively*

complicated, a distillation both of what is finest in our natures,
and of what is most dangerous.[19]

Because her manias, in their milder forms, in the early days, were intoxicating states that gave rise to an incomparable flow of thoughts and a ceaseless energy, she refused both help and medication. Later she was able to say, 'The major clinical problem in treating manic-depressive illness is not that there are not effective medications – there are – but that patients so often refuse to take them.'[20]

It was only when she had been almost submerged by the illness, and by the personal knowledge that manic depression distorts moods, destroys rational thought, incites destructive behaviours and erodes the desire to live, that she herself sought medical help.

Jamison, like Wolpert, had many concerns about writing this book. Clinicians have always been reluctant to make their psychiatric problems known publicly. When she wrote the book she had no idea what the consequences might be for either her personal or her professional life. 'But, whatever the consequences, they are bound to be better than continuing to be silent.'

She says she was tired of hiding, tired of misspent and knotted energies, tired of the hypocrisy of acting as though she had something to hide. 'One is what one is,' she says bravely. 'And the dishonesty of hiding behind a degree, or a title, or any manner and collection of words, is still exactly that: dishonest.'[21]

She remains concerned about the effects on her life of the book's openness. But the advantage of having had manic-depressive illness for more than thirty years is that, finally, very little seemed insurmountably hard. 'Much like crossing the Bay Bridge when there is a storm over the Chesapeake, one may be terrified to go forward, but there is no question of going back.'[22]

At the start and the conclusion of the book, she found herself comforted by Robert Lowell's crucial question: *Yet why not say what happened?*[23]

There is a fifth (and my final) writer, who is not a scientist but who has explored the grey and challenging areas between brain, intellect and body, between truth and confabulation, and between consciousness and reality. She has recently demonstrated a nearly complete mastery (by a non-specialist) of the extremely specialised field of neuropsychiatry. She is the gifted **Siri Hustvedt**, novelist, essayist, literary non-fiction writer, who is also writing-tutor for patients at New York's Payne Whitney Psychiatric Clinic.

Her recent book *The Shaking Woman or A History of My Nerves* is a quest to understand her own mysterious condition, an intermittent syndrome, a violent seizure from the neck down to her feet, which first attacked her when she was speaking at a memorial event for her father. Her arms faltered, then flapped, then waved. Her legs shook so hard she thought she would fall over. Every limb was out of control. Her mother later described it as watching an electrocution. Yet throughout this extraordinary performance by her body, her mind was steady and controlled.[24] Determined to discover whether this attack, repeated on several occasions, was triggered by emotion, nerves or something else entirely, Hustvedt began her quest for understanding, if not for cure.

She takes readers on a thought-provoking and mind-enhancing journey through philosophy, psychiatry, neuroscience and medical history in search of a diagnosis. She goes to an array of disillusioned, often disbelieving doctors. None of them has a satisfactory answer. She has MRI scans. There seems to be nothing wrong with her brain. She talks to neurologists and psychologists. She has no recognisable illness. The shaking is not nerves. It is not a panic attack. It is not epilepsy. It is not even conversion disorder, the twenty-first-century name for nineteenth-century hysteria. She is a medical mystery.

But while she investigates her own frightening symptoms, she also treads the murky space between psychological and neurological disorders and enquires about what lurks there.

She begins to ask more urgent questions than her medical advisers do. How does physiology affect personality? What is pain? What is suffering? Can we abstract it from its social and cultural context? What part do memory and language play in our chemical or physiological reactions and responses? Where does the self begin or end?

Hustvedt, who is one of this book's distinguished guest contributors, decides to write about it. Not in order to master her illness – indeed, she is never able to do that. The book ends, but the shaking continues. She writes in order to own her illness. Every good memoir is an act of ownership. Writing helps her to accept that her illness is both a mystery and a part of her.

Hustvedt above all is a storyteller with a moving capacity for empathy. She is a pure novelist who trades in narratives. But she is also a sceptic with a deep knowledge of neuroscience and medicine. Her findings are complex and difficult, but she has an enviable ability to reframe them in bracing, clear prose. She brings a writer's insight to a scientific challenge, and even more significantly to the awesome dangers of the inner life.

Notes

1. Virginia Woolf, 'The Art of Biography', in *The Death of the Moth and Other Essays*, Harcourt Brace Jovanovitch, 1939, pp. 187–97. Virginia Woolf, struggling to write a biography of the artist Roger Fry, suggested that facts were hindering her attempt to get at a real life which in her view was an inner life.
2. Oliver Sacks, *The Mind's Eye*, Picador, London, 2010, p. ix.
3. Oliver Sacks, *Awakenings*, Picador, London, 1973.
4. Oliver Sacks, *The Man Who Mistook His Wife for a Hat*, Picador, London, 1986.
5. Sacks, *The Man Who Mistook His Wife for a Hat*, epigraphs.
6. Sacks, *The Man Who Mistook His Wife for a Hat*, p. ix.
7. Sacks, *The Man Who Mistook His Wife for a Hat*, p. x.
8. Rebecca Skloot, *The Immortal Life of Henrietta Lacks*, Pan Books, London, 2011, p. 1.
9. Skloot, *Henrietta Lacks*, p. 3.
10. Skloot, *Henrietta Lacks*, p. 5.
11. Skloot, *Henrietta Lacks*, p. 4.
12. Kay Redfield Jamison, *Touched With Fire: Manic-Depressive Illness and the Artistic Temperament*, Free Press Paperback, Simon and Schuster, New York, 1993.
13. Wolpert, *Malignant Sadness*, p. vii.
14. Wolpert, *Malignant Sadness*, p. viii.
15. Wolpert, *Malignant Sadness*, p. ix.
16. Wolpert, *Malignant Sadness*, p. 185.
17. Kay Redfield Jamison, *An Unquiet Mind. A Memoir of Moods and Madness*, Alfred Knopf, New York, 1995; Picador, London, 1997, p. 3.
18. Jamison, *An Unquiet Mind*, p. 4.
19. Jamison, *An Unquiet Mind*, p. 5.
20. Jamison, *An Unquiet Mind*, p. 6.
21. Jamison, *An Unquiet Mind*, p. 7.
22. Jamison, *An Unquiet Mind*, p. 8.
23. Quoted in Jamison, *An Unquiet Mind*, p. 8.
24. Siri Hustvedt, *The Shaking Woman or A History of My Nerves*, Sceptre, 2010.

Part 2:
Tips and tales

Guest contributors

Lisa Appignanesi

Lisa Appignanesi is the author of *All About Love: Anatomy of an Unruly Emotion* **and** *Mad, Bad and Sad: A History of Women and the Mind Doctors from 1800 to the Present,* **and among other non-fictions, the acclaimed family memoir** *Losing the Dead.* **She has also written several novels. She is a former President of English PEN, Chair of the Freud Museum London, and Honorary Professor in English and Medical Humanities at King's College, London.**

The term 'non-fiction' has always seemed to me a strange sort of negative beast, as if fiction, the making up of stories, always came first and was the primary form of putting words together. It's a catch-all category, of course, and makes about as much sense as defining all prose as non-poetry. It's also peculiar to English classification. The French speak of 'essais', which at least has the grace of harking back to Montaigne and forefronting an attempt to think about the world.

In my writing life, I seem to have navigated an odd course between fiction and its negation, always half-wishing when I'm immersed in one that I were embarked on the other. I want the free flight of story when I'm hunkered down in facts and wish for a character who could offer a statement contradicted by another character. Authority is such a difficult place. On the other hand, when I'm writing fiction, I often enough find myself wishing that I could fill the blank page with some meaty matter that didn't demand the difficult act of creating a scene which then had to leave most of the matter out in order to live. And so on it goes . . . Non-fiction depends on remembering your research, fiction on forgetting it.

Over the years I've noticed that my non-fiction has learned not a little about storytelling, narrative energy and scene-setting from my fiction and has been enlivened by it. As I was pondering the writing of my family memoir, *Losing the Dead*, I realised that 'voice' was as crucial here as in fiction. I just hadn't been able to write the memoir, though all the research was in place, until the voice of the book came to me. It's my own, of course, but translated into words ownership is always a creation.

My last two books have been non-fictions and I'm rather proud of them because, like *Losing the Dead*, they seem to work well read aloud and have a certain pace. In *Mad, Bad and Sad*, I traced a history of two hundred years of the growth of the mind-doctoring professions and changing understandings of the mind, madness and normality. Facts, argument and speculation were nurtured by story, in this instance by the cases and lives of women.

In *All About Love*, my anatomy of that unruly emotion – and the last space where 'madness' is still permitted in our normalising society – once again I got nowhere until the voice of the book finally revealed itself. Then ideas, analysis, interviews, stories and history began to fall into place.

It may be just a negative, but I'd say the writing of non-fiction has become as much of an adventure for me as the writing of fiction.

Rosemary Bailey

Rosemary Bailey is an award-winning travel writer of three books about the French Pyrenees. *Life in a Postcard* describes her life in a mountain village, *The Man who Married a Mountain* is about a romantic nineteenth-century mountaineer and his quest for the sublime, and *Love and War in the Pyrenees*, an investigation of the Second World War, was described by the *Jewish Chronicle* as 'a quiet triumph of historical reconstruction'. In 1997, she wrote *Scarlet Ribbons: A Priest with AIDS*, the story of her brother and the remarkable support he received from his Yorkshire mining village parish. She is a regular tutor for the Arvon Foundation.

I sometimes feel a fraud being called a travel writer, since all I have ever done is go to one place and write about that. France. South of, more specifically the Pyrenees. In truth, one particular valley. But actually that I think is the point – real travel writing requires total immersion. The immersion of writers like Gerald Brenan, in *South from Granada*, who lived the life of the village high in the hills of Andalucia in the 1920s, or Colin Thubron, who says when he travels he never even takes another book with him. Nor camera or recording equipment. The best travel writing demands dedicated observation and total engagement with place and people. It is more about place than about the journey, though no doubt many are initially compelled by wanderlust. For Freya Stark, it was her passion for the Arab world, her deep fascination for its people, that motivated and informed her travels. She learned Arabic, of course.

Her level of observation – making notes from the back of a camel as often as not – was almost forensic. She took photographs too but it is her assiduous daily notes that form the basis of her writing. Journals written at the time, drawn on sometimes many years later, have proved invaluable for me too. Though written without thought to style, they yield a freshness and immediacy that re-creates the moment. I once made the mistake of thinking on a particularly rushed exploratory trip that I could take photos and write it all when I got home. Not so. There was nothing there. No texture, no detail, critically no response.

Thus, I am convinced that travel has to be written. Photos help, of course. But I want not just the information gleaned by the explorer but also their response to the experience. How else could that be conveyed except by writing? Format doesn't matter, and the huge number of travel blogs today means that anyone can do it. But TV travel does not do it for me. It is too superficial. There are too many layers between the presenter and the audience – the film crew lurking somewhere, however much they try to convince us that the traveller is soulfully alone in the middle of the desert; the researchers who have prepared the information. There is no authentic response to the place.

Not only do the best travel writers offer a knowledgeable and authentic experience of the place they observe, I think they also fill an important gap of reportage. No longer do we have foreign correspondents in Uzbekistan and every far-flung corner of the world. We need writers who travel and embed themselves in order to inform us. And better indeed that they should be independent and not paid for by governments or media barons. Of course, modern technology means the locals can tell us what is going on these days and this empowerment is vital, but we also need writers with knowledge and experience of these worlds, writers who have been there and observed and recorded before the precious mosque was destroyed, the Roman bridge blown up, the tribal village obliterated by floods.

Gillian Beer

Dame Gillian Beer has been the King Edward VII Professor of English Literature, University of Cambridge, and most recently the Andrew W. Mellon Senior Scholar at the Yale Center for British Art, 2009–2011. Among her books are Darwin's Plots **(3rd edition 2009) and** Virginia Woolf: the Common Ground **(1996). She has twice been a judge for the Booker Prize and has also judged the Orange Prize and the David Cohen Prize. She is on the Board of Writers' Centre Norwich and on Arts Council England, East. Her collected and annotated edition of Lewis Carroll's Poems is forthcoming from Penguin and she is completing a study of the** Alice **books,** Alice in Space.

Sometimes I think I write for the twenty minutes of euphoria when a piece is finished, and that might explain why I so like writing essays (twenty minutes' reward for seven thousand words, instead of the delayed gratification of eighty thousand book-length). But that's not all of it. I love the immersion of writing and the curiosity of research. It's strange to enter another person's mind and discover there further reaches of time, different rhythms of thinking, new kinds of knowledge and emotions grappling the writer, forcing form, held by form. Words on the page take us past the page into other communities as well as other individuals. We come to know the past from the inside, inside the head, and yet palpable. Reading gives us intimate encounters with experiences we could not otherwise have shared and it does so through detail and, more surprisingly, through abstraction. Literary critics are the reader as writer: we write to plumb and to garnish the text, to expand its meaning for readers now, though it may have been written in quite unfamiliar circumstances that we can never quite recapture. We can't turn ourselves into past readers intact but we can play between our own assumptions and theirs, learning the means of their experience.

I'm fascinated by how we come to have new ideas. How do writers turn language, which is communal and soaked in history, in a new direction that can encompass thoughts quite out of kilter with the society's current assumption? Ideas don't fully exist until they are communicated. They can't thrive in an idiolect; they need an audience. The writer has to show his or her readers how to read anew, how words can be pressed into fresh shapes for meaning, how old metaphors can be turned over to reveal their underside, those unconsidered consequences that reveal connections we'd not foreseen. That's one reason why I've spent so much time reading and thinking about Darwin's language. Darwin worked with an open non-technical vocabulary: the great family, the struggle for life, the face of nature, natural selection, contingency, imperfection. This open language generated contradictory stories in which leftover elements in metaphors began to work out new narratives: the descent of man, the ascent of man, the interdependence of all forms of life, the struggle and destruction. In order to understand how he controlled the ebullience of his imagination, I had to learn much about nineteenth-century habits of thought among theologians, natural historians, political theorists, humourists, economists and family dynamics. I realised more than I ever had done before how books are always in conversation with other books of the time and the past as well as with imagined readers. That sense of the thick present of the past is what I most try to communicate when I write. These people were as alive as we are. And writing mercifully allows some of that experience and that thinking to survive, close up to the present reader. I write to find what lies latent and available, as well as for the pleasure of what's manifest.

Bidisha

Bidisha, writer, broadcaster, critic, was writing for international magazines at 14 and had her first book published at 16. *Venetian Masters* **(2008), her third book, became a bestselling travel memoir. Most recently published is** *Beyond the Wall: Writing a Path Through Palestine.* **Bidisha presents and appears on arts programmes for radio and TV, including** *The Word, Nightwaves, Saturday Review, The Strand, The Review Show, Front Row* **and** *Woman's Hour.* **She has judged the Orange Prize (2009) and the John Llewellyn Rhys Prize (2010).**

I feel I write such dismal, hectoring articles. In place of wit, I have hollow sarcasm. Instead of insight, carping complaint. I write pressed against the glass ceiling, joints aching, cold from the disdain that flows from above. I should be quiet about women's issues – we are only 52 per cent of the world after all. If I rock the boat, it will remain intact but I will topple out, drown and die.

Yet something happens when I write. The small oblong of the article carves a door into the universe and thousands of women charge through it. For every one of my vignettes about sexism and whatnot, women write to me with dozens of their own. All over the world we are living, thinking and suffering exactly the same things to a greater or lesser degree.

Our fire comes from our fatigue of the past and our fear that the future will be no different. We have nothing to lose. Society as it is cannot do anything worse to us than what it has already done and continues to do. We are tired of feeling the same rage and despair about the same things. We want to walk with indecorous grins, not at the edge of the world but at its heart. We want to walk unpunished, not leered or jeered at, not harassed, not purchased or coerced, not hounded out, not in fear of being followed, beaten, raped, judged.

It does not matter what the gentlemen of science, the captains of industry and the pillars of society think about feminism. We fight the casual rage of their misogyny with the precision of our truthfulness and the dignity of our pacifism. We recount our experiences, describe our emotions, express our hopes, identify our fears and gift to the perpetrators an unvarnished representation of the effects of their sabotage. They may not like it, but there it is.

Testimony, witness, confession, history, account. These names are given to the words of prisoners, the unfairly accused, the tortured, victims and survivors, people who have seen or experienced something terrible, people with an unspoken past, people whose knowledge weighs on their conscience or their heart, those who petition for justice and those who have come to understand a transcendent spiritual truth. Women are all this and more. I will not go on about 'the need for feminism' because it is obvious, but here's a brief, unpoetic rundown: domestic violence, rape, harassment, sexual and labour exploitation, victim-blaming, stalking, discrimination, marginalisation, objectification. The classics.

And still we fight. The women's movement is the most successful and widespread non-violent revolution in world history. Every woman who writes and speaks about what is happening to her, her sisters, her mother and grandmothers, her daughter, makes it easier for the next woman to write and speak. Every woman who stands up catches the light so that other women may see. Every drop of ink takes the shape of a woman's footprint, walking to freedom.

Lizzie Collingham

Lizzie Collingham is the author of *Imperial Bodies: The Physical Experience of the Raj, Curry: A Tale of Cooks and Conquerors* **and** *The Taste of War: World War II and the Battle for Food.* **Having taught History at Warwick University, she became a Research Fellow at Jesus College, Cambridge. She is now an independent scholar and writer.**

I write history from the position of someone who as a child dreamed of becoming a novelist. History may be what fascinates me now but the pleasure I derive from research and writing is related to what I find satisfying in fiction. Research, when it is going well, becomes, like a good novel which draws one into its world, a form of escapism. I spent many hours in the India Office archive working on my first book on the physical experience of the British living in India. Here I read the letters and diaries of members of the Raj and lost myself in their lives. It was easy to form an image of Fanny Wells, so oppressed by the heat that she flouted nineteenth-century convention and risked her morality by leaving off her drawers and wore only one petticoat under her muslin dress. Another letter writer kept me on tenterhooks as to her fate as the pile of her letters I had not read dwindled, and there was talk of a move to Cawnpore just as the date for the terrible events of the Indian Mutiny began to draw closer.

During the research for my latest book, on food during the Second World War, hours would pass unnoticed in the library as I pored over dry tomes full of lists and figures. I was surprised to find that the dullest of books could be absorbing. A study of Japanese agriculture, which was apparently tediously detailed, became a source of fascination as it enabled me to understand how little room for manoeuvre there was within the Japanese food system under the circumstances of total war. Figures for vegetable production meshed with the complaints of a diarist I had been reading whose family's vegetable ration consisted of just two large radishes for a week. A Japanese soldier's account of the discovery of an American GI's discarded chewing gum on a leaf he was about to eat brought home the figure that, for every four tons of supplies the Americans shipped to their ground troops, the Japanese received only two pounds. What interests me as a historian and a writer is the process of analysing material in an attempt to explain the driving forces in history and, in conjunction with this, the creation of a narrative which connects the broad sweep of history with individual lived experience.

William Dalrymple

William Dalrymple was born in Scotland but has lived in Delhi on and off for the last twenty-five years. He is the author of seven books about India and the Islamic world, including *City of Djinns* (Thomas Cook Travel Book Award and *Sunday Times* Young British Writer of the Year Prize), *White Mughals* (Wolfson Prize for History and SAC Scottish Book of the Year Prize), *The Last Mughal* (Duff Cooper Prize and Vodafone Crossword Award for Non-Fiction) and *Nine Lives: In Search of the Sacred in Modern India* (Asia House Literary Award). He is one of the founders and a co-director of the annual Jaipur Literary Festival.

Everyone goes about writing a travel book in a different way. For me, the biggest mistake was to try to keep a logbook when I was exhausted at the end of the day. I think it is absolutely vital to scribble constantly: not so much full sentences, so much as lists of significant detail: the colour of a hillside, the shape of a tulip, the way a particular tree haunts a skyline. Creating fine prose comes later – back at home at the keyboard.

Getting it down is especially important when writing dialogue – the key to any half-decent travel book: you simply can't remember the exact words even half an hour later, never mind at the end of an exhausting day. The travel writers I really admire all keep exceptionally detailed notes: Theroux, Thubron, Chatwin.

If nineteenth-century travel writing was principally about place – about filling in the blanks of the map and describing remote places that few had seen – I think that some of the best twenty-first-century travel writing is about people: exploring the extraordinary diversity that still exists in the world beneath the veneer of globalisation.

The second golden rule is to try to enjoy yourself. If you lose interest in your own journey, the reader can tell immediately and soon loses interest himself.

The third golden rule is to be open to the unexpected. In 1990, I went up to Simla to interview two old Stayers On who had lived in Delhi in the 1930s and would, I hoped, be able to re-create that lost world of the Raj. In the event, I arrived ten years too late: both had gone senile and now imagined they were being persecuted by Jewish prostitutes who popped up from beneath the floorboards to put dope in their food. I failed to get anything at all useable about 1930s Delhi, and left disappointed that I had wasted an afternoon. It was only when I told my wife, Olivia, that she pointed out that the bizarre afternoon would make an excellent sequence in itself. It became one of my favourite sections in *City of Djinns*.

You often come across the best stories when you have ticked off your interviews and visits for the day and settled down to have a drink in a bar or have dinner. It's often when you close your notebook and relax that you stumble across the most intriguing characters.

A final rule: capture all the senses. When you write about place, include significant sounds and smells. How your body responds to a particular location – the roll of perspiration down the forehead, the grit of sand in your shoes, the grind of cicadas or the smell of frying chillies.

The same is true of building up a character: the way someone smells, or the timbre of their voice. Most important of all is dialogue: a well-chosen snatch of conversation can bring a person to life in a single sentence.

CITY AND ISLINGTON
SIXTH FORM COLLEGE
283-309 GOSWELL ROAD
LONDON EC1V 7LA
TEL 020 7520 0652

Stevie Davies

Stevie Davies is Professor of Creative Writing at Swansea University, her home town. She is a Fellow of the Royal Society of Literature and a Fellow of the Welsh Academy. Stevie has published widely in the fields of fiction, literary criticism, biography and popular history. *The Element of Water* **(2001) was longlisted for the Booker and Orange Prizes and won the Arts Council of Wales Book of the Year. Her new novel,** *Into Suez,* **set in the years leading up to the Suez Crisis of 1956, was published by Parthian in 2010. Her website is www.steviedavies.com.**

Strange meetings take place in antiquarian libraries: in their silence we catch the echo of voices stilled for centuries. This experience was especially powerful as I researched *Unbridled Spirits: Women of the English Revolution, 1640–1660.* The extraordinary women radicals had managed to escape the rigid bondings of gender and caste, in the name of spiritual equality. They raised defiant voices in a world disrupted by fratricidal civil war where, briefly, press censorship was overturned, the newspaper was born, print became cheaper and Puritan sects gained a public theatre. Women fleetingly gained control of the pen to state their opinions on a range of public subjects, from tithes to the state of the army, from the theory of magistracy to nice calculations of the end of the world. Although the pen was wrenched away from them at or before the Restoration, they had spoken loud and clear. Antiquarian collectors saved rare copies of these ephemera.

And what voices, militant, apocalyptic! In the British Library I listened in to Lady Eleanor Davies, the anagrammatical, anti-grammatical prophetess, vilified as 'Abominable stinking great simnel-faced excrement'. In Chetham's Library, Manchester, I met Katharine Chidley, Leveller and Puritan iconoclast, the first woman into print in 1640. Katharine was all for razing the churches of England to the ground, especially anathematising those 'old Chiming chimneys of the drunken Whore of Babylon' (bell towers). For Thomas Edwards, heresiographer and author of *Gangraena*, Katharine was 'the brazen-faced audacious old woman, likened unto Jael'. In the John Rylands Library of Manchester I met Anna Trapnel, the notorious Fifth Monarchist, specialising in twelve-hour trances and catatonic doggerel prophecies, taken down at her bedside by scribes. And in the Friends' Meeting House Library I made the acquaintance of the magnificent Quaker women: Barbara Blaugdone, Mary Fisher (who walked alone to Turkey to convert the Sultan), Mary Dyer, hanged at Boston, Margaret Fell, the movement's 'nursing mother'. Most moving of all: Dorothy Waugh, ex-serving maid of Westmoreland and the only woman in history to write about the experience of wearing the scold's bridle.

The leaves of their tracts bear all the signs of time; their voices remain with their dissident energy. The writer of biography or history learns a new language in which to participate, a vernacular English in which Bible English, Early Modern English and local dialect meet. It's only when one is thinking in this tongue that the full connection is made.

Colin Grant

Colin Grant is a historian and BBC radio producer. He is the author of *Negro with a Hat: The Rise and Fall of Marcus Garvey* **and** *I&I, The Natural Mystics: Marley, Tosh & Wailer*. **His account of life with his father in 1970s Luton,** *Bageye at the Wheel*, **was published by Jonathan Cape in June 2012.**

Naipaul's ghost

'There are no facts,' Jamaicans will tell you, 'only versions.' In the same breath, locals will add that the laws of the land are not to be trusted as those laws are written in pencil and are forever being rubbed out. Travelling round the island, you're left with the feeling of history eclipsed. The national newspaper, the *Gleaner*, not long ago considered it bad manners to reflect on the country's troubled past. 'Colour questions are not permitted in these columns,' it trumpeted in an editorial. Yet colour and the idea of a pigmentocracy are central to any serious writing on Jamaican history.

Writing about the Caribbean has vexed many people, especially its inhabitants. Though illuminated in literature, the region has remained an area of darkness. A succession of British writers from Anthony Trollope through to Patrick Leigh Fermor and latterly Ian Thomson has cast the islands in a very gloomy light: the attitude struck sometimes seems patrician and dismissive.

About the pearl of the Antilles, Trollope concluded: 'If we could, we would fain forget Jamaica altogether.'

As the child of black Jamaican parents, what stance should I take? The temptation is to try to leaven past literary insults by revealing a gentler, more humane side of the country. Though I've been travelling back and forth between England and Jamaica for twenty-five years, I've settled on an approximation of the innocent abroad. With this insider/outsider approach, I hope to elicit a revelatory and rewarding tension.

Both my books have been framed by dramatic events which pose a question in the opening to be answered in the text. The first was the image of the Black Nationalist leader Marcus Garvey reading his own obituary and then falling down dead; and in *I&I: The Natural Mystics* it was the vision of Bunny Wailer, one of the giants of reggae, at a comeback concert, being bottled off stage.

I've embraced narrative techniques that are more commonly found in novels – tension, drama, denouement. The narrative of *Negro with a Hat* centres on the rivalry and 'narcissism of minor differences' of Marcus Garvey and his nemesis W.E.B. Dubois. The lasting tension from *I&I* comes from the elevation of Bob Marley over his compadres, Peter Tosh and Bunny Wailer, as first among equals.

Finally, when embarking on any non-fiction work on the contemporary Caribbean, one must come to terms with V.S. Naipaul. I've laughed and squirmed in equal measure when reflecting on the Trinidad-born writer's exploration of Caribbean life. More than any other, Naipaul's is the literary ghost abroad in the land. It's time to uncouple the freight of negativity associated with him.

When I sit down to write, rather than Naipaul it is the nineteenth-century Jamaican journalist John B. Russworm at my elbow. Russworm wrote that he was determined to give readers a more accurate portrayal of black life, because 'too long have others spoke for us [such that] our vices and our degradations are ever arrayed against us, but our virtues are passed unnoticed'.

Rahila Gupta

Rahila Gupta is a freelance journalist, writer and activist. With Kiranjit Ahluwalia, she wrote *Circle of Light* **(reissued as** *Provoked***), the story of a battered woman who killed her violent husband, and co-scripted the feature film:** *Provoked,* **which was based on the book and released in 2007. She has edited a collection of political essays on the issues faced by black women in Britain,** *From Homebreakers to Jailbreakers: Southall Black Sisters.* **Her last book,** *Enslaved: The New British Slavery,* **tells the stories of five undocumented migrants and explores the role of immigration controls in enslaving people with no formal status here. She writes for** *The Guardian* **and** *openDemocracy* **among other papers and websites.**

Is non-fiction really fiction parading as the truth once it has been given a literary makeover? I write about the voiceless, mainly women and young girls, who have been through the most horrific abuse and degradation. I am driven by the desire to change the system that left them open to abuse. I know that I have to play on the readers' heartstrings so that they are more open to the radical political solutions that I may propose. In order to do this, I must build a character, find a voice, decide at which point to begin her story so that the hooks have sunk firmly into the reader's brain. These are 'literary' decisions made in order to progress a political project. But are the political and the literary in conflict or is the literary a handmaiden to the political?

It is from a political impulse that I want to make the subject of my auto/biography (I will explain the slash in a minute) more than the sum of her victimised parts. I want her voice to rise above the quaver in which she describes her genital mutilation and tell us about the music she likes and the dreams she has for her future. So far, the political and literary aims are in harmony.

But when I return the 'I' to her, I immediately introduce fiction into the relationship between reader and subject. She is not talking directly to them; I mediate that conversation. I could maintain the fiction by squashing my authorial voice completely. But no! I am so committed to the integrity of her voice that I do not want to put any information in her mouth that she could not have possessed, say, a knowledge of the homicide legislation, which is critical to an understanding of the story, so I insert factual passages in the third person which interrupt her story, perhaps upsetting the reader by breaking into their tête-à-tête. Hence the slash: my books are both autobiography and biography.

How far can I push the truth in the portrayal of her character? Literature demands a flawed, contradictory character which elicits a complicated response. Political objectives dictate that our sympathies must not be alienated. In my book *Provoked*, the story of an Asian woman who sets her husband on fire when she can no longer stand his brutality, she mourns the loss of her expensive velvet curtains in the fire that gave her husband 40 per cent burns. I thought long and hard about including it in the final draft. In the end I left it in – part of the anguish of that relationship was located in the long hours of factory work that she did, trying to make ends meet, managing both children and work, while her husband played the field and then came home and beat her.

And before I shape that voice, she too shapes it, motivated by self-justification, self-preservation or even glorification. We should not make the mistake of thinking that the subject has no agency. We tell stories to ourselves about who we are, stories that allow us to sleep at night. Imagine how much more shaping goes on when you know that story is to be presented to society at large. And if that shaping holds together her crumbling self, do I have the right to allow my search for the truth, for non-fiction, to destroy the defences she has created? There are many fictional black holes in which auto/biographies can capsize.

Philip Hoare

Philip Hoare is the author of six works of non-fiction: *Serious Pleasures: The Life of Stephen Tennant* **(1990),** *Noël Coward: A Biography* **(1995),** *Wilde's Last Stand: Decadence, Conspiracy, and the First World War* **(1997),** *Spike Island: The Memory of a Military Hospital* **(2000) and** *England's Lost Eden: Adventures in a Victorian Utopia* **(2005). His latest book,** *Leviathan or, The Whale,* **won the 2009 BBC Samuel Johnson Prize for non-fiction.**

An experienced broadcaster, he presented the BBC 2 film *The Hunt for Moby-Dick*, and directed three films for BBC's *Whale Night* in 2008. He was writer-in-residence at Ruskin College, Oxford, 2010, and is currently Leverhulme artist-in-residence at University of Plymouth/The Marine Institute, 2011.

A couple of years ago, at the back of a cupboard, I found a journal I'd written when I was in my mid-teens. It was a hardback notebook, brought back by my father from his job as a cable tester in a factory in Southampton. I'd filled it with writings and paintings, testaments to my teenage obsessions. On one page, I'd painted a killer whale; on another, I'd written an adolescent fantasy about a dandy. Discovering this book after four decades was a shock. Each page seemed to predict my future 'career', like an Ordnance Survey map of my imagination.

Writing is a vulgar art, an immodest way of calling attention to one's self. But, of course, it's a diversionary tactic too, an indulging of one's fantasies. I wrote my first book, a biography of the aesthete Stephen Tennant, because I wanted to enter his world, albeit at one remove.

The brightest Bright Young Thing, patron of Cecil Beaton and lover of Siegfried Sassoon, in 1986 Tennant was still living in the Wiltshire manor house in which he was born eighty years before. I'd made three pilgrimages to his door; only on the last was I finally conducted by the housekeeper through rooms filled with polar bear skin rugs, multicoloured fishing nets and, strewn across the floor, the manuscript of *Lascar: A Story of the Maritime Boulevard*, a salty tale of tars and tarts destined never to be finished, since once the author had reached the end he just began all over again.

That day, at Tennant's bedside, when he held out his beringed hand from a darkened room filled with the memories of his past, was the spark that impelled me to re-create his life. I've since come to realise that all my books owe their genesis to the effect of a single day, encounter, event. Fast-forward twenty years to another memorable encounter, this time off the coast of Pico in the Azorean archipelago where, after five years' pursuit of the cetaceans which had become my new obsession – yet were one of my oldest – I came face to face with a sperm whale. Possessed of the largest brain in the animal kingdom but also of the largest teeth, this great predator swam directly towards me as I snorkelled in the three-mile-deep ocean.

I felt utterly terrified. The animal did not appear to stop. I imagined it was either going to hit me, or open its huge jaws at the last moment. At that point I lost control of my bodily functions. Then I felt – rather than heard – the whale's echo location moving through my body like an MRI scan – *click–click–click*. It was using its sonar to discern what kind of creature I was. How ironic: I'd spent five years trying to describe whales, and now here was a whale trying to describe me. The result, my most recent book *Leviathan or, The Whale*, was as much an attempt to map an obsession as my first.

From aesthetes to whales may seem a long leap. Yet, as my teenage journal shows, our imaginations are sown early. From fantasy to reality, we may live the life we plan for ourselves, making it happen, turning 'non-fiction' – such a curiously negative term – into something else. And, without such passion, you might as well be writing entries in an encyclopaedia.

Siri Hustvedt

Siri Hustvedt is the author of a book of poetry, five novels, two collections of essays and a work of autobiographical non-fiction. She lives in Brooklyn, New York.

An Enumerated Catalogue of Thoughts and Questions About the Writing of Non-fiction

1. Because the characters inside a work of non-fiction also exist or once existed outside the pages of the book you are writing, you have a responsibility to them or to their legacy.

2. You are not supposed to lie.

3. Lying is double consciousness: you write one sentence on the page while concealing another sentence you believe to be true.

4. What is true?

5. Even though there may be no truth with a capital T, there are some facts that can be verified – birth and death dates, places where particular events

took place, etc. As a writer of non-fiction, you must do your best not to garble documentary facts.

6. That is the easy part.

7. What is the hard part?

8. The hard part is that much of writing non-fiction is not about relating documentary facts. A memoir, for example, is an act of remembering, and remembering is a slippery business. We never retrieve an original memory. We retrieve the last time we brought that particular memory to consciousness. Memories shift over time.

9. A seventy-year-old woman sits down to write her memoir. Her father died when she was eight. She cannot relive the reality of her eight-year-old self; she can only evoke the child she was through the mind of her aging self. Still the memory of that painful time burns inside her. Emotion colours memory. It also consolidates memory. Our writer has a vivid recollection of her father's funeral. Our writer's sister, however, remembers the day entirely differently. The sisters tell two different stories. Not only do their feelings diverge, they quarrel about what actually happened on that day. The truth of memory is not documentary truth. It is subjective truth. A complex, searching memoirist might include her sister's version of the funeral in her book as well as her own.

10. Even with subjective truths, the writer of non-fiction should not knowingly lie.

11. Many memoirs read like bad fiction. They borrow the tired conventions of journeyman novels. They contain page after page of dialogue no ordinary human being could possibly remember. You should think twice before you invent long conversations between characters in a book of non-fiction. It forces the reader to 'suspend disbelief'. This may not be what you want.

12. Every good book, fiction or non-fiction, is written out of necessity.

13. What does that mean?

14. It means that your reader can feel when you're bored with your subject. A necessary book had to be written, and your urgency is conveyed to the reader.

15. Montaigne is a tonic for the creative non-fiction writer. Note especially his transitions.

16. In the essay, the motion of thought becomes form.

17. The best forms are not preordained but arrive during the act of writing itself.

18. Is that all?

19. No, but that's all for now.

Alice Kessler-Harris

Alice Kessler-Harris teaches American History and Women's Studies at Columbia University. Her research focuses on labour, women and gender, and social policy. Much of her scholarship explores these arenas through the experience of wage-earning women and utilises comparative and interdisciplinary frames. She is the author of books including *Out to Work: A History of Wage-Earning Women in the United States* **and** *In Pursuit of Equity: Women, Men and the Quest for Economic Citizenship in Twentieth Century America.* **In recent years, she has turned to biography as a way of interpreting the past.** *A Difficult Woman: The Challenging Life and Times of Lillian Hellman* **was published by Bloomsbury Press in the spring of 2012.**

Historians, of whom I am one, have a rather odd place in the panoply of non-fiction writing: a dual mission that places us on the cusp of two audiences and two forms of writing. As professionals, our goal is to contribute to the sum of scholarly knowledge, if not by unearthing new information then by re-interpreting and revising the old. The result, we believe, is to come ever closer to an elusive and objective truth. In this vein, we tend to write for each other. Our prose precisely tuned to articulate nuance and subtlety, our work laden with footnotes, we seek the adulation of peers who will assign our books to generations of graduate students.

But we flatter ourselves, as well, that much of what we have to say will intrigue and fascinate a general public and contribute to its broader education.

We believe, many of us, that our deeply rooted knowledge, our resonant views of the past, will introduce large audiences to new insights, and perhaps even persuade ordinary folk to think anew about issues and problems that confront them today. Is there a fiscal crisis? How were such crises resolved in the 1930s? Does a wide public believe that less government is better government? What does the past tell us about how governments have ameliorated the lot of ordinary people, and fended off or provoked revolutionary change? Our knowledge, we think, might help to change the world. Our problem is how to convey it without losing credibility among other historians.

Here we find ourselves walking a fine line. In my most recent work, an effort to rethink twentieth-century history through the life of playwright Lillian Hellman, I try to write without jargon, without repeated reference to the dozens of scholars who have approached my subject before me. I try to evoke empathy for a historical period, to challenge my audience to grapple with the dilemmas that faced real people caught up in historical circumstances not of their own making. My job is not to judge, but to explain. And yet, as I do so, I find myself turning to footnotes to argue with my predecessors. After all, my credibility rests on my persuasiveness in refuting their interpretation. I eliminate conditional sentences: might, could, possibly, perhaps become suspect words used only with caution. To add drama, I construct my narrative around exciting people and adventures. I highlight conflict. I slip into hyperbole.

As the form of my writing changes, I move further and further from the historian's craft.

I stop questioning myself, my interpretations, my conclusions. I find myself, albeit unconsciously, searching for information that supports my story. I begin to lose the scepticism that underlines every historical narrative. I tell myself that I have something so important to say that I can justify saying it as forcefully as possible. The search for knowledge has become less important than the articulation of a point of view. Before long, I find that I have set aside my historian's robes; in seeking a public, I have become a part of the audience I want to reach. And I wonder if I am still the historian I once was, and whether this is a natural evolution.

Barry Lopez

Barry Lopez is the author of thirteen books of fiction and non-fiction, including *Arctic Dreams*, for which he received the National Book Award. His most recent book of fiction is a series of inter-related stories called *Resistance*. He has written for numerous magazines and periodicals in the United States and abroad, and has travelled to more than sixty countries. More at www.barrylopez.com.

My travel is often to remote places – Antarctica, the Tanami Desert in central Australia, northern Kenya. In these places I depend on my own wits and resources, but heavily and more often on the knowledge of interpreters – archaeologists, field scientists, anthropologists. Eminent among such helpers are indigenous people; and I can quickly give you three reasons for my dependence on their insights. As a rule, indigenous people pay much closer attention to nuance in the physical world. They see more. And from only a handful of evidence, thoroughly observed, they can deduce more. Second, their history in a place, a combination of tribal and personal history, is typically deep. The history creates a temporal dimension in what is otherwise only a spatial landscape. Third, indigenous people tend to occupy the same moral universe as the land they sense. Their bonds with the earth are as much moral as biological.

Over time I have come to think of these three qualities – paying intimate attention, a *storied* relationship to a place rather than a solely sensory awareness of it, and living in some sort of ethical unity with a place – as a fundamental human defence against loneliness. If you're intimate with a place, a place with whose history you're familiar, and you establish an ethical conversation with it, the implication that follows is this: the place knows you're there. It feels you. You will not be forgotten, cut off, abandoned.

As a writer, I want to ask on behalf of the reader: How can a person obtain this? How can you occupy a place and also have it occupy you? How can you find such a reciprocity?

The key, I think, is to become vulnerable to a place. If you open yourself up, you can build intimacy. Out of such intimacy may come a sense of belonging, a sense of not being isolated in the universe.

My question – how to secure this – is not meant to be idle. How does one actually enter a local geography? (Many of us daydream, I think, about re-entering childhood landscapes that might dispel a current anxiety. We often court such feelings for a few moments in a park or sometimes during an afternoon in the woods.) To respond explicitly and practicably, my first suggestion would be to be silent. Put aside the bird book, the analytic state of mind, any compulsion to identify, and sit still. Concentrate instead on *feeling* a place, on deliberately using the sense of proprioception. Where in this volume of space are you situated? The space behind you is as important as what you see before you. What lies beneath you is as relevant as what stands on the far horizon. Actively use your ears to imagine the acoustical hemisphere you occupy. How does birdsong ramify here? Through what kind of air is it moving? Concentrate on smells in the belief you can smell water and stone. Use your hands to get the heft and texture of a place – the tensile strength in a willow branch, the moisture in a pinch of soil, the different naps of leaves.[1]

Richard Mabey

Richard Mabey is the author of some forty books, including *Gilbert White*, winner of the 1986 Whitbread Biography Prize, the memoir *Nature Cure*, and *Flora Britannica*, a National Book Award winner in 1996. He received an honorary DLitt from the University of East Anglia in 2011, and is Patron of the John Clare Society. He lives in Norfolk.

Roots and ruts: on writing about home

Publishing autobiography can be a perilous business, apt to provoke visitations from the past you've conjured up. Old teachers, one-time neighbours, forgotten girlfriends – all, sometimes, hapless participants in your plot – suddenly manifest themselves in front of you in distant lecture halls. These are usually the happiest of reunions, but can be challenging, too. And, when part of your story is the abandonment of your home country for some feckless new arena, they can, I've found, come close to being rebukes. I'd written about flitting

1. Extract from an article that appeared in the Summer 1997 issue of *Portland* magazine.

from the cosseting hills of Chilterns to the flatlands of Norfolk after a long illness, but that didn't excuse me. How could I do it, my shocked enquirers protested – leave such a nourishing, bosky heartland for a featureless desert?

But I sensed that it wasn't the place itself that was the issue, rather the severing of roots. I was being disloyal, treacherous, deserting my responsibilities to the place that, as John Clare said of Helpston, had 'made my being'. Worse, I was having a lot of fun in my new *terroir*, and was therefore guilty of a kind of promiscuity.

But are deep attachments to a place ever so exclusive, so fragile? Ronald Blythe, writing of his own roots in the niggardly flints and muddled field-corners of East Anglia, wonders whether 'landscape enters the bloodstream with the milk'. Quite likely so, and builds itself just as firmly into your persona. John Clare's madness was aggravated when he was moved out of his birthplace, his mother lode. But, as often as not, the indigenous eye survives translocation by becoming a way of seeing *other* places. If I think of what half a lifetime in the Chilterns has left in my bloodstream, beyond the indelible images of particular woods and childhood dens, there is a whole grammar and lexicon of the experience of place: the fuzziness of commons, the deepness of green lanes, the conciliatoriness of old trees, the knack of short cuts. All these are discoverable, close-to, in my new home among Norfolk's vast fields and marshes. To know one place intimately is to have a way of knowing all places.

When I first explored limestone country, a landscape made from the dissolution of rock by water, it made instant sense to me by having the same patterning as the creek-riven marshes of north Norfolk. When I discovered the cork-oak *dehesas* of central Spain, one of the most distinctive places in Europe, their plains and pollard trees were so like Windsor Forest, moved south a thousand miles, that I found myself strolling about with my hands behind my back, like Prince Philip. The three-course meal I had there one day, layered in a single pot, seemed like a metaphor for all the last, non-globalised places on the planet: *pot au feu*, local variations on a universal theme.

In his writings on nomads, Bruce Chatwin suggested that an urge to wander was as much a part of our biological inheritance as the need to settle, and have territory. Roots – and routes – are both necessary and rewarding, until they become ruts.

Robert Macfarlane

Robert Macfarlane is the author of *Mountains of the Mind* (2003), winner of *The Guardian* First Book Award, the *Sunday Times* Young Writer of the Year Award, and a Somerset Maugham Award. *The Wild Places* (2007) won several prizes, including The Boardman-Tasker Prize for Mountain Literature. *The Old Ways* was published in 2012. He is a Fellow of Emmanuel College, Cambridge.

On writing as reading

Writing is a craft. It is learnt in the way that cabinet making is learnt, or a musical instrument is learnt, which is to say by practice and the often effortful acquisition of technique. Richard Sennett, in his brilliant book on the idea of craft, estimates that it takes 10,000 hours to learn to play the violin well or to make an admirable cabinet. It takes even longer to become a writer, because before you become a writer you must first become a reader. Every hour spent reading is an hour spent learning to write; this continues to be true throughout a writer's career.

Reading bad writers can be as useful as reading good writers. To continue the cabinet-making analogy, reading good writers shows you how to achieve the verbal equivalent of the tongue-and-groove joint, the well-bevelled edge, the countersunk screw, the mahogany inlay or the beeswax polish. Reading bad writers, you see how the chisel can leap and gouge the wood, how joints can be left unflush and how hinges can creak.

You don't have to read within your tradition or form, of course. J.G. Ballard, for instance, read almost no fiction, preferring what he memorably called the 'grey literature' of technical manuals, medical journals and police reports. I happen to like to read as much as I can from the tradition in which I supposedly work. All of the books in my writing room are either travel literature, or nature writing, or a mix of the two. On the lower shelves, within grab-able reach, I've got my favourites: Jonathan Raban, Italo Calvino, Rebecca Solnit, Antoine de Saint-Exupéry, Hugh Brody, Annie Dillard, John Muir, Gretel Ehrlich, Tim Robinson, J.A. Baker, Barry Lopez . . .

It's these last two writers who have influenced me more than any others: Baker, the author of *The Peregrine* (1967), and Lopez, whose masterpiece is

Arctic Dreams (1984), but whose essay collections *Crossing Open Ground* and *About This Life* are also magnificent. In *The Peregrine* I saw how to describe the rapid actions of nature, and I experienced the power of Baker's metaphors: what an early reviewer called their 'magnesium-flare intensity'. Lopez's hymn to the Arctic revealed to me the possibility of twining cultural history, anthropology, epiphany, travelogue, science and elegy. Lopez also convinced me that lyricism was a function of precision – and that exact and exacting attention to the natural world was a kind of moral gaze.

Encountering is different from mastering, of course. I've not come close to perfecting any of these modes or manners. But discovering them in other writers has made me aware of their possibility as effects. I feel no awkwardness in laying out my influences and teachers like this. No writer should. The vision of the isolated artistic visionary, striving in his garret, blissed out on laudanum, feeding off inspiration, is pensionable – and also historically inaccurate. Keats's line about poetry needing to come 'as naturally as leaves to a tree' is given the lie by his manuscripts, which show as many inkblots and crossings-out as one of Molesworth's notebooks.

Sara Maitland

Sara Maitland's first novel, *Daughters of Jerusalem*, won the Somerset Maugham Prize in 1979. Since then, she has written five more novels and five collections of short stories as well as several works of non-fiction including *A Book of Silence* (Granta, 2008). She is now working on *Gossip from the Forest* about forests and fairy tales (forthcoming Granta, 2012). Her story 'Moss Witch' was runner-up in the 2009 BBC Short Story Competition.

On lying

If you are a journalist, or a historian, you are supposed to write only facts – externally verifiable, demonstrable realities. You are not allowed to make anything up.

If you are a fiction writer, you are meant to make things up. Even if you are a historical novelist, or in some other way your story is grounded in 'real' events, you would be selling your readers short if you did not make anything up.

This is not a difference between truth and lies, it is about different sorts of truth. Readers know the difference, and so do publishers, booksellers and even jacket designers. Sometimes, though surprisingly seldom, the cover of the book will spell it out: under the title will be a comment, 'A novel'. Usually this is not necessary. A whole set of codes guide us in working out what we are reading, and we agree, so to speak, to accept whichever kind of truth we are being offered.

But with literary non-fiction these rules are far less clear. There are some conventions to assist the writer – for example, we are allowed to 'invent' direct speech. In a memoir it is completely impossible to remember accurately what a particular person said twenty years ago, but 'invented' conversations in direct speech are permitted, to give life and energy to the story: no one expects these to be 'quotations' in the journalistic sense.

There also seems to be an agreement that, at least in certain circumstances, you can compress time to make a tidier story. This happens a lot in 'nature writing'. In her wonderful *Pilgrim at Tinker Creek*, Annie Dillard arranges her chapters into the shape of an unfolding year. We know for a fact that she spent three years in her valley, but we do not mind that three winters are merged into a single one.

Readers also seem happy to accept that background research was not actually done at the moment of an experience: if you describe a building as fourteenth century, you do not have to say whether you learned the date before, during or after the time at which you visited it.

But often it is not clear. In creative non-fiction, writers are walking a delicate boundary between the two sorts of truth. Stories seldom come in the same patterns and rhythms as 'real life'. We never actually know what someone else thought or felt (we hardy know what we thought or felt last year) – and yet the truth of the story drives us to write with confidence. We know that memory is dodgy and truth uncertain, but we write with authority – and note the connection between 'author' and 'authority'. We apply a writerly intelligence as we negotiate our way through different kinds of truth. We bend and wriggle our way between the clumsy facts and a strong story. To reveal the emotional truth we may have to warp the factual truth.

Film has found a solution to this problem: 'Based on a true story' the advertisements say boldly. Perhaps writers of non-fiction need to claim that freedom too. As it is, we often have to lie in order to tell the truth.

Neil McKenna

Neil McKenna is the author of *The Secret Life of Oscar Wilde* **(Century London, 2003) and** *Fanny and Stella: the Scandalous Lives and Extra-ordinary Trials of Two Victorian Cross Dressers* **(Faber, 2012).**

You can't win. Your writing is too this or too that. Too literary. Or not literary enough. Overwritten and over-blown, or underwritten and underwhelming. Too tight, too loose, too much, too little, too long, too short.

People aren't reading any more. And even when they do read, they don't want your book. It's been done. 'It's not in the zone,' they say. But trying to ascertain exactly what or where the zone is is a hopeless grail quest, because it's like a dancing moonbeam, or the pot of gold at the end of a rainbow.

Or it's about you. You're too old or too young, or too dreary or too middle class or not sufficiently middle class. Or not sexy enough to look good in profiles and interviews. So you hang your head in shame and apologise to the world because you and your writing don't quite fit. You can't win.

Writing doesn't come with a money-back guarantee. There is no law which says that effort equals reward, and that the pain of writing, the deep, dark pain of writing, is always and perfectly assuaged by literary success. Whatever success means. As Truman Capote once said, 'Honey, don't let me *commence . . .* ')

But in the midst of all the deep and dark pain of writing, there is always *Hope*. Hope that what we write will be good, that it will work, that people will read it, that they will get it. Hope for my writing (and emphatically not hope for myself) has kept me going through the darkest of dark passages.

Hope and Truth. The very worst thing that any writer can do is to deviate from the truth of their writing. Truth in writing is hard to define and is probably different for everyone. For me, truth in writing means several things. It's about staying true to your idea, even when the nay-sayers and the sowers of doubt and the mewlers and the pukers tell you otherwise. It's about finding the authentic voice of the book you're working on. Every book is different and every book has a true and unique voice. Finding that voice and staying with that voice (even if it's not always the voice you wanted to hear) is essential to the truth of a book. And it's about not allowing yourself to accept work that isn't up to scratch, about knowing when you're fooling yourself, about being ruthless in the pursuit of your craft.

Most of all, truth in writing is about courage: the courage of your conviction, the courage of your passion, the courage to create something from the void, the courage to risk failure, to experience reverses of fortune because you hope and believe that what you want to write and what you will write with all the verve and vigour and passion you can summon will be worth reading. You can win! And you can and must win on *your* terms. *Bon courage!*

Caroline Moorehead

Caroline Moorehead is a biographer, the author of lives of Bertrand Russell, Freya Stark, Martha Gellhorn and Lucie de la Tour du Pin. She has written an account of refugees in the modern world, *Human Cargo*. Her most recent book is *A Train in Winter*, about the French Resistance.

In praise of archives

One of the worst fears of my life is this: that, between them, the internet, microfilm, scanner, email and Kindle will, gradually and inexorably, do away with one of the great – perhaps the greatest – of the non-fiction writer's pleasures – life in the archives. Nothing has ever given me more delight than the buff folder, slid across a desk, full of mysterious promise and unimagined secrets. A never-before-seen letter? A remarkable discovery? The answer to some perplexing riddle in a character's life? It hardly matters. What counts is that delicious moment when the folder arrives and you take it in your hands and gently, slowly, pull back the flap.

I have worked in many archives over the last thirty years. Some I have cursed for being too far away, too inhospitable, too cavalier towards visitors from abroad. Researching a life of Bertrand Russell, I arrived at McMaster University, one and a half hours outside Toronto and the library to which

Russell's papers were sent, in the middle of a week in late May when the students had left. What I had not done was to find out that the campus was dry, that the only canteen shut at 6 p.m., and that I had arrived on the eve of a four-day national holiday. The library shut at 4.30 p.m. on Thursday; it reopened at 9 a.m. on the Tuesday. It rained every day, all day. It was the longest weekend of my life.

I have looked at papers in the vaults of French mansions, in the attics of chateaux in Belgium, in libraries both large and small in Washington, Rome, Paris, Bordeaux, Amiens, Albany, Bamako, Turin, Brussels and Arolsen. I have rifled through cupboards and lofts and trunks in shuttered holiday cottages, in the manuscript sections of historic houses and in school libraries. But one archive stands out for me as the single happiest working experience of my life.

In 1989, I was asked by HarperCollins (then William Collins and Sons) to write a history of the International Committee of the Red Cross, the guardian of the Geneva Conventions and the arbiter of the behaviour of nations at the time of war. The ICRC, founded in 1863, run entirely by the Swiss and based in Geneva, has always been a famously secretive institution. At the end of the 1990s, its archives remained closed.

Before taking on the book, I visited Geneva and asked whether I might read in their archives. The reply was non-committal: the request needed to go before the board. Foolishly assuming this meant yes, I set about my initial researches. From time to time, I asked how soon I might begin work in Geneva. Not yet, soon perhaps, sometime. The months passed, then a year, then another. Fortunately, there were enormous numbers of documents which were not in the archives, but there were still questions that I was desperate to answer.

One morning, while I was reading in the library of the ICRC, a man appeared at my desk. 'You may enter the archives,' he announced, with great solemnity. 'Last night, we voted to open them to researchers. You can be the first.'

The archives consisted not of a single room but of an entire floor: 140 years of papers, reports, documents, the records of missions, all immaculately catalogued, a vast and meticulous chronicle of war. My first reaction was one of horror. .

But, having been at work for over three years, I knew now what I was looking for. I wanted confirmation of episodes I only had references to, of deals I dimly understood. I wanted to know and understand why certain things had happened.

It was midwinter and snowing hard. They gave me a key. I arrived every morning at six, walked through the deserted building and into a small office they had set aside for me, where I found the papers I had requested the night before. All day, until late at night, I read. I have never felt happier.

This is what frightens me: that such experiences will vanish.

Susie Orbach

Susie Orbach is a psychoanalyst and writer. She co-founded The Women's Therapy Centre in 1976 and is the author of many books including *Fat is a Feminist Issue*, *Hunger Strike*, *On Eating*, *The Impossibility of Sex* and *Bodies*. Susie has a clinical practice seeing individuals and couples.

Writing non-fiction

If I know exactly where I am going, I am not interested in writing it. I want to be surprised by my own thoughts and connections. I don't want an outline or a conclusion before I start. I need to be far away from the school essay I could never do. It is only if I get in a muddle that I have to retrospectively outline what I have and see what I was wanting to say and where the arc of my argument fails.

There's a why and there's a how.

The why is to understand and to share.

The how demands an entry point, a first sentence, or a title that lets me invite the reader into a way of considering something anew.

Like my day job as a psychoanalyst, writing forces my words to slow. What's the emotional, psychological, or political tale I want to be telling? Is it truthful? Is it sufficiently complex? Is there enough space for the reader?

Some writing is emphatic, rhetorical, uses repetitions. Other writing aims for ambiguity and space.

In the morning there is nothing. Hours later there will be something; an assemblage of words that will represent a personal confrontation with what I think and believe for now. When the thoughts and words don't come, the process of writing hurts. It takes a lot of self-steadying to remind oneself that sentences will arrive.

The materiality of writing is always a surprise. The words make a story or a polemic. In psychoanalysis, the words which enable a person to feel alive to her or himself are private and untouchable. Writing is concrete. It is a product that didn't previously exist. It can be ignored. Its effects can be subtle or profound. But it is there.

Writing is for me and it is for you. It is a relationship. I make an offering. You find something different there than what I thought myself to be saying. The reader is not passive. Digesting what is written is an act of transformation.

Writing ignites new thoughts and emphasises old ones. It is a public yet intimate way of having a conversation with others known and unknown.

Jennifer Potter

Best known as a horticultural historian, Jennifer Potter has written three novels, two works on gardens, a biography (*Strange Blooms, The Curious Lives* and *Adventures of the John Tradescants*, longlisted for the Duff Cooper Memorial Prize in 2007), and most recently *The Rose, A True History*. A former Royal Literary Fund Fellow, she is an Honorary Teaching Fellow on the Warwick Writing Programme.

I want my writing to take me by surprise. After starting out with fiction – set variously in Martinique, the Yemen and France – I reinvented myself as a garden historian, inspired by a course on landscape and garden conservation at London's Architectural Association, where I wrote my thesis on capturing the spirit of place. Then came books about gardens and landscape, biography, and most recently a cultural history of the rose. Whatever the genre, all my writing dabbles in 'truth', and I look for the story that will take flight.

Places matter, too. They have a feel and a smell that alter your perceptions, so whenever humanly possible I visit the ones I describe in my books, although publishers rarely pay travel expenses, so better writing comes at a cost. But I love travelling with a book in my head, and the obsessive focus that is oddly liberating. I have visited Virginia as an early colonist, the Yemen as an Edwardian woman traveller, Iran and the White House Rose Garden in pursuit of the rose.

Suggested originally by my editor, *The Rose* took five long years from proposal to publication. At first I hesitated: so much has been written about the rose, did we really need another book? But a little investigation soon had me hooked and I wrote an elegant proposal, imagining that I could simply work my way through it in a couple of years.

After just a few months, I threw away the plan I had so diligently mapped. Most rose histories endlessly recycle the same old 'facts' without interrogating the evidence, and my synopsis had meekly followed their lead. More problematically, the rose has permeated western culture so comprehensively that ploughing my way from the Sumerians through to the present was proving a monumental chore. I write best from a sense of danger and turning my proposal into a book was like trying to pad a short story into a novel by multiplying words.

I wouldn't recommend writing without a plan, but it worked for me this once. I had to find a narrative that made sense chronologically and thematically, and a shape that would encompass the whole. The six-part structure − which now seems obvious − emerged slowly and organically, and I came close to losing my nerve. That was scary, but I formulated a question that turned my exercise into a quest: what makes the rose so special to so many cultures around the world? As in all the best mysteries, the answer came to me only at the end.

Calling my book a true history was asking for trouble, and I left the deadliest task till last: checking that all my facts are true. Revisiting every scrap of research took me three horrible months. I'm trying with the new book to check as I go along, but, in the tension between creating and revision, the surprise of discovery invariably triumphs.

Susan Sellers

Susan Sellers is an editor and translator, and the author of several books of non-fiction, including a study of the writer Hélène Cixous and an exploration of myth and fairy tale in contemporary women's fiction. She edits Virginia Woolf for Cambridge University Press and has also written a novel about Woolf and her painter sister Vanessa Bell, entitled *Vanessa and Virginia*. She is a Professor of English and Related Literature at the University of St Andrews.

When writing *A Room of One's Own* Virginia Woolf chose to tell stories. She described the meals she ate while visiting two Oxbridge colleges. At a male college she feasted on sole in cream sauce, partridge, and a confection for dessert that defied description, but at a woman's college she sat down to plain gravy soup, humdrum beef, and prunes and custard.

Her story is more than a way of engaging attention. She uses it to make a serious point about the differences between men's and women's education. The men's colleges benefit from centuries of endowment and so can fund luxuries such as fine wine at lunch, while the recently created women's colleges can afford only water.

A Room of One's Own is a marvellous instance of good essay writing, drawing on a range of literary devices. In another story Woolf invents the character of Judith Shakespeare, whom she imagines to be as intelligent and gifted as her brother. Unlike William she is not permitted to attend school, but she teaches herself to read and write. When a husband is picked out for her she protests and runs away to London. Like William she tries to earn a living by acting. Women, however, are not allowed on the stage. Finally, pregnant and in despair, she kills herself.

These stories are far more powerful than any statistic about women's education. As readers, we empathise with the plight of the imaginary Judith Shakespeare and feel angry and frustrated at the waste of her life.

Woolf deploys language with the care and precision of a poet. She understands that words are powerful: that when they ricochet and dance together they have the potential to make us see the world anew. When she is chased from the forbidden lawn of the men's college, she doesn't simply invoke an irate porter, she paints for us 'the gesticulations of a curious-looking object in a cut-away coat and evening shirt'. She is not content to list the menu at lunch but engages all our senses in her depiction of partridges with 'their retinue of sauces and salads, the sharp and the sweet, each in its order; their potatoes, thin as coins but not so hard; their sprouts, foliated as rosebuds but more succulent'.

There is a popular image of Woolf as relying on flashes of inspiration to fuel her writing. Yet her detailed, almost daily diary entries and voluminous correspondence prove she was a voracious reader and a thoughtful planner. She read French and Russian literature as well as English, classical authors alongside her contemporaries, books from many other disciplines. Ideas were tried and scratched out and slowly replaced by better ones; word choices were revised over multiple drafts. She was a great walker and frequently came back from an hour out of doors with a fresh perspective.

Woolf's work and her way of working have inspired me as a writer. She was a consummate wordsmith, with an incessant delight in the potency and possibility of language.

Dava Sobel

Dava Sobel, a former science reporter for the New York Times, **is the author of** Longitude, Galileo's Daughter, The Planets **and** A More Perfect Heaven. **She still hears occasionally from her old friend Carolyn, and enjoys looking at the Moon.**

During the glory days of the Apollo project, a young astronomer who analysed Moon rocks at a university laboratory fell in love with my friend Carolyn, and risked his job and the national security to give her a quantum of Moon dust.

'Where is it? Let me see!' I demanded at this news. But she answered quietly, 'I ate it.' After a pause, she added, 'There was so little.' As though that explained everything.

I was furious. In an instant I had dropped from the giddy height of discovering the Moon right there in Carolyn's apartment to realising she had eaten it all without leaving a crumb for me.

I still envy Carolyn her taste of the Moon. I've heard the old wives' tales advising women to sleep in the moonlight to regulate their menstrual cycle or heighten their fertility, but no folklore describes special powers to be won from the Moon by eating its dust. Carolyn's deed is a Space Age story, unthinkable when her mother and mine were new wives.

I heighten the romance of the incident in my reverie, so the Moon dust enters Carolyn's mouth to ignite on contact with her saliva, shooting sparks that lodge in her every cell. Crystalline and alien, it illuminates her body's dark recesses like pixie powder, and thrums the senseless tune of a wind chime through her veins. By its sacred presence it changes her very nature: Carolyn, the Moon goddess. She has mated herself to the Moon somehow by this act of incorporation, and that is what makes me so jealous.

In reality, I know Carolyn is married now to a veterinarian in upstate New York and has three children. She doesn't glow in the dark or walk on air. She has long since lost all traces of that Moon morsel, which no doubt passed through her body in the usual manner. What could it have contained, anyway, to preoccupy me all these years?

A few grains of titanium and aluminium?

Some helium atoms borne from the Sun on the solar wind?

The shining essence of all that is unattainable?

All of the above, probably, all rendered the more extraordinary for having travelled to her across 240,000 miles of interplanetary space, in the belly of a rocket ship, and then hand-delivered as the love token of a handsome man. Lucky, lucky Carolyn.

I imagine the tall astronomer's surprise at the way his gift was received, for he did not yet know her well. I'll bet she surprised him again the very next moment, by clasping him to her with the same hasty rapture and devouring him along with the Moon dust.

I'm not angry any more. I sense Carolyn's same primal hunger myself at least once every Blue Moon.

After dark, when even the slightest sliver of the Moon's silver presence spreads luminescence and magic, I murmur the names of the features on his face – Mare Crisium, Mare Serenitatis, Mare Tranquilitatis – like some Latin incantation to still the longing in my heart. Moonstruck with my lunatic fantasies, I watch him change shape by the hour, like one bewitched. Waxing and waning, whining for my attention, he reminds me that I was born to wonder.

Diana Souhami

Diana Souhami is the author of many highly praised books: *Edith Cavell* **(winner of the EDP-Jarrold East Anglian Book Award);** *Coconut Chaos, Selkirk's Island* **(winner of the Whitbread Biography Award);** *The Trials of Radclyffe Hall* **(shortlisted for the James Tait Black Prize for Biography and winner of the US Lambda Literary Award); the bestselling** *Mrs Keppel and Her Daughter* **(also winner of the Lambda Literary Award and a** *New York Times* **'Notable Book of the Year');** *Wild Girls; The Lives and Loves of Natalie Barney and Romaine Brooks; Gertrude and Alice; Greta and Cecil;* **and** *Gluck: Her Biography.* **Her latest book,** *Murder at Wrotham Hill,* **will be published by Quercus in 2012.**

I wince to admit I'm the author of a book with the title *Wild Girls*. Its cover photo is of a bodice being tightly laced by grubby fingers. The invitation is to back-alley sleaze. I intended a humorous but high-minded book about Natalie Barney and Romaine Brooks and those wonderful lesbians in Paris between the wars whose lives and work were intrinsic to modernism. To associate with them and their freethinking ways I interpolated fictional snippets of contemporary lesbian life.

The title I chose, and that was in my mind as I wrote, was *A Sapphic Idyll*. It was meant as ironic because the relationships in the book are sometimes alarming and far from idyllic. It was also a reference to a memoir by Liane de Pougy, one of Natalie Barney's more flamboyant lovers, called *Idylle Sapphique*.

I liked the initial design for the jacket of *A Sapphic Idyll*. It showed portraits by Romaine of herself and Natalie. It was put to the sales team, the marketing lot. Pitched, was the word used. They hated it. No one, they said, would know what Sapphic meant. Particularly the booksellers. Someone came up with 'Wild Girls'. The sales team liked that. Booksellers know what girls mean. Particularly when they're being laced into bodices. I consoled myself that at least in America I'd be allowed my Sapphic Idyll. But they said no one would know what Idyll meant and that they loved Wild Girls.

The reps, the sales pitch, the bookselling chains – it's a shame when they become our cultural arbiters. They are so wedded to dividends, and profit and loss. They want the same as they had before, and are not keen to be playful or break moulds in the way that, between the wars in Paris, the little presses, often privately funded by lesbians, 'died to make verse free'.

I ran into problems with the next book too, *Coconut Chaos*. In it, I hovered between fact and fiction. My allegiance was to what I viewed as literarily rather than literally true. The underpinning idea was of chaos theory – that one small act, in this case the taking of a coconut by Fletcher Christian on 27 April 1789 from the heap piled on board the *Bounty* by Captain Bligh, could have ramifications that echoed through time. I abandoned a linear narrative, linked past and present, action and far-reaching consequence, fact and imagination. I produced a hybrid of history, autobiography, fiction, travelogue and police procedural.

It did not please the booksellers or the reps. It got shelved in Travel, under S for Souhami where only the intrepid might find it.

When it came to the next commission, I was taken to lunch by one of the publishing bosses and given what he called 'a reality check'. This time, he suggested, not unreasonably maybe, I should write something more straightforward – 'so that we can all get on the bus'.

Dale Spender

Dale Spender has been a reader, writer, educator and feminist for most of her life. And loves change. She has wanted to change the world – but suspects she is running out of time.

Gone are the days when there was a distinction between fiction and non-fiction: when it was clear that novels were stories – that were made up. But non-fiction – well, that was something entirely different!

Of course, fiction could be serious, realistic – and even insightful. But it was at the creative end of the spectrum. In contrast, non-fiction was meant to be informative, authoritative – substantive and convincing.

Non-fiction writers were supposed to keep the records, to verify information, check things out and avoid unnecessary flights of fancy.

Personally, I always had difficulty with such a division. As a feminist non-fiction writer who was interested in the way knowledge was constructed so that women were marginalised or left out, I was well aware that the victor and the gatekeeper not only kept the records, they also made them up!

My convictions were reinforced when I started on the research for my (non-fiction) PhD on women and men talking. I had been reading the work of Otto Jespersen – the father of linguistics – who consistently asserted that women talked too much, went round and round in circles – and never finished their sentences.

This rather surprised me, as I had not noticed such behaviour. How did he know? I wondered. And then I understood full well. He had made it up, of course! And his non-fiction – which was entirely fiction – had stood unchallenged for years! His was the authoritative text. No transparency in the print era.

It wouldn't happen today; not with the new technologies. We are all authors – of all genres – in the digital era. And all up for international questioning. We know that everyone can make up anything in the twenty-first century. Books were the democratisation of reading – but the internet is the democratisation of writing. And as a writer, you don't even have to start with a blank page any more: you have the world's best sources at your fingertips – to cut and paste. And mash and remix.

I must admit that I prefer the level playing field and the presence of genuine and international peers – and the blurring of the barriers between writer and reader. (Twitter comes into this.)

Even the dividing line between fiction and non-fiction is more difficult to draw as enhanced novels include commentary, criticism, graphics, animation and sound – along with a choice of ending. Non-fiction, insofar as it is distinctive, has become the online art of combining the 'search' and the 'solution'.

Unlike my writing of the past, my online writing today is always a work in progress – always in need of an update! Otto Jespersen wouldn't have lasted five minutes on Wikipedia!

Different of course, but no less demanding – and often far more satisfying. And there's no going back!

Francis Spufford

Francis Spufford is the author of four books of literary non-fiction, which have all crossed genre boundaries. *I May Be Some Time* (1994) mixed travel writing and cultural history; *The Child That Books Built* (2002) fused memoir with literary criticism and child psychology; *Backroom Boys* hybridised science writing and politics. *Red Plenty* (2010), the last, was a halfway house between fiction and non-fiction itself. He has won prizes including the Somerset Maugham, the Banff Mountain Book Award, and the *Sunday Times* Young Writer of the Year. In 2007, he was elected a Fellow of the Royal Society of Literature.

It's always struck me as unfair that writing has so little sensation when it's going well.

When it's going badly, then you feel it: there's the gluey fumbling of the attempts to gain traction on the empty screen, there's the misshapen awkwardness of each try at a sentence (as if you'd been equipped with a random set of pieces from different jigsaws). After a time, there's the tetchy pacing about, the increasingly bilious nibbling, the simultaneous antsiness and flatness as the failure of the day sinks in. After a longer time – two or three or four or five days of failure – there's the deepening sense of being a fraud. Not only can you not write bearably now, you probably never could. Trips to bookshops become orgies of self-reproach and humiliation. Look at everybody else's fluency. Look at the rivers of adequate prose that flow out of them. It's obvious that you don't belong in the company of these real writers, who write so many books and oh, such long ones. Last, there's the depressive inertia that flows out of sustained failure at the keyboard and infects the rest of life with grey minimalism, making it harder to answer letters, return library books, bother to cook meals not composed of pasta. All vivid, particularised sensations, familiar from revisiting though somehow no less convincing each time round.

But there's no symmetrical set of good feelings when the work goes well. I find that hours pass without my being aware of myself enough to be in the business of having sensations; at least, of having any marked, distinct ones. It isn't just that the dyer's hand is stained the colour of what it works on. The dyer's elbow follows it in, the dyer's arm, the dyer's whole body: plop into the vat, to disperse into my attention to the thing being made. When things are going right, almost all I notice is the fiddly half-created structure of the writing, with all the mutual dependences of the pieces of it upon each other, including the delicate dependence of written parts upon parts not yet written, and vice versa; and the whole thing in motion, or at least in a kind of state of responsiveness, ready to flow into new positions and new configurations as the possibilities alter. To try to attend to my own state of mind while this is happening would be to throw myself abruptly out of it, back to a place where there's nothing to feel but that I'm cold from sitting still so long, and wouldn't mind visiting the cottage cheese pot in the fridge, with a teaspoon. So far as I can look at my own mind at all, it is in a state of flow mirroring the responsive flux I feel in the writing. What I know, from a thousand books read and conversations had, works itself together as if by itself; what I need next comes to my hand without being forced, ready to be turned, examined, compared, remoulded, adjusted, smoothed until it aligns itself in parallel with the other pieces of what seems at this moment to be the design.

Why do I write? From selfishness. Because this state of liquefied, complex concentration, however faintly and dimly I'm able to perceive it, is the greatest pleasure I know.

Daniel Swift

Daniel Swift is the author of *Bomber County*.

On non-fiction and swimming

For a long time the only breaks I took from writing were to go swimming in a grand tree-ringed lake about half an hour's drive from the house where I was living. This was in Saratoga Springs, in upstate New York, on the southern edge of the Adirondacks, the best stretch of wilderness on America's east coast; I was living there because I was teaching at a college in town, and I was finishing my first book. To get to the lake you have to know about the lake, because it isn't marked, as such. You park your car on the curve of a country highway and cross the road and then through a border of trees, no path, and out on to the rocks into the lake, brown water, clear.

I didn't like to take many breaks as I wanted to live for the time of writing inside the world about which I was writing. In this case, it was 1943 and an RAF bomber base in Lincolnshire, but it could have been anywhere; a man and a writer I very much admire once wrote a book about all the events in one year of Shakespeare's life, and I remember him challenging me, Ask me about the weather. Ask me what the rainfall was like in April of that year. So when I was writing my Second World War book I was really counting my days against the rhythm of then, thinking the bombers out on their night raids, thinking them back in. I don't know what it's like to write a novel – maybe you can take a holiday from a novel – but the imaginary kingdom I was writing was not wholly mine so I distrusted any great break in the spell.

The lake was all right, though. When there were men fishing there, or families swimming – I once was shocked to go on a day when the ice had hardly melted, and I considered myself brave to go that day, and then when I got there a family with two children, flushed pink little girls, were there already, and they said sure, we've been coming here for a couple of weeks – then I resented the intrusion into my imagining, but the lake was worth it. The colours there are pale and agreeable, they concur with one another, and the sky knows the water.

I made a mistake, not long ago. I looked up the lake on a map. It isn't a lake at all; it's a bend in a river, in the Hudson river.

Colin Thubron

Colin Thubron is a travel writer and novelist. His classic travel books have been about the land mass that makes up Russia and Asia, and include: *Behind the Wall*, *In Siberia*, *Shadow of the Silk Road* and, most recently, *To a Mountain in Tibet*. He has won many prizes and awards, and is currently President of the Royal Society of Literature.

Whenever rules are laid down for a genre, somebody is sure to come along and creatively break them. That may be the best service guidelines can do: to challenge the talented transgressor.

Travel writing is a particularly complex genre because it demands contradictory qualities from its practitioner: the toughness to make a good journey, and the sensitivity to write it.

The foundation of the journey is curiosity. There are those works, of course, which teach about a foreign culture from prior knowledge. But more excitingly a travel book can convey a sense of personal discovery that is unique to the genre. This is understanding as much through the senses as through the intellect.

The first challenge to the travel writer is the establishment of motive. Why is the journey necessary? What is its aim? To give a forward thrust and shape to the narrative, it needs to hint at some other purpose than the haphazard accumulation of experience. This has led many writers into strained expressions of motive. But you only have to look at a few successful travel books to witness the sheer variety of impulses, whether it's the delight of Patrick Leigh Fermor marching across Europe in *A Time of Gifts*, William Dalrymple following the trail of two Byzantine monks in *From the Holy Mountain* or Bruce Chatwin's fascination with a sloth-skin that kick-starts *In Patagonia*.

Then there is the question of research. It is often from research that the motive – or thread – of the journey springs. Something about the material arouses a special enthusiasm – or elicits questions in the mind – and already the journey is starting in the writer's head.

Uniquely, outside autobiography, the traveller includes himself. And this 'I' in the narrative can be a source of both riches and embarrassment. It is this 'I' who gives the illusion of unity to a narrative that may not obviously have any: for the stuff of the typical travel book is a melange of description, history and incident. But the 'I' is the person who is common to them all, as narrator or participant: the person who must emerge naturally out of the narrative.

In the field, everybody has different ways of recording experience. Some make lavish notes as they go along. This can make for too self-conscious a journey, but the amount of detail recorded – and it is often detail that gives life to a description – is invaluable. Unless a writer's memory is phenomenal, all but the bare bones of a scene will have been forgotten after several months of intense experience. But the notes recover it.

Finally, of course, travel foments prejudices as well as dispelling them. An open mind is more important than any technique. Robert Louis Stevenson wrote: 'There are no foreign lands. It is the traveller only that is foreign.'

Natasha Walter

Natasha Walter is the author of *The New Feminism* (1998) and *Living Dolls: the Return of Sexism* (2010). She is a journalist and broadcaster, having worked for *Vogue*, the *Independent* and *The Guardian* as a feature writer, reviewer and columnist. She is also the founder and director of Women for Refugee Women, a charity that supports the rights of women who seek asylum. In 2008, her verbatim play *Motherland*, based on the experiences of women and children in immigration detention, was performed at the Young Vic, directed by Juliet Stevenson.

Extract from *Living Dolls*[1]

Although opportunities for women are still far wider than they were a generation ago, we are now seeing a resurgence of old sexism in new guises. Far from giving full scope to women's freedom and potential, the new hypersexual culture redefines female success through a narrow framework of sexual allure.

What's more, alongside the links that are made between this kind of exaggerated sexual allure and empowerment, we have recently seen a surprising resurgence of the idea that traditional femininity is biologically rather than socially constructed. A new interest in biological determination now runs throughout our society. Indeed, the association between little girls and everything that is pink and glittery is being explained in many places not as a cultural phenomenon, which could therefore be challenged, but as an inescapable result of biology, which is assumed to be resistant to change . . .

I think it is time to challenge the exaggerated femininity that is being encouraged among women in this generation, both by questioning the resurgence of the biological determinism which tells us that genes and

1. Natasha Walter, *Living Dolls: The Return of Sexism*, Virago, London, 2010, pp. 10, 11, 14, 15.

hormones inexorably drive us towards traditional sex roles, and by questioning the claustrophobic culture that teaches many young women that it is only through exploiting their sexual allure that they can become powerful. Of course, it has to be a woman's own choice if she makes a personal decision to buy into any aspect of what might be seen as stereotypically feminine behaviour, from baking to pole-dancing, from high heels to domestic work. I am just as sure as I ever was that we do not need to subscribe to some dour and politically correct version of feminism in order to move towards greater equality. But we should be looking for true choice, in a society characterised by freedom and equality. Instead, right now a rhetoric of choice is masking very real pressures on this generation of women. We are currently living in a world where those aspects of feminine behaviour that could be freely chosen are often turning into a cage for young women . . .

Above all, this is no time to succumb to inertia or hopelessness. Feminists in the West have already created a peaceful revolution, opening many doors for women that were closed to them before, expanding opportunities and insisting on women's rights to education, work and reproductive choice. We have come so far already. For our daughters, the escalator doesn't have to stop on the doll's floor.

Sara Wheeler

Sara Wheeler's books include the bestselling *Terra Incognita: Travels in Antarctica* and the prizewinning *The Magnetic North: Notes from the Arctic Circle*, which was chosen as Book of the Year by Will Self, Michael Palin, A.N. Wilson and others. *Access All Areas: Selected Writings 1990–2010* appeared this year. She is working on a book about Fanny Trollope and North America.

The happiest moment of my life presented itself one cool February afternoon in the Transantarctic mountains, many years ago. I was hiking up a valley. Fearful of losing my bearings, I stopped to fish a USGS map from my pack and spread it on the ice. Tracing my route by topographical landmarks (including an especially pointy mountain glaciologists had baptised The Doesn'tmatterhorn), my finger came to a straight line drawn with a ruler and marked *Limit of*

Compilation. Beyond that, the sheet was blank. I had reached the end of the map.

Travel writing is a house of many mansions. A journey – it has always seemed to me – loans a vehicle in which to explore the inner terrain of fears and desires we stumble through every day. Writing about travel allows flexibility and freedom within a rigid frame of train journeys, weather and a knackered tent. The creative process is an escape from personality (Eliot said that), and so is the open road. And a journey goes in fits and starts, like life.

I often hear it said that tourism has murdered travel writing. I don't think so. Mass travel has liberated the form. No amount of package tours will stop the ordinary quietly going on everywhere on earth. The end of the map has become a metaphor for fresh ideas, new connections. When I lived in Chile in the early nineties I found my weekly trawl round the supermarket gripping beyond belief: watching women decide between this jar of *dulche de leche* or that one, weighing out their chirimoyas, loading up with boxes of washing powder. Don't you sometimes find daily life almost unbearably poetic? Minute curiosity is a requirement of the travel writer – and of the biographer, novelist and poet. The significance of the trivial is what makes a book human. Out there on the road, I have often found that the most aimless and boring interludes yield, in the long run, the most fertile material.

In short, the notion that all the journeys have been made is just another variation of the theme that the past exists in Technicolor while the present has faded to grey – that everything then was good, and everything now is bad. A theme, in other words, as old as literature. The writer must forget that, and instead strive to be true to life and faithful to the world's multiplicity. Maps can end. Landscapes go on for ever.

Simon Winchester

Simon Winchester, a former geologist and foreign correspondent now living in New York, is a writer of non-fiction. He is currently working on a new book about the United States, of which he became a citizen on Independence Day 2011.

I want to get something off my chest. I have to be careful, because I don't want this to seem like a rant: I feel more puzzled than cross. But in truth it does trouble me – an Englishman in New York – that, while my books do enormously well here in America, they do rather indifferently back home. I am coming to accept that I am far less known – and here's the bit that will prompt the stifled laugh – than I feel I ought to be.

It began with *The Surgeon of Crowthorne*, a book I wrote in 1998 about the involvement of a mad killer in the making of the *Oxford English Dictionary*. In America, with a different title (*The Professor and the Madman*) it sold millions, was on the bestseller list for more than a year, and still sells well in hardback. In Britain, while it was pleasingly reviewed, fewer copies were sold than in Australia (where, most oddly, I am very well known, and sell well). Since then, every title of mine has performed according to a similar pattern: brilliantly in America, very well indeed in Canada, Australia and New Zealand, yet in what I can only describe as respectably lacklustre fashion in my homeland.

I am of course thrilled to have done well anywhere. I was taken to task once in America when I grumbled that one of my books had slipped briefly off the *NYT* list (*Have you any idea how lucky you are?* the store manager asked). Yet I do find it strange indeed that my storytelling falls on such generally infertile ground – if such mixing of metaphors is allowed – back where I belong.

My British reviews have been generally good, though often curiously brief (my most recent book, *Atlantic*, got three full pages in the NY *Review of Books*, only half a column in the *Sunday Times* here). Honours have been generous, and gratefully received – especially an OBE four years ago; the British Ambassador telling me that such are given to Britons living abroad 'for bringing honour and glory to our country', somewhat flies in the face of what I am arguing.

Except that it really doesn't. For what I am puzzled about is not the want of honour and distinction, nor the want of pleasing reviews. It is, simply, the want of sales. It is puzzlement over the fact that, while half of the audience after a lecture in Houston will line up to buy the book, only five per cent will in Britain. It is puzzlement that chain booksellers have little real idea of who I am.

Maybe, as a friend in London says, it is because my sentences are too long. Maybe it is because I am not on TV (having, as the same friend said, *a face made for radio*). Or maybe it is as an Oxford Festival lady said to me: *You've gone to America. We think you're a traitor.* Oh yes. She was serious. And didn't buy my book.

Part 3:
Write on

Planning

1: Planning the writing
by Sally Cline

Important general points for all literary non-fiction writers:

- Learn from good writers in the area you are interested in.
- Read, read, read in that particular area – be it sport, history, science, nature, whatever.
- Also read widely in all areas of non-fiction, noting how authors enliven their texts with exciting examples.

> **TOP TIP**
>
> *Travel writing may be different from food writing but both must highlight what is special and of interest to the author. That way it will not only inform but also entertain your readers.*

Issues and challenges to take into account

In Part One, we discussed a number of crucial ideas, issues, enigmas and snags. These were some of the main challenges we mentioned, plus some new ones:

- Who owns the story behind your non-fiction?
- How do you re-create the past if you weren't there?
- How do you make familiar subjects appear fresh?
- What do you do when witnesses offer different versions of the same event/place/person?
- How close to fiction can literary non-fiction get?

- How can you ensure that your subject stands for more than itself?

- How do you ensure that suspense and tension feed into your writing?

- What are the ethical and legal problems of writing about real people including your own family?

- How can you tell if a theme is ephemeral or if it will last?

- How do you tell complex stories in a readable way without oversimplifying?

- What are the problems of memory and myth-making in some forms of literary non-fiction?

- Should there always be a story and an interpretation or is a simple record of facts sufficient?

- How safe is it to blur the distinctions between one genre and another?

How to plan the writing for all genres
(e.g. travel, nature, feminism, history, etc.)

TOP TIP

When you first choose your subject and the angle you wish to write from, check out whether anyone has done something similar. You can always offer a new treatment but first read what has already been written.

Referential matter
This is the material that goes before and after the main text. It needs careful, accurate planning.

- The dedication comes at the start.

- The preliminaries go before the main text.

- Preliminaries include contents table, illustrations list, preface or prologue or introduction. In a piece of life writing you may also need a family tree.

- Preliminaries (up to or including the preface) are paginated separately, in lower-case roman numerals. This shows the difference between the preliminaries and text proper.

- The concluding material comes after the main text.

- Concluding material includes endnotes, bibliography, index. Some genres may need a subject index and an author index. Other genres may only use one.

- Acknowledgements can go before or after the main text. They are appreciations to people and organisations who have helped, funded or supported you.

- Permissions can go before or after the main text.

Preface and prologue in literary non-fiction

The preface

- A preface is a good introduction to your book.

- It gives readers a brief, clear summary of the goals, the themes and the content of your book.

TOP TIP 1

Some literary non-fiction is lengthy. Some reviewers are idle. They have no time to read your whole book. Your preface with its clear summary will help them. Make it readable. Ensure it says what you want people to quote from.

TOP TIP 2

Most authors write the preface when they have finished the book and can finally stand back and say: 'Oh, so that's what it's about!'

The clever author writes the bulk of it in rough at the start in order to give herself a memorable account of the book's aims and a prop to hang on to as she writes.

PREFACE EXERCISE

You are writing a travel memoir about a walking holiday through the Pyrenees. Halfway through the book and the holiday, you stop at a ruined cottage and decide to buy it.

Write the preface, giving enough of the contents to excite readers but not so much that you give away the storyline and denouement.

The prologue

The prologue is the introduction to the whole book. It is optional, but useful to give readers a sense of the book's tone, atmosphere, contents and aims.

The prologue could include an account of why you wrote it or what your aim is. It could open with an exciting introductory scene. This would work well in travel or nature or life writing. Here are some examples:

- In a book about birds it might be a scene featuring a particular bird about to become extinct.

- In a food book the scene might take place in an exotic foreign country where you are invited to sit down and eat a strange creature that you have never encountered before.

- If it is a memoir or autobiography the scene might take place during a key moment in the subject's life, such as witnessing a murder or being bullied at school.

Prologues also serve other functions:

- In travel books they can point ahead to the countries under scrutiny, methods of travel, what the traveller might expect and the reader might find.

- In neuroscience studies a prologue could help readers understand problems that occur in syndromes of the brain.

- In social history books a prologue might vividly set out the period and the range of key historical characters.

Footnotes and endnotes

Here are some particularly useful points from Midge Gillies.

Notes are used for citing references or for any extra information you want to supply but which would interrupt the narrative. They are usual in genres such as history and serious biography in which the reader will want to know where you obtained your information, but rarer in other types of non-fiction such as memoir.

You can put notes at the bottom of the page to which they refer ('footnotes') or gather them together as 'Notes' either at the end of the chapter – as in this book – or at the end of the book ('endnotes').

Most works of literary non-fiction, if they have notes at all, use endnotes and place them at the back of the book. A footnote sends a strong signal that the book is academic in tone and can put many readers off. However, you might choose to use the occasional note at the bottom of a page to make a comment that otherwise might be in brackets – for example, explaining how to pronounce an exotic word, or saying what happened to a character you don't intend to mention again.

Bibliography

The word 'bibliography' originally meant the academic study of books as physical cultural objects. But we use it in its current sense: a systematic list of books (usually in alphabetical order) and possibly also of the journal, newspaper or magazine articles referred to in your particular text. The bibliography comes at the end of your book after the subject material is finished.

A bibliographic citation of a book usually contains the following information:

- Author
- Title
- Publisher
- Place of publication
- Date of publication

The entry for a journal or periodical article will contain this information:

- Author(s)
- Article title
- Journal title
- Volume number
- Date of publication
- Page reference

Index

The earliest reference to an index dates from 1593, in Christopher Marlowe's *Hero and Leander*:

> *Therefore, even as an index to a book*
> *So to his mind young Leander's look.*

An index is a list of words or phrases (or both) termed 'headings' and associated pointers sometimes called 'locators'. Pointers in a non-fiction book are typically page numbers. In an academic index a pointer might also give paragraph numbers or section numbers.

An index is a very useful guide to where in your book readers can find material related to each heading. If you plan to use a single index then headings will include subjects, i.e. names of people, places, events, and also concepts, e.g. Victorian religious beliefs. Concepts must be relevant to the subject material and of interest to the range of readers likely to read your book.

If a single index seems too unwieldy you could devise two indexes, one for subjects and one for authors.

Indexes take a very long time to research, categorise and finally write. You may prefer to hand the job over to a member of the Society of Indexers who will draft your index for a fee. From January 2011, the Society recommended indexing rates of: £21.50 per hour, £2.40 per page, £6.50 per thousand words.

These rates are for an index to a straightforward text. An experienced indexer working on a complex book may charge more.

Contact: The Society of Indexers, Woodbourn Business Centre, 10 Jessell Street, Sheffield S9 3HY; 0144 244 9561 or 0845 872 6807; info@indexers.org.uk; www.indexers.org.uk. In the USA contact: The American Society for Indexing, 10200 West 44th Avenue, Suite 304, Wheat Ridge, CO 80033; (303) 463-2887; info@asindexing.org; www.asindexing.org.

2: Planning social or cultural history
by Midge Gillies

Writing a work of social or cultural history can take years and turn out to be an expensive enterprise. Before you embark on it, make sure it's something that stands a good chance of being published, and that will keep you entranced through the years of writing and research.

- Find out what's already been written about the subject and think about how you could produce something fresh. Do you have a new angle, new sources, a different viewpoint? Perhaps you want to write about a particular subject from the viewpoint of someone whose voice hasn't been heard before – for example, a female perspective, or that of an ethnic minority.

- What type of book do you want to write? Something definitive, or something that focuses on an element of a bigger topic? This will help to determine the length of the book and the level of research.

- What 'voice' will you write in – chatty or more distant? You may not know yet, but it will help if you have an idea of the kind of reader you're aiming at.

- What is your timeframe? If you're writing a history of bicycles, will you begin before their invention and end with how they might develop in future, or stick to some more limited period?

The skills audit

You don't have to be an expert in your subject — in fact, someone who is learning about a subject may be best placed to frame telling questions. But you do need the skills to understand the subject. As the proud owner of an 'O' Level certificate in Maths, grade C (gained with extra tuition), I could never hope to write anything involving sums. I feel dizzy just thinking about the subject of Alexander Masters' book *The Genius in my Basement*, which is about a mathematical prodigy.

But while I know my limitations well enough to steer clear of blackboards crowded with equations, I am prepared to fill the gaps in my knowledge if the rest of the subject interests me enough. I'm not an engineer, but I had sufficient knowledge of how ailerons and joysticks work to tackle the pioneering pilots of the twentieth century in my biography of Amy Johnson.

Before you commit yourself to an historical subject, ask yourself the following:

- Do you need to be fluent in another language? And if you don't already speak that language, do you have the linguistic talent, and the time, to learn that language? Alternatively, do you have a friend who can accompany you on your research trips, or translate documents? This, or the services of a professional interpreter or translator, will be expensive.

- Does your subject require a certain amount of technical knowledge and, if so, how easy would it be to acquire? If, for example, you want to write about the Pre-Raphaelite painters and you're not already an art historian, you will need to be prepared for the criticism of professionals who may feel you have encroached on their field. If, on the other hand, only one of the people in your book is a Pre-Raphaelite model, you may not need an in-depth understanding of the movement.

- Are there any courses you could take that would increase your knowledge? When I was researching the life of Amy Johnson, my husband bought me an hour's lesson in a Tiger Moth. It gave me an invaluable insight into the courage of the early aviators.

TOP TIP

During your research, keep an eye out for someone who is particularly knowledgeable and sees themselves as responsible for accuracy in their subject. They may be an archivist, librarian or someone who runs a study group.

Once you have built up a relationship of trust with them, you will be able to ask them questions, and they will probably let you know if any new material appears.

You may decide to ask them to read your final manuscript. It's usually advisable not to ask someone who is writing their own book on the subject, as they may be motivated by jealousy, or have their own agenda.

What and who do you need to know?

It is helpful to keep a notebook listing the people you need to interview, places to visit, books to consult or simply questions to which you need the answers.

● Draw up a list of books to read. Your starting point might be to photocopy the bibliography at the back of a book that covers the period or subject you're interested in. You will add to this as your research progresses.

● If you want an overview of a period or subject, find a biography or autobiography of a politician, monarch or key player. Or you might be fortunate enough to find a book that covers the period. For example, if you want to write about some aspect of the 1930s, Piers Brendon's *The Dark Valley* or Juliet Gardiner's *The Thirties* are both wonderful. For more recent history, Andy Beckett writes about Britain in the 1970s, e.g. in *When the Lights Went Out*.

● Make contact with any special interest groups that cover your period. The Researching Far East POW History Group (www.researchingfepowhis tory.org.uk/) led me to veterans I wanted to interview and academics, archivists and experts who helped me clarify points and explore new sources, as well as to the group's conference of international speakers.

EXERCISE: WHAT'S YOUR BOOK ABOUT?

Writing a blurb for the back of your book requires a certain style of writing. Sometimes your publisher will do this, but having a go yourself can be a useful way of focusing your mind. Aim for 500 words or fewer. What is your book about? Why would someone want to read it? In what ways is it different from other books in that genre?

Know your sources

This is an important consideration when it comes to planning your time and applying for travel grants. There may be some archives that it would be sensible to look at straight away because they provide the basic facts. Others may be more specialist and can wait until you have a more intimate knowledge of your subject. If an archive is a long way from home, you will have to make sure you make the most of your visit. Don't forget that new information may become available during your research as official files are released, descendants bequeath material to archives, or witnesses feel ready to share their experiences.

- Gather as many official documents as you can: birth, death and marriage certificates, wills and census returns. These will help you pin down your characters and provide a framework for your story.

- Where appropriate, draw up a family tree.

- If you want to interview someone, make sure you are on top of the subject before you approach them, but, if they are elderly, don't leave it too late.

- It's never too early to think about photos and other illustrations. Take photocopies where possible, or even see if you can obtain high-resolution scans of material you are likely to want to reproduce.

- Look out for temporary exhibitions about your subject – for example, at places like the Wellcome Institute in London – and keep an eye out for television documentaries.

TOP TIP

A timeline of events in your story will help you to see a structure and make you feel in control. A second timeline of events happening at the same time in the wider world will put your story into context. Put both side by side in a folder, or on your computer, to help you feel more confident about the period you're focusing on.

So, for example, if you're writing a history of space travel, you might have:

Space Travel

1963
16 June, Soviet Valentina Tereshkova
first woman in space

Wider world

1963
The Bell Jar (Sylvia Plath)

EXERCISE: CAPTURING A SENSE OF PLACE

Visit somewhere strongly connected to the people you are writing about or an event you are describing. Have a good look round and jot down what would have been there at the time and what has been added. Look out for any dates on buildings. What has changed? Would it have been noisier or quieter then? Would there have been more or less light? Would it have smelled different?

3: Planning travel writing and writing about nature and landscape

by Midge Gillies

Books about travel, nature and landscape are often more personal than other forms of literary non-fiction. Typically, their authors write from experience and from the heart. They don't have to search around for a subject; they already have a passion they want to explore on paper – whether that passion be a place, a bird or an animal, or a landscape. Usually they will write in the first person.

This sort of writing demands a distinct voice. Of course, it also helps if you have a different 'angle' on a familiar subject. In *Waterlog*, for example, Roger Deakin found an unusual way of writing about the British landscape by embarking on a series of swims. But his book was successful mainly because of his unique writing style.

The travel or nature writer is not in search of facts in the same way as someone writing about history or sport. The *experience* of nature or travel forms the backbone of this writing, so it is important to take notes throughout the journey. Facts about how the Taj Mahal was built can be gathered later; your impressions on first catching sight of it will be hard to remember even a day after the event.

You may start out with a theme in mind, or your writing may be part of a quest to reach a certain place (literally or spiritually). However, often the themes that emerge as you travel or observe are more interesting than the original impetus for your search.

TOP TIP

Frequently, it's the things that go wrong – the missed train, the rare bird that shows itself on the one day you decide to take a rest from the hide – that make the best writing. Even boredom can be entertaining for the reader – if written unboringly.

Read before you start writing

Apart from research, there are two reasons to read before you begin your book. The first is to help you to find your voice; to know what you like and don't like in a writing style. The second is to discover what has been written about your subject before.

- Reading will help to ensure that what you produce is new and fresh – but don't only read contemporary accounts.

- Looking at old books will show you how some attitudes have changed and others have become part of our accepted view, for example of a place. Consider how a Victorian traveller might describe India, and how someone visiting it today might.

- The same is true of animals. There are often commercial and cultural reasons why creatures such as whales and tigers have become endangered.

- Seek out rare books that give insights into a place's history: the battles it saw, how its landscape has changed and whether it was once sustained by a trade that has long since vanished.

- Don't just pick the obvious titles. Read about the food connected to a region, its religion and its geology. Think about how artists and novelists have seen it, and the wildlife that lived there.

EXERCISE ON RESEARCH AND ADDING LITERARY ALLUSIONS

Probably the most unusual animal I've ever held is a mole. I was stunned by the size of its feet, and at how muscular it seemed compared to the docile image fixed in my mind by Kenneth Grahame's *The Wind in the Willows*.

Choose an animal or bird (or a place if you're a travel writer) you're particularly interested in. Research any references to it in literature or folklore and incorporate these into your description.

Planning the journey – for travel and nature writers

Whether you're writing about a journey or nature, you have to decide whether you are aiming for exoticism or the familiar – but with some twist that makes the reader want to travel with you. You may choose to study your back garden or your own cat, or alternatively head for the Himalayas or take a year off in search of a rare bird.

Obviously, expense is going to play a big part in your decision about where you go and how long you can afford to spend away from paid work (see below). If you want to write about a place you've already visited or a creature you've already studied, there shouldn't be gaps in your knowledge. Is there someone you need to interview or an archive or picture library you need to consult?

> **TOP TIP**
>
> *Even if you think you have all the information you need in your head or in notebooks, an extra bit of research can help pep up your prose. Looking at a map, reading a new book or talking to someone in your field is a good way of preventing you from becoming stale.*

Funding

For most writers of literary non-fiction, travel is the single biggest expense, but if you think laterally you may discover ways of spreading the cost.

- Would an airline or ferry company pay your fare, or a hotel put you up for free? (You need to be sure this won't make you feel obliged to write something favourable about them.)
- Are there any conferences that might be interested in hearing you speak – and paying your fare?
- If you have a track record and can prove your commitment to a project, you might be able to become a writer in residence. The British Antarctic Survey, for example, has in the past run a scheme for writers and artists.
- If you are able to build workshops around your book, you could earn money by visiting schools and colleges.

4: Planning a biography or autobiography
by Sally Cline

Planning a biography or an autobiography is an exciting but complex process.

Volume 1 of this series, *The Arvon Book of Life Writing: Writing Biography, Auto-biography and Memoir,* gives readers detailed information on planning all types of life writing. If you want to write a biography, autobiography or memoir, do consult it. Here in Sections 4 and 5 I summarise the key points.

Planning a biography

- Choose a subject from an area you are interested in, such as sport, politics or literature.

- Check out whether anyone else has written a biography of your subject. If so, when.

- Write a proposal. This is useful for securing an agent, or for fundraising for your project. And to focus your mind.

- Problems of cost and the availability of funds are vital to your planning process. Few authors can afford to start researching a biography without either a commission or a grant/award, or both.

- Look in advance at other help, e.g. courses, mentoring, literary development agencies. (See details in Section 8.)

- Most crucial is a plan for the structure.

How to choose a subject

Ask yourself:

- Should your subject be unknown and new or already written about or indeed famous?

- If the subject is unknown, think of a slant that is provocative and original. If your subject has already been written about, you need either new research in one area or a new angle.

- Should your subject be a single person or do you want to write a group study?

- Today publishers are more interested in group portraits (for example, a study of three sisters or two lovers) rather than the classic single subject. If you have set your heart on a birth-to-death life of a single person, you will definitely need an original take on it.

- Should you choose a subject who is alive or dead?

- The dead are much easier to write about. Biographies of the living often encounter problems and conflicts with family and friends, or indeed the subject him/herself, who can criticise or even try to control your work. Be wary.

- Remember that you cannot libel the dead. So choosing a dead subject can be a good idea.

TOP TIP 1

A frequently asked question is: Do you have to like your subject? The quick answer is that it helps if you do! You will be more sympathetic and more dedicated. However, you can take on a subject who seems interesting but at first dislikable. After two or more years, they may become dear to you.

TOP TIP 2

What happens if you dislike your subject?
You might end up loathing your subject, as did Roger Lewis, biographer of Anthony Burgess. But somehow you have to make him or her authentic and believable to readers, or they will be put off.

TOP TIP 3

What if you fall passionately in love with your subject? To avoid boring your readers, however much you love your subject, please look at their flaws too.

Who are your readers?

It is always useful to have your main readership in mind. This will also help you decide on the level of your material. Your main choices are:

- An academic audience
- A literary mainstream audience
- A popular mainstream audience

Academic readers will include fellow university scholars, researchers and postgraduate students. They will be happy with scholarly apparatus and specialised vocabularies.

Literary mainstream readers, such as those who read *The Times, Guardian* or *Observer* in the UK or the *New York Times* or the *Los Angeles Times* in the USA, are the target audience for writers of literary non-fiction. They will be interested in thought-provoking subjects, and excellent to great literary writing of a non-specialised kind.

A popular mainstream readership might find more pleasure in biographies of celebrities, entertainers or sport stars, and will require first-rate storytelling and entertainment skills.

What type of biography should you write?

Biographies can be authorised or unauthorised, commissioned or uncommissioned.

COMMISSIONING: TOP TIP 1

If you are commissioned by a publisher, you will probably get one-third of your advance on signing your contract. This is useful as research is expensive, especially if archives and contacts are abroad.

TOP TIP 2

Uncommissioned biographies present major problems of funding and also of time. To get financial help, see Section 8.

AUTHORISATION: TOP TIP 1

Authorised biographies have the advantage of unique access to family files and other private materials. If the estate and family are on your side, they can give you many more close contacts than you would otherwise find easily.

The disadvantage is that family and friends can interfere.

TOP TIP 2

Freedom and independence are the advantages of non-authorised biographies. You can go where you like for information and ask whom you like for interviews.

But you can be wrong-footed if the estate or family absolutely refuse to help you. They can, moreover, prevent other relatives and friends from aiding you.

SALLY'S NOTE

I have managed to avoid both the above traps. My books have been neither authorised nor unauthorised. The estates and families have had no contract with me or my publisher, so they could not control my work and findings. On the other hand, they have always known what I am doing and have all been very helpful. I have been lucky, however; the risk is always there.

Who chooses?

Subjects of biographies can be chosen by you or your agent, or suggested by the publisher or the subject her/himself, if alive. If you choose the subject, you must write a proposal to sell your idea to agents and publishers.

Proposals

In Section 7, Midge offers all writers of literary non-fiction ideas on how to write proposals. Here are a few suggestions on planning proposals specifically for *biographies*.

Elements to include:

- Introduction to your biography
- Timeliness of your book
- Why a publisher would want to commission this topic
- Your literary intentions (where relevant)
- Your subject's life (include timeline)
- Your subject's work (where relevant)
- Limitations of previous biographies
- Research programme and travel
- Estimate of costs

- Estimate of length of time needed

- What preliminary research has been done

- Which contacts you have already established

- Relevance of your previous books

- Relevance of your interests, passions, other research

- Competition with other books in the same area

TOP TIP 1

Though it may feel too early to include in your proposal a full outline of the book with a chapter or section breakdown, it can be helpful to commissioning editors and it is definitely helpful to you. It will form the backbone of ideas that need structuring.

TOP TIP 2

Give your work a racy, interesting or memorable title. Put that title in your proposal. It is a selling point to agents and publishers. A good title will help your book to sell.

Titles for biographies

Some biographers put the subject's name first as a title, then give it a sub-title, e.g.

> *Mary Wollstonecraft: A New Genus*
> *Amy Johnson: Queen of the Air*

Other biographers put an explanatory line first as the title, then under it the sub-title has the subject's name, e.g.

> *Savage Beauty: The Life of Edna St Vincent Millay*
> *The Invisible Woman: The Story of Nelly Ternan and Charles Dickens*
> *Burying the Bones: Pearl Buck in China*

Costs

Section 8 will help you work out funding problems. But writing a major biography involves massive costs.

- There is the cost of research: often travelling to archives abroad.
- There are costs for textual permissions. You have to clear copyrights for all quotations beyond short phrases.
- Costs for illustrations and for illustration permissions.
- Costs for the index, often paid for out of your royalties and organised by the publisher.
- There are legal risks to bear in mind and, if you are unfortunate, these might be expensive.

Structure of biographies

For general guidance on structure see Section 6, where Midge deals with the structure of all kinds of literary non-fiction including life writing.

For detailed advice on biographical structure, see pages 177–83 in *The Arvon Book of Life Writing.*

Planning an autobiography

If autobiography is your aim, reading the section on planning a biography will be useful as certain things are similar, e.g.

- The necessity of reading in your genre as much as you can to give you a clear feel for the subject
- Checking out: all research plans, list of interviewees (if needed), ethical and legal problems, etc.
- Deciding on the level of work
- Titles

Much, however, is unique to autobiography.

Questions autobiographers need to ask

- How good is your memory? Many autobiographers fall into myth-making. Try to tell the 'truth' as you genuinely recall it.

- How will your family and friends react to your autobiography? You should check with them any parts that might attract ethical or even legal problems.

- What role does the notion of 'truth' play in your autobiography? How factual should it be?

- Is there a special event you cannot forget? If so, that can be a good trigger for starting your autobiography.

TOP TIP

Facts alone won't make a good story. Your interpretation is needed too. But the facts you decide to use – and autobiography is always a matter of selection – should be verifiable.

Special stories and angles

If you are an ordinary writer rather than a celebrity, a famous politician or movie star, you need to ensure that you have a special story to tell, e.g.

- Have you been adopted and then set out to find your birth parents? Now you want to tell the tale of the trail.

- Perhaps you were a child of travelling parents who never lived in one country longer than three months. One of those countries might have been of immense importance to you.

Focus on the angle that will interest an agent and publisher and later your readers.

Whole or part?

Do you want to write a classic autobiography, i.e. a review of the whole of your life up to the point of writing? If so, you might choose to write it chronologically, picking out interesting incidents from each part of your life.

Or would you prefer to concentrate on themes that have run throughout your life? Or a particular period or experience? If the latter, you are probably moving towards *memoir*. Decide why you have chosen to write it now. Did something spectacular or scary happen to you this year? Did a cache of memories that you thought were hidden spring up? Are you thinking of an autobiography or of a more narrowly focused memoir? For the differences between autobiography and memoir, see Section 5, and *The Arvon Book of Life Writing* (passim).

AUTOBIOGRAPHICAL EXERCISE

Imagine you have been a fortunate and famous ice skater. For many years you have reaped awards and prizes. Suddenly, at 27, at the peak of success, you are involved in a terrible car crash. One leg is damaged beyond repair. It must be amputated.

Decide before writing how you dealt with that news and what the rest of your life was like.

• Write out the structure of the autobiography.

• Write the four opening paragraphs of Chapter 1 in 300 words maximum.

Costs of writing an autobiography

● In comparison with a biography, a much shorter time is usually needed.

● Time and money for textual permissions, photograph permissions, legal risks will be similar to those for biography.

● You can save time in autobiographies by not using endnotes.

● Indexes: save money by not having lengthy subject and place indexes and therefore not needing to use professional indexers.

● You will need a name index. This can either be done by a professional indexer or you can compile one yourself and save costs.

Titles and other selling points

Titles must attract readers' attention. They can either give a hint as to the content, e.g. Virginia Woolf's *A Room of One's Own* (1929), or they can intrigue as in *Knots in my Yo-Yo String* by Jerry Spinelli.

First and last lines are important. For a discussion of the skill of writing opening and closing lines, see *The Arvon Book of Life Writing*, pages 235–7.

Here are some titles I find arresting:

Blankets
A Long Walk to Freedom
I Know Why the Caged Bird Sings
Dreams from My Father
The Year of Magical Thinking

EXERCISE ON TITLES and FIRST SENTENCES

Give your autobiography the best title possible. Write it now.

Write the first sentence of your autobiography.

5: Planning a memoir
by Sally Cline

Read as many memoirs as you can. Remember, most memoirs are either written by extraordinary people or by ordinary people who have some extraordinary, special or interesting experience, theme or subject they wish to share.

Types of memoirs

Memoirs can be subject or theme-based. They can be woven around people, places, adventures or experiences, and around childhood, old age, sickness, even death.

At present the bookshops are crammed with celebrity memoirs and misery memoirs, as well as memoirs on subjects as diverse as bereavement and holidays in Venice. Many of these are exciting, interesting and honest.

A few are fakes and frauds, such as James Frey's addiction memoir *A Million Little Pieces* or the Holocaust memoir *Fragments*. These books betray the trust between writer and reader. That *trust is essential and is based on truth*.

How to plan

If you want to write a memoir, first scrutinise Section 4 on Autobiography, as certain elements are similar.

But though memoirs are a form of autobiographical writing, not all auto-biography is memoir, because it does not follow the same criteria.

Autobiography encompasses an entire life (up to the point of writing), is usually told chronologically in the first person and focuses on development of personality.

Memoirs are more focused and more flexible. They can take a portion of a life, half a life, significant memories during a life.

- A memoir is a first-person account of one experience, aspect, place or period in someone's life.

- Autobiographers focus as much or more on self. Memoirists focus more on others.

A WRITER'S DEFINITION

Author Gore Vidal in his own memoir, Palimpsest, *gave a personal definition:
'A memoir is how one remembers one's own life, while an autobiography is history, requiring research, dates, facts double-checked.'*

EXERCISE

Find three memoirs that adhere to Vidal's definition and three memoirs that do not.

Write down their titles and give a two-paragraph outline for each one.

Questions to ask yourself

● Do I want to record a particular place, event, person or time?

● What was fascinating/curious/fateful about any of these? Did it change my life in some way?

● Would that place or that period be interesting to others?

● Remember, if you get relevant facts wrong (such as historical dates or names of statues in a foreign plaza), your readers will stop trusting you.

TOP TIP

You can begin and end your memoir where you like. This is because by their nature memoirs are partial. But you can't invent what you like. Memoir readers must believe in you and your material. They will expect a strong link to reality.

Outlines

Memoirists, like autobiographers, are less likely to get publishing commissions in advance, unless they are famous or writing about a famous event such as 9/11. But what you can do is to write a sturdy outline, which shows the selling points of the memoir's contents and the reasons why you should be paid to write it.

Titles

Here are some memoir titles that woke me up:

> *Impossible Motherhood: Testimony of an Abortion Addict*
>
> *Bird Cloud: A Memoir*
>
> *Amen, Amen, Amen: Memoir of a Girl Who Couldn't Stop Praying (Among Other Things)*
>
> *A Child Called 'It'*
>
> *You Don't Look Like Anyone I Know: A True Story of Face Blindness and Forgiveness*
>
> *An Unquiet Mind: A Memoir of Moods and Madness* *

If you are famous or well loved, you may not need to find a clever title, e.g.

- Bill Clinton called his memoir *My Life*
- Bob Dylan called his *Chronicles: Volume 1*

Both became bestsellers.

In a competition organised by *Smith Magazine* which set out to find racy memoir titles in only six words, several famous writers suggested these:

- *Revenge is Living Well Without You* (Joyce Carole Oates)
- *Well, I Thought It Was Funny* (Stephen Colbert)
- *Fifteen Years Since Last Professional Haircut* (Dave Eggers)

---

* Details of these titles are: Irene Vilar, *Impossible Motherhood: Testimony of an Abortion Addict*, Other Press, New York, 2009; Annie Proulx, *Bird Cloud: A Memoir*, Scribner, New York, 2011; Fourth Estate, London, 2011; Abby Sher, *Amen, Amen, Amen: Memoir of a Girl Who Couldn't Stop Praying (Among Other Things)*, Scribner, New York, 2011; Dave J. Pelzer, *A Child Called 'It'*, HCI Books, Florida, 1995; Orion, London, 2012; Heather Sellers, *You Don't Look Like Anyone I Know: A True Story of Face Blindness and Forgiveness*, Riverhead Books, New York, 2010; Kay Redfield Jamison, *An Unquiet Mind: A Memoir of Moods and Madness*, Alfred Knopf, New York, 1995; Picador, London, 1997.

EXERCISE

Here are four titles of well-known memoirs:

Memoirs of a Dutiful Daughter

Memoirs of a Not So Dutiful Daughter

The Three of Us

This Is Not About Me[*]

- Write each title on the top of a page.
- Pretend you are the author of each book.
- Under each title invent and write a three-paragraph synopsis.
- Then write down the first line of each book.

Cost of writing memoirs

Memoirs are less costly than biographies. They also take much less time to research and write.

The research is limited, as it is in autobiography. You will already have the main documents to supplement your memories: birth and death certificates, maps and guides to places visited, possibly old diaries. Unlike in autobiography, you are not covering your whole life, so again less research and probably less writing time.

You will have the costs of interviews – tape recorders, cassettes – and all printing and computer costs. You might need a travel budget if you wish to revisit certain places or people. Expenditure on courses, mentoring, permissions for quoted text or any illustrations will be similar to what you would have in biography and autobiography.

TOP TIP

If you want to write about something with a special appeal for you and, you hope, for many others, go ahead – read the guidelines and enjoy yourself!

---

* The authors of these memoirs are: Simone de Beauvoir (1959), Jenni Murray (2008), Julia Blackburn (2008) and Janice Galloway (2008).

6: Structure for all types of literary non-fiction
by Midge Gillies

What is 'structure'?

The structure of a book is the order in which you present your facts or tell your story.

Consider the structure of a house. The architect has to decide how the rooms will fit together. Every part of the building must have a good reason to be where it is. The architect will consider the best way into the house and, for both aesthetic and practical reasons, where he or she should put the bedrooms, study, bathroom, etc. The writer's job is the same.

Most writers, however, find that the structure of their book changes and evolves once they start writing.

- Your research may take you in a different direction, either to a dead end or to a whole new treasure trove of facts.

- People – even dead ones – have a habit of staking a claim to inclusion. Some characters become more interesting; others, on closer inspection, prove to be dull.

- You may find that you can't quote from a particular source: either the estate won't let you or you can't afford the fees.

- A theme may develop that you would like to pursue, but hadn't considered at the start of the book.

- As you reread, you may feel that the order is wrong and chapters need to be moved around.

Luckily, most of us write on a word processor these days, making it easy to move text.

I keep detailed plans of how I envisage a book developing and where I intend to put information. I update it regularly, sometimes several times a day. I find this very useful to refer to – especially when I'm writing a long book and struggling to keep on top of mountains of notes and legions of characters.

TOP TIP

If you're not sure about the right place for a particular passage, highlight it in a different colour and leave a note in square brackets to yourself. For example: '[Is this the right place for a paragraph on the popularity of seances in Edwardian Britain, or does it belong in Chapter Two?].' This will allow you to make the final decision without breaking the thread of your writing.

Looking for inspiration when planning your structure

Everyone has a different way of planning their book. You could try drawing a 'mind map', or putting different chapters on index cards and spreading them out on the floor. If you're musical, you might see your story as a tune that needs variety and changes of mood and pace. Others think in a more visual way and imagine their story in cinematic terms. As I mentioned earlier, Rebecca Skloot borrowed techniques from several different disciplines, including fiction and film, to construct *The Immortal Life of Henrietta Lacks*.

The Writers' Rooms feature in *The Guardian* (www.guardian.co.uk/books/series/writersrooms) provides a fascinating insight into how writers work, including how they plan their writing. Will Self, for instance, says that his books start life in notebooks, and then move on to Post-it notes pinned on to his office walls, before being transferred into scrapbooks.

See: www.guardian.co.uk/books/2007/apr/06/writers.rooms.will.self

As you burrow further into your writing, you will need this sort of 'writer's nest' from which to work. Unless you are the sort of person who is able to keep everything in their head, you will probably want to have your plan close to hand. Some people pin it on a wall next to maps, photos, family trees and timelines.

When you're planning your structure consider the following:

- The first chapter will set the tone for the book. It also needs to grab the reader's attention.

- Try to vary the length of your chapters. Short ones can be very effective – especially at the end of a section, or to create a shift in pace or mood.

- Think carefully about the dramatic peaks in your story: for example, a death, a battle, a moment of danger. Make sure they aren't all crowded together, and that you make the most of them.

- Vary the pace. If your story is too breathless, it will be difficult to appreciate the most thrilling moments. Every piece of dramatic writing needs quiet moments as contrast.

- What themes do you want to introduce, and how will you do it?

- Is there anything technical you need to explain to a lay audience? How will you achieve this? And how soon do you need to do it – too soon and they might be put off, too late and they might not understand what you're saying.

- How much of yourself will you include in the story and when, if ever, will you write in the first person?

- You might also consider introducing some fictionalised sections, if you want to be slightly more daring and imaginative in your approach, or in areas where there are few facts. Peter Ackroyd does this in his biography of Dickens and Alison Light adopts a similar technique in *Mrs Woolf and the Servants*.

SPOTTING DRAMATIC POINTS EXERCISE

Cut out an obituary of someone who interests you and make a list of the dramatic points in their life, together with the dates. For a famous Russian ballet dancer, this might be their death, the first time they performed, their first major success; and dates of injuries, exile, retirement. Make a list of the themes in their life. (The two most obvious ones in this case would be dance and politics.) Finally, make a list of the cast of people in their life.

Pick up any work of literary non-fiction and flick through it. Glance at the contents page. That will give you some idea of how this particular writer structured their book.

The most common approach is to arrange the story in a chronological order – the author's year in the Antarctic, the life story of a famous writer, the history of a food. But, once you start to read, you will probably find that the author has jumped backwards and forwards in time, gone off on tangents and woven various ideas or themes into the narrative. It would be a dull book – and probably not literary non-fiction – if they hadn't done so. Part of their skill is that the reader is not aware of the fine planning that went into the book, but simply reads for pleasure and edification.

You will know from your own reading what you think works as a structure, but once you start planning you may have to find your way into the structure through trial and error. When I was writing about prisoners of war in the Second World War, I first considered basing the chapters on subjects such as art, learning, performance, sport. But this didn't seem to give the men whose stories I was telling a chance to be heard. Next I considered basing them on particular POW camps – but that didn't work either, because the prisoners were moved around so much. And how did I distinguish between camps in Europe and the much harsher regime in the Far East?

After much experimenting, I took a broadly chronological approach. This had the advantage of using the war's inbuilt drama – its start, the Allies' major defeats, then the gradual turnaround and the end in victory. I began in Europe, where the war started, and in Part Two switched to the Far East, with all the drama of the surprise attack by the Japanese. I then switched back again. I hoped this would give the reader the urge to read on, in order to find out what

MIDGE'S NOTE

The occasional lean chapter can be extremely effective. In Kathryn Hughes's The Short Life and Long Times of Mrs Beeton *she introduces a number of 'interludes' in which she pauses from the main biography to discuss specific themes or topics, such as what 'dinner' meant to the Victorians, or Mrs Beeton's understanding of the link between health and diet.*

On this model, at the start of The Barbed-Wire University *I included three short chapters on 'Uses for a Red Cross Parcel' as a way of changing the pace.*

happened to the men. I wove my themes, such as the extraordinary role of art and learning, into this human story.

As Sally has said in her chapter on planning your book, it can be very helpful to have a reader in mind. It could even be someone you know. This will allow you to gauge how they might react to your structure: would they enjoy it and keep reading, or would they find it confusing, or too slow? If they are a good friend, you could even ask them to read it.

7: Writing a proposal
by Midge Gillies

Very few authors enjoy writing a book proposal, but it can be an extremely useful exercise – not just in securing a publishing deal, but also in forcing you to stop and think about the structure of your work.

Writing a proposal or 'pitch' requires different skills from writing a book. This difficulty is increased by the fact that most of us only write a proposal every few years. When I write a proposal, I try to imagine a room full of 'Sales and Marketing' people who are constantly looking at their watches and who may not even read many books – and certainly not the sort I want to write.

First contact

● Whether you're approaching a publisher or an agent (see below), make sure your proposal is going to the right place. Consult the *Writers' & Artists' Yearbook* or *The Writer's Handbook* to see which agent or publisher prefers the sort of book you want to write. The latter will also tell you whether an agent or publisher is willing to accept unsolicited approaches. Many publishers will only consider a manuscript or proposal from an agent.

● Always send your proposal to a specific, named person. 'Commissioning editor' is too vague, and your letter may be lost, or end up in 'chick lit' when you were trying to reach the head of the history list. A quick phone call should put you right. Remember to check the spelling of the person's name and their correct title.

- Agents and publishers are busy people; your covering letter should be brief and businesslike. Don't be obsequious or aggressive, or try to be funny. Always send a stamped addressed reply envelope, and, unless specifically requested, send a 'hard copy' rather than an electronic version.

- Never send an original document, whether the proposal or the full manuscript.,

---

TOP TIP

Although there is no copyright in an idea or facts, copyright in a work exists as soon as it is recorded. The Society of Authors recommends that you include © [Your Name] 20** when you send in a typescript (although, if you forget, it doesn't mean you've forfeited your right).

The Society also suggests adding a line in your covering letter saying that you own the rights to your proposal, and that you are showing it to the publisher or agent in confidence.

Marketing your idea

Those hard-nosed people in Sales and Marketing (and your editor before agreeing to take it to a sales meeting) will want evidence that your idea can become a commercial success.

Make sure your proposal includes:

- A convincing argument about why there is a market for your book. Perhaps there's never been a modern biography of a certain crime writer, but he/she has a huge fan base; or maybe a Facebook site about a certain subject has thousands of followers, suggesting there's a demand for that subject.

- The competition. What books have already been written on the subject and why will yours be different? If there aren't any books on the subject, could there be a good reason why not? Perhaps people who enjoy horse racing don't tend to read books on the subject (although *Seabiscuit* showed that the story of a horse can have wide appeal).

- Your Unique Selling Point. Perhaps you have spoken to the last survivor of a particular disaster, you're related to an important figure in your story, or you've spent the last ten years living with snow leopards.

- Why you are the best person to write this book. What skills and advantages do you have? Do you have a track record? If you're a New Yorker and the book has a strong link to the city, this could help build a local readership. Are you a good public speaker? Do you write for publications where you could promote the book? Or are you a blogger with a loyal following? Do you know a well-known name who might give you a quote for the back of the book?

TOP TIP

Writers aren't always good at selling themselves. Ask a friend – preferably a writer – to write a paragraph about why you are the best person to produce this particular book.

EXERCISE (FOR GROUPS)

Divide into pairs and pick a book (or, if you're feeling brave, use an idea of your own). Each pair prepares a presentation of their book for a sales and marketing meeting, as if it were still at the proposal stage. Why is the book a good idea and what makes the author marketable? The rest of the group can ask questions, and, when all the sales pitches have been delivered, the group votes on which book they would offer a contract.

The proposal

Your finished book is likely to look quite different from your initial proposal. Unless you deliver a children's novel when your publisher was expecting a travel book about Peru, this shouldn't matter too much. Very few writers can tell once they embark on a manuscript which way the story will take them. And even when you submit what you think is a finished book, your editor or agent may have ideas about how you can improve it.

Your proposal should include the following:

● An overview showing what your book's about. This will also give a flavour of your writing style.

● A chapter breakdown, explaining what you intend to cover in each. (Again, don't worry if this won't resemble the finished book.)

● Illustrations. Will the book have maps, photos, sketches? Will you need to pay any copyright fees? Remember that colour illustrations will push up production costs, and the publisher should have a budget for illustrations.

● Word length. This can be difficult to foresee, but the book won't feel 'real' unless you include an estimate in the proposal. You should also check to see whether a publisher only publishes books of a certain length.

● A deadline. Only you know how much you have already written, or how much material you have gathered. Be realistic, but don't allow yourself too much time or your project will be forgotten. For one book, which took me two and a half years, I went through four different editors.

TOP TIP

If it looks as though you are likely to miss a deadline, or that your manuscript will be much longer or shorter than you had expected, you should speak to your agent and publisher as soon as possible. Schedules are worked out a long time in advance and a sudden change in delivery time or length can cause trouble.

What's in a title?

Sometimes titles come first. I settled on *Waiting for Hitler* as soon as I began to think about what it would be like to live under the threat of Nazi invasion.

The title for my book about Second World War POWs went through a much more painful pregnancy. I came up with all sorts of lacklustre ideas, until my editor suggested *The Barbed-Wire University*.

Many POWs used this expression to describe what they had learned from their experience of captivity, and one camp even referred to its education section in this way. It had the advantage of being quirky and memorable, but I wasn't sure. I finally agreed after my publisher said it had had a strong response from booksellers, and I'm glad I did. It now seems exactly the right title to me. I have resisted the temptation to take the credit for it – so far.

TOP TIP

Remember the internet and search engines such as Google when you're thinking of titles.

Some part of your title should make it as easy as possible for people to stumble across your book if they're interested in the subject. The subtitle for The Barbed-Wire University *is* The Real Lives of Allied Prisoners of War in the Second World War. *'Prisoners of War' and 'Second World War' should alert anyone who's interested in these two subjects. 'Real Lives' hints that this will be a book about social rather than military history.*

One of my early, and least successful, suggestions for the main title was Prisoner's Pie *(a reference to a magazine produced in one camp). I thought this gave a sense of the creativity among POWs – until my agent pointed out that the book might end up in a cookery ghetto somewhere on the internet.*

8: Mentoring and other matters
by Sally Cline

In this section, we consider writers' groups, courses, literary consultancies, mentoring, grants, literary prizes and organisations.

Among the many plans writers of literary non-fiction must make, one of the most crucial is to decide what (if any) financial and literary support you may need.

All writers at one time or another need help from other writers who have travelled the same path, and non-fiction writers, most particularly those engaged on long research-heavy books, may also be in urgent need of finance.

Writers' groups, circles, workshops
Informal **writers' groups** can be found today in most big cities and many smaller towns and can be most helpful. Each member brings material to read out and discuss with the others. Groups are generally run in libraries, in bookshops or at members' homes, rather like book clubs. They have a friendly, encouraging atmosphere which helps new writers become adventurous.

- *Directory of Writers' Circles, Courses and Workshops* contains contact details for the UK's 1,000 groups and courses: 39 Lincoln Way, Harlington, LU5 6NG (01525 873 197); Diana@writers-circles.com; www.writers-circles.com. Within this central directory you can find a special section for Travel Writers.

- For a comprehensive list of writers' groups and courses use *The Writer's Handbook 2011*, ed. Barry Turner, Macmillan, London, which is excellent on USA courses and groups as well as those in the UK, and/or *Writers' & Artists' Yearbook 2012*, ed. Jo Herbert, A&C Black, London (revised yearly). These books both have useful material to add to that set out in this chapter.

Courses in the UK

- **Creative Writing MAs** are now offered by many universities in the UK (and in the USA: see below). Most offer either full- or part-time courses, some both. The best university MA courses employ as tutors published writers who are also good mentors. Only go for those. Also ensure the course gives you plenty of time for your own writing. An MA in Creative Writing that is dominated by literature modules may be interesting academically but will be less useful for the practical business of writing.

- **Online writing MAs** are springing up. Though there is no personal contact, they do offer communication with fellow writers from other backgrounds and disciplines.

- **Undergraduate creative writing degrees or diplomas**. Many universities have writing programmes (more and still better in the USA, although the UK is catching up) for people without undergraduate degrees. These can be taken on their own or in conjunction with English Literature or Media Studies courses. Diplomas might take one or two years; degrees will require the standard three years full-time.

- **Creative writing classes**. Some courageous local councils still run these. Track them down by approaching your local Literature Development officer, or ask in the library. It is also worth phoning all the community colleges in your region. Very well worth investigating if you are over 50 and not in full-time employment is the University of the Third Age. Many U3As run highly successful writing classes directed and taught by established writers.

Courses in the USA

There is an excellent section on American writers' courses in *The Writer's Handbook 2011*.

Some of them are university courses, others are at Film Institutes or Arts Institutes, several are at small liberal arts colleges that run high-level courses in the community. The MFA Creative Writing Programs can be found in most large city university departments. Undergraduate courses are also run. Always try to establish who is tutoring on them and go for highly established published writers rather than academics wherever possible. Three courses I would recommend highly are:

- **Eastern Washington University** MFA Creative Writing Program, Inland Northwest Center for Writers, Eastern Washington University, 501 N. Riverpoint Blvd./Suite 425, Spokane WA 99202 (001 509 359 4950); prussell@ewu.edu

- **The James A. Michener Center for Writers**, University of Texas at Austin, 702 East Dean Keeton Street, Austin, Texas 78705; mcw@www.utexas.edu. There are three-year interdisciplinary courses on the MFA programme in fiction, screenwriting, poetry and playwriting. Students are supported by annual fellowships of $25,000 dollars plus remission of tuition and fees. The program is highly competitive.

- **Hunter College of the City University of New York**, 605 Park Avenue, New York 10065 (001 212 772 5164); mfa@hunter.cuny.edu. MFA programme in Creative Writing in the Department of English. Two-year programme in fiction, memoir and poetry. Hunter's Distinguished Writers Series brings world-class writers to teach and give readings. The Hertog Fellowship in Fiction and Memoir pays students to work as researchers for such writers as Toni Morrison, Jonathan Safran Foer and Jonathan Franzen. Other scholarships pay students to work for established poets.

Literary consultancies and writing development groups

The following UK agencies and consultancies have strong reputations for helping writers from diverse backgrounds, all ages and most writing genres to achieve their full potential and become recognised professionally.

- **Spread the Word.** This development agency provides support through networking events, publisher and agent talks, advice surgeries, online literary help, community programmes and mentoring. Their aim is to develop and showcase writers to ensure both they and their communities benefit. Programme Coordinator: Annette Brook, 77 Lambeth Walk, London SE11 6DX (0207 735 3111); Annette@spreadtheword.org.uk

- **Writers' Centre, Norwich**. This literature development agency based in Norwich is dedicated to supporting creative fiction and non-fiction writing not only in the eastern and south-eastern area but also nationally and internationally. 14 Princes Street, Norwich NR3 1AE (01603 877177); info@writerscentrenorwich.org.uk; www.writerscentrenorwich.org.uk

- **The Literary Consultancy** is the best-known agency which offers both critiques of your writing for a fee, and also online and by-post mentoring. Founded and directed by Rebecca Swift, herself a writer, it uses highly qualified critics and writers and gives detailed feedback in a reasonable time: info@literaryconsultancy.co.uk

- **New Writing South**. This organisation works through the south-east to create environments where creative writers can flourish. It offers development, resources and partnerships between writers and those able to produce or project their work. Emerging, aspiring and professional writers can all apply. Director: Chris Taylor, 9 Jew Street, Brighton BN1 1UT (01273 735353); www.newwritingsouth.com

- **Susan Grossman Writing Workshops & Media Coach**. Susan Grossman is an established travel writer, media coach, trainer, editor and journalist who also lectures at universities. She runs workshops for authors looking to focus ideas and approach editors. She runs regular Travel Writing workshops in central London. She also runs one-to-one mentoring sessions online and by phone: 0207 794 0288; susangrossman@tiscali.co.uk; www.susangrossman.co.uk

Mentoring

One-to-one face-to-face mentoring is probably the greatest help aspiring and even established writers can have. It is not easy for any writer today to acquire an agent or break into the publishing world on their own. However talented you are as a writer, both you and your work will benefit from guidance.

- **Gold Dust Writers' Mentoring.** This professional scheme founded and directed by the novelist Jill Dawson is the one we have both chosen to mentor for. Gold Dust only uses well-known writers with fine reputations as mentors and judges. New writers can work with experienced authors in their chosen specialist area. They receive face-to-face tutoring advice, and their manuscripts are read and reviewed in advance of each mentoring session: PO Box 247, Ely, Cambs. CB7 9BX; webenquiry@gold-dust.org.uk; www.gold-dust.org.uk

- **The Jerwood Foundation** organises mentoring and also offers various writing schemes: info@jerwood.org

Grants

Many grants for writers have recently been cut and more cuts are due. However, these contacts are worth trying.

- **Arts Council England**: www.artscouncil.org.uk
- **New Writing North**: www.newwritingnorth.com
- **New Writing South**: www.newwritingsouth.com
- **British Academy**: www.britac.ac.uk
- **Leverhulme Research Fellowships**: www.Leverhulme.ac.uk/grants_awards
- **The Royal Society of Literature, Jerwood Awards** gives grants to unpublished writers. These have in the past included general non-fiction writers and biographers: www.jerwoodcharitablefoundation.org
- **The Biographers Club** offers prizes to new literary non-fiction writers of biographies, autobiographies or memoirs: www.biographersclub.co.uk
- **Winston Churchill Memorial Trust** offers travel fellowships in different categories every year. It is worth checking each year to see whether writers are included: www.wcmt.org.uk
- **Hosking Houses Trust** offers women writers over 40 (non-fiction or fiction) a time of financially protected peace to write: 33 The Square, Clifford Chambers, Stratford upon Avon CV37 8HT; www.hoskinghouses.co.uk

Other grants and fellowships can be found in *The Writer's Handbook 2011* (details above). This is the last year the print version of the Handbook is to be produced. But all information in the 2011 volume will hold for 2012–2013.

TOP TIP ABOUT GRANTS 1

Go to the public library. Ask for two books – they are massive – containing an amazing amount of information about funding sources for writers. They are: The Grants Register (Palgrave Macmillan, published annually) and The Directory of Grant Making Trusts (Directory of Social Change). Spend two hours browsing and you could be a winner.

TOP TIP ABOUT GRANTS 2

When you need funds for your project, think laterally. Think about what subject areas your project could fit into: landscape, travel, feminism, history, food, nature, etc. There are grants available under many subject titles, not only under the category 'funds for writers'.

International awards for literary non-fiction

The importance of literary non-fiction as a category has been recognised for many years in Great Britain, the United States, Canada and Europe. In America, the nation's pre-eminent literary prizes for non-fiction (as well as for fiction, poetry and young people's literature) are given by the National Book Awards. The literary non-fiction category includes among its many genres religion, science, biography, history, politics, culture, memoir and autobiography.

Each of the four categories has a panel of judges who pick out 20 finalists and award the winner with a $10,000 cash prize and a bronze sculpture. Each finalist wins $1,000 plus a medal and a citation from the judges.

Previous National Book Award winners include Joan Didion for *The Year of Magical Thinking* in 2005, Tim Weiner for *Legacy of Ashes: The History of the CIA* in 2007, T.J. Stiles for *The First Tycoon: The Epic Life of Cornelius Vanderbilt* in 2009, and Patti Smith for *Just Kids* in 2010.

The UK has been blessed for many years with prestigious prizes for literary non-fiction. Among these are the Samuel Johnson Prize for current affairs, history, science, sport, politics, autobiography, biography, politics, travel and the arts; the Hessell Tiltman prize for works of historical content and high literary merit; and the Duff Cooper Prize for the best work of biography, history or political science.

In Canada, literary non-fiction has been recognised and generously rewarded since 2000. Under the auspices of the Charles Taylor Prize for Literary Non-Fiction, an annual award of $25,000 has been offered.

Organisations

There are many writing organisations that can help you during the writing process or even before it begins. Look into these:

- **The Arvon Foundation**. This book, like the two volumes before it, has grown out of the non-fiction and life-writing courses run at Arvon. At Arvon up to 16 students write for five dedicated days helped by two professional writers in one of four idyllic settings. See page 257 for more details. The Arvon experience is among the most imaginative and creative a new or experienced writer can enjoy.

- **British Guild of Travel Writers**: Chairperson: Melissa Shales; Secretariat: Robert Ellison; 335 Lordship Road, London N16 5HG (0208 144 8713); secretariat@bgtw.org. They can also put British travel writers in touch with the Society of American Travel Writers.

- **International Food, Wine and Travel Writers Association**: admin@ifwatwa.org

- **Outdoor Writers & Photographers Guild**: 07530 317348; secretary@owpg.org.uk

- **The Leon Levy Center for Biography**. This important new centre, founded in 2008, aims to study and support biography, and offers paid residencies to three biographers a year. It is part of the Graduate Center at New York's City University (CUNY): biography@gc.cuny.edu

- **The Centre for Life History and Life Writing Research**. This centre houses the Mass Observation Archive and contains the original Mass Observation papers (1937–1950s) on the daily life of Britain as well as a continuing Mass Observation project from 1981: www.sussex.ac.uk/clhlwr

For memoirists, biographers and autobiographers, further details of helpful organisations can be found in The Arvon Book of Life Writing, pp. 173–4.

9: Agents and publishers
by Midge Gillies

Do I need a literary agent?

As few of us are lucky enough to secure a six-figure advance, it can be tempting to see the services of a literary agent as the first place to save money. Most agents charge ten to fifteen per cent of any deal they secure, and in the UK will add VAT on top of that. But a good literary agent, like a good accountant, is well worth their fee.

What does an agent actually do for their money?

- Many publishers will refuse to consider an unsolicited approach. If a respected agent comes to them with an idea, they will take it seriously, because the agent is putting their reputation on the line.

- A good agent will know which publisher has money to spend, what type of book they would be interested in, and whether they would be likely to warm to you and your proposal.

- An agent should be able to protect your interests around the world and in different media such as film and television, either in-house or via sub-agents.

- Your agent should keep up to date with developments that might affect you. This could be changes to Public Lending Right, or how an electronic version of your book should be marketed.

- They will negotiate on your behalf and make sure the contract is watertight. As most contracts are impenetrable, this is very important.

- They should check your royalty statements and make sure that you receive any money owed to you.

- An agent should be a buffer between you and your publisher – particularly if something goes wrong. If you don't like the cover, or the way your book has been edited, you can discuss this with your agent, who will intervene if they think you have a fair point.

- The terms of your agreement should be clearly laid out in a contract between you and your agent.

TOP TIP

There are two types of agent. One only handles financial matters and contracts. The second does the same, but also acts as a first-stop editor. As publishers do less editing in-house, it can be invaluable to have an agent who sees this as part of their role. Many agents began their career as editors and are highly skilled at this aspect of publishing.

When you meet a prospective agent, ask them about their editing experience and how much of it they do for their clients. It can be a great benefit to have an agent who is not just familiar with your work but has read each book carefully. An agent can offer the continuity that a publisher may not be able to.

Finding an agent who's right for you

Choosing the right agent is a matter of personal taste. Would you feel happier with a one-person agent who's very 'hands-on' and works out of their attic? Or do you hanker after a swanky office in London's Soho, and an agent who may not always answer your calls but who tempts you with the promise of a large advance?

Of course, choices are never that simple. The one-person agency may work much harder for you, and secure that fat deal because they know their livelihood depends on it. And you may be able to find an individual within a large agency who really cares about your work. The important factors are whether you trust the person, have a good rapport and are happy for them to represent you.

Draw up a list of potential agents, listing their pros and cons. You can find them through the many books and directories online or by personal recommendation.

You might decide to approach someone whose clients include an author you particularly admire. The author's website or publisher will tell you who represents them, and they will probably mention their agent in the acknowledgements section of their book.

Think carefully about approaching an agent who has no authors in any field close to yours; or equally one who has an author whose work is very close to your own: why would they want to take on someone who's similar, and as yet unproven?

Find out as much as you can about each agent and then write to the most promising. If they are interested, agree to meet them for a chat.

If you approach more than one, you might find yourself in the awkward, if flattering, position of having several agents interested in you.

The publisher

Your agent will have suggestions about which publisher to approach, but you should also be able to tell them which books in your genre you admire. This will give them more ideas about who might make a good fit for you and your book.

The publisher you first meet may not be your editor. If they pass you on to a more junior editor, this is not necessarily a bad thing. They may be on their way up and will have more time to spend with you and will be keen to make the book a success.

Try to build up a good working relationship with your editor. Stand your ground if you think your artistic integrity is being challenged, but always be prepared to listen. If you've been working on a book for years, you won't be as objective about it as someone who has seen it for the first time.

TOP TIP

Keep an open mind about small, independent publishers. They won't be able to offer you a huge advance, but they may devote more time to certain aspects of publishing, such as cover design and – most important of all – publicity.

Research

1: Where to go

Basic printed resources

Many of the following can be accessed free of charge from public libraries, in some cases from your own computer.

- *The Dictionary of National Biography*. There is a Concise DNB, and since 2004 an online edition.

- The equivalents elsewhere include: *American National Biography, Allgemeine Deutsche Biographie* and *Neue Deutsche Biographie, Dictionnaire de Biographie Francaise, Dizionario Biografico degli Italiani,* etc.

- *Who's Who* for contemporary biography, and *Who Was Who* for past figures. *Who's Who in America, Who's Who in France, Who's Who in Italy, Wer ist Wer?* and *Who's Who in Germany.*

- There is also an *International Who's Who* and an *International Who's Who of Women.*

- Group directories: *Debrett's Peerage and Baronetage,* the Palgrave Macmillan *Dictionary of Women's Biography,* etc.

- Professional directories: *Who's Who of British Members of Parliament,* the *New Grove Dictionary of Music and Musicians,* the *Medical Register,* the *Army, Navy* and *Air Force Lists, Crockford's Clerical Directory,* the *Writers' Directory* and many others.

- Business directories; e.g. the *International Directory of Company Histories* and *Who Owns Who.*

- Obituaries: in national newspapers such as *The Times, Daily Telegraph* and *The Guardian* in the UK, and *New York Times, Washington Post* and *Los Angeles Times* in the US. Local papers are also useful; they are often held in local libraries, many are online and, in Britain, in the Newspaper Library in Colindale.

National Archives

The main national UK archive is the National Archives (formerly the Public Record Office) at Kew. Its website – www.nationalarchives.gov.uk – has links to its catalogue and to guides relating to particular subjects such as slavery or the transportation of convicts. There's a direct link to its online catalogue at: www.pro.gov.uk/catalogues/default.htm

The National Archives give advice on tracing people, for example, through birth, death and marriage certificates, occupation, adoption: see www.national archives.gov.uk/records/looking-for-person/

Scotland and Northern Ireland have their own National Archives. The General Register Office for Scotland has merged with the National Archives of Scotland to become the National Records of Scotland (NRS). Its most recent website address is: www.gro-scotland.gov.uk. The Public Records Office of Northern Ireland can be found at: www.proni.gov.uk

Births, deaths and marriages

The General Register Office (GRO) keeps all certificates of births, marriages and deaths in England and Wales since 1837. Indexes to these registrations can be searched online via www.freebmd.org.uk and ordered from the GRO or the local register office. Some libraries, archives and record offices have indexes on microfilm.

The General Register Office (England and Wales) is at: www.direct.gov.uk/en/ Governmentcitizensandrights/Registeringlifeevents/index.htm

In Northern Ireland it is at: www.nidirect.gov.uk/gro

For Scotland see: www.gro-scotland.gov.uk

Birth, marriage or death records before 1837 may be found in parish registers kept by churches (also chapels, synagogues, etc.) or in local archives. See *Phillimore Atlas and Index of Parish Registers*, 3rd edition, edited by Cecil R. Humphrey-Smith (Phillimore, 2003).

Wills

The National Archives website offers advice on finding wills before and after 1858.

The National Probate Calendar provides information on wills and probate records created in England and Wales between 1861 and 1941. It can tell you where and when people died and reveal the value of the estate they left. The six million names can be searched online, for a fee, at: www.ancestry.co.uk/probate

An up-to-date guide to will research in the UK is *Wills and Probate Records* by Karen Grannum and Nigel Taylor, published by the National Archives in 2009.

Local archives

Most local libraries have good local history sections, the bigger city libraries (e.g. London, Manchester, Liverpool) very extensive ones.

Local authorities' records offices contain documents going back centuries on local government matters – health, welfare, education, housing, burial grounds.

These local archives will typically contain:

- Census and electoral registers
- Valuation rolls (property registers) and local tax records
- School, church and welfare records (e.g. workhouses)
- Local business and institution records
- Local publications (e.g. newspapers and magazines, directories and business directories, books and pamphlets)

Many schools, businesses and local newspapers (especially old established ones) will have their own archives.

Other important records include, for example:

- *Hansard: Parliamentary Debates* from 1803 onwards
- *All England Law Reports* from 1558 onwards
- Parish records of baptisms, marriages and burials from 1538
- Other denomination records (e.g. Nonconformist and Catholic churches synagogues, mosques)

- The National Sound Archive at the British Library, for broadcast speeches and interviews; also Parliamentary sound recordings

- Shipping records, e.g. Lloyd's Shipping Index and the P & O Company records at the National Maritime Museum. The National Archives hold passenger lists both inward-bound and outward-bound from the UK up to 1960. There is also a website called AncestorsOnBoard.com on which you can search for your fortune-seeking ancestors.

There are many tools, both printed and online, to help you navigate the vast world of archives. There is also the Access to Archives project, which aims to put all UK archive catalogues on the Net; see www.a2a.org.uk

There are countless books, websites, courses, television programmes and organisations devoted to genealogy, from the Society of Genealogists in London to websites like www.findmypast.com and www.ancestry.com. Among the most famous and assiduous genealogists are the Genealogical Society of the Church of Jesus Christ of the Latter Day Saints, the Mormons, who have compiled the International Genealogical Index, the IGI, containing over a billion names from birth, death and marriage records around the world. The IGI is too vast to be consistently reliable, but it is an excellent starting point. It is accessible, free of charge, at www.familysearch.org. You can also access the online catalogue directly at www.familysearch.org./Search/searchcatalog.asp

Libraries and museums

The Copyright Libraries: the most complete because they are entitled to a copy of every book published in the UK and the Republic of Ireland (as is the Library of Congress for the USA).

- The British Library, London

- The Bodleian Library, Oxford

- Cambridge University Library, Cambridge

- The National Library of Scotland, Edinburgh

- National Library of Wales, Aberystwyth

- Trinity College Library, Dublin

Most catalogues are online, for example, the British Library is directly accessible at http://catalogue.bl.uk

Their catalogues are also listed online by Copac, the National Academic and Specialist Library Catalogue. Copac contains over 34 million records from the national and main university libraries, plus many specialist libraries, such as the National Art Library at the V&A. Its website is at www.copac.ac.uk

University libraries
Most other universities, especially the larger and older ones, have excellent libraries. If you have a publisher, or proof that you are a *bona fide* scholar (often a letter from a current library member will do), it is not usually difficult to obtain a membership card for a limited period.

Public libraries
If you have more time than transport, the Inter-Library Loan Service means that any book in the UK system can be delivered to your local library. Some will even extend the service to libraries abroad if necessary, although the charge can make it worthwhile to buy a second-hand copy of the book instead.

Other libraries
There are all kinds of specialist libraries, including:

- Picture libraries, such as the famous ones: the Mary Evans Picture Library still exists, while the Hilton Picture Library is now a special archive at Getty Images. All the national museums, and the Birmingham and Manchester Art Galleries, have picture libraries, as have the National Archives and the British Library, all of which can be accessed online. There are many picture libraries in specialist institutions such as English Heritage, the British Geological Survey, the Scott Polar Institute and the RSPCA. These and dozens more can all be found through the website of the British Association of Picture Libraries and Agencies (www.bapla.org.uk). Google Images and Getty Images are both well-known online sources. Don't forget that most paintings and photographs are subject to copyright and/or owners' fees.

- Manuscript libraries. The main manuscript depository in England is the Manuscript Department of the British Library. However, manuscripts are also held in many other libraries and archives. Check the ARCHON (Archive Contacts) facility of the National Archives: www.nationalarchives.gov.uk/archon/ or the Historical Manuscripts Commission: www.national archives.gov.uk/information-management/projects-and-work/hmc.htm. There are reference books like *British Archives*, already mentioned, or *The ASLIB Directory of Information Sources* in the United Kingdom.

- For literary manuscripts, consult the Location Register of English Literary Manuscripts and Letters at the University of Reading: www.reading.ac.uk/library/about-us/projects/lib-location-register.aspx

- Newspaper libraries. The main one is the British Library Newspaper Library in Colindale in North London, which holds over 50,000 newspapers, periodicals, magazines, comics, etc. The newspaper catalogue is a subset of the main British Library catalogues and clearly signposted on the BL website.

- Subscription libraries. The London Library is the biggest and best known with over a million books. Others include the Bath Royal Literary and Scientific Institution, the Central Catholic Library in Dublin and the Nottingham Subscription Library. The Association of Independent Libraries lists them all (www.independentlibraries.co.uk).

- Special interest libraries, for example:

  - The British Architectural Library of the Royal Institute of British Architects
  - The British Film Institute Library
  - Companies House for company records
  - Horniman Library for musical instruments and ethnography
  - Lindley Library, the Royal Horticultural Society
  - Royal Geographical Society Library
  - Society of Genealogists Library
  - Wellcome Institute Library for medical history

- Wiener Library for Jewish history
- The Women's Library for women's history and women's studies
- and these are just in London.

Museums

Museums, often with their own libraries, are also a precious resource. Apart from the National Gallery, Tate Modern, Tate Britain, the city galleries of Birmingham and Manchester, etc., here are just a few:

- Ashmolean Museum, Oxford
- British Museum
- Courtauld Institute of Art Library
- Fitzwilliam Museum, Cambridge
- Imperial War Museum
- Museum of Transport
- National Army Museum
- National Maritime Museum
- National Monuments Record
- National Portrait Gallery Library and Archives
- Royal Air Force Museum
- Science Museum Library
- Theatre Museum
- Victoria and Albert Museum Library

- and hundreds of others.

TOP TIP

Start to make a list of sources and acknowledgements from the very start of your research. Three years down the line, you won't remember everyone who's helped you, or every library, museum or archive you've visited.

Online sources

The British Library and the Library of Congress both have websites on which you can check their holdings (www.bl.uk and www.loc.gov). The website based at Northwestern University in the US (www.libraryspot.com) will locate and link to the online catalogues (if available) of public and academic libraries around the world. The complete OED (Oxford English Dictionary) is at www.oed.com. and Encyclopedia Britannica at http://www.britannica.com; both are free at some libraries. The famous 1911 edition of the latter is browsable free at www.1911encyclopedia.org. The Columbia Encyclopedia is at www.encyclopedia.com, Merriam-Webster at www.merriam-webster.com and Microsoft's Encarta encyclopedia at www.encarta.msn.com.

Through the many internet search engines you are connected to the biggest libraries in the world. Everyone knows Google and Yahoo; other main ones are AltaVista, Ask Jeeves, Excite, Hotbot and Lycos. Once you've learned how to refine your search with AND, OR and NOT, quote marks, brackets and so on, you can find anything you need. If you still haven't found the answer, you can go to www.mimas.ac.uk, a research information site maintained by the University of Manchester. Their website, www.mimas.ac.uk/portfolio/current, lists their most useful projects, for example, archiveshub.ac.uk, which locates archives; a link to www.jstor.org, which gives academics access to over 1,000 journals; and zetoc.mimas.ac.uk, which gives access to the BL's electronic tables of contents of journals and links to the texts.

As you'll know, Google is proposing to put every book ever published on the Web, and, despite some resistance from authors, has already begun. Project Gutenberg has been digesting the contents of archives and libraries for nearly 40 years, and now has nearly 30,000 free e-books available on its website, www.gutenberg.org. Amazon now has the Look Inside facility for millions of new books. You can even get translations (though not very good ones) and quotations on the net.

For US research, the list could be as long again. For a more than comprehensive guide, consult the website of the Center for Biographical Research at the University of Hawai'i at Manoa, the longest-established life writing centre: www.hawaii.edu/biograph.

Useful addresses for literary non-fiction

Feminism

African American Women's Organisations, allied to
The National Council of Negro Women Inc
633 Pennsylvania Ave NW
Washington DC
Tel. 20004 202 737 0120
Membership@ncnw.org

Barnard Center for Research on Women
Organisation for feminist action and scholarship
Barnard Center for Research on Women
101 Barnard Hill, 3009 Broadway
NY 10027
Tel. 212 854 2067

National Alliance of Women's Organizations (NAWO)
Umbrella organisation for many Women's Centres, European Unions,
Asylum Aid, Abortion Rights, etc.
admin@nawo.org.uk

National Organization for Women (NOW)
Political and social organisation campaigning for equality
PO Box 1848SALMerrifield
VA 22116-1848
Tel. 202 628 8669

UK Feminista
A movement of ordinary women and men who campaign for gender equality
info@ukfeminista.org.uk

London Feminist Network
Networking and campaigning organisation
londonfeminist@yahoo.co.uk

The Fawcett Society
UK's leading campaign organ for gender equality
The Fawcett Society
1–3 Berry St
London EC1
Tel. 0207 253 2598

Food

UK Food Group
Principal UK network for non-governmental organisations working on global
food and agricultural issues
UK Food Group
94 White Lion St
London N1 9PF
ukfg@ukfg.org.uk

Institute of Food Research
Researches harnessing food for health and preventing food-related diseases
Institute of Food Research
Norwich Research Park
Colney
Norwich NB4 7UA
ifr.communications@ifr.ac.uk

Food Standards Agency
Research into food and science
Food Standards Agency
Aviation House
125 Kingsway
London WC2 B6NA
Tel. 0207 276 8000

History

As well as the above:

British Library: St Pancras, 96 Euston Road, London NW1 2DB.
Tel. 0843 208 1144. Customer-Services@bl.uk

Imperial War Museum: Lambeth Road, London SE1 6HZ.
Tel. 020 7416 5000. mail@iwm.org.uk

Library of Congress: 101 Independence Ave, SE, Washington, DC 20540.
Tel. 202 707 5000

Mass Observation: The Mass Observation Archive, Special Collections,
The Library, University of Sussex, Brighton BN1 9QL.
Tel. 01273 67 8157. library.specialcoll@sussex.ac.uk

RAF Museum: Grahame Park Way, London NW9 5LL.
Tel. 020 8205 2266. london@rafmuseum.org

The National Archives: Kew, Richmond, Surrey TW9 4DU.
Tel. 020 8876 3444. www.nationalarchives.gov.uk/contact/

Nature (see also Science and Travel below)
BirdLife International: Wellbrook Court, Girton Road, Cambridge CB3 0NA.
Tel. 01223 277 318. birdlife@birdlife.org

The Zoological Society of London: Regent's Park, London NW1 4RY.
Tel. 020 7449 6293. library@zsl.org

Science

British Medical Association: BMA House, Tavistock Square, London WC1H 9JP.
Tel. 020 7383 6625. bma-library@bma.org.uk

Natural History Museum: Cromwell Road, London SW7 5BD.
Tel. 0871 971 6105. www.nhm.ac.uk

Science Museum: Exhibition Road, London SW7 2DD.
Tel. 0870 870 4868. www.sciencemuseum.org.uk

Wellcome Collection: 183 Euston Road, London NW1 2BE.
Tel. 020 7611 8722. library@wellcome.ac.uk

National Air and Space Museum Library: Room 3100,
6th Street and Independence Avenue SW, Washington, DC 20560-0314.
Tel. 202 633 2320. libmail@si.edu

Travel

Pitt Rivers Museum in Oxford cares for the university collection of anthropology and world archaeology. http://www.prm.ox.ac.uk/thesiger.html

It also includes the Thesiger Collection of photographs from the travel writer Wilfred Thesiger. Many images can be viewed online at: www.prmprints.com

The Royal Geographical Society organises lectures and offers travel grants. See http://www.rgs.org

For polar research see: Scott Polar Institute. http://www.spri.cam.ac.uk and British Antarctic Survey (BAS) at http://www.antarctica.ac.uk

Stanfords' past customers include explorers such as Amy Johnson, David Livingstone and Captain Scott. It offers a wide range of maps, travel books and gadgets in its UK stores or online. See: www.stanfords.co.uk/

EXERCISE

What does the internet say about your subject?

Remember that information on the internet, unlike that in a book, is constantly changing. Use a search engine such as Google to find out what is available online. What information is false and what do you need to check out? Are there any new archives worth visiting? What does Wikipedia say today? Repeat this exercise every few months.

2: Other things to do in the research period

Copyright research

For all quotations, you will have to clear, and often pay for, all the copyright material you use. You can start the process now.

Copyright in published material extends to 70 years after the author's death in the USA and Europe, including Britain (but not, for example, in Canada, where it extends for only 50 years).

Copyright in unpublished material is more complicated. See the Society of Authors' Quick Guides to copyright and permissions, downloadable free from www.societyofauthors.org/guides-and-articles.

Note that, though most material on the web is free to download, everything on the internet is under copyright, and you require permission to quote from it as you would from a printed book. And don't forget that letters are also subject to copyright.

You must seek permission from the author's publisher or agent, or from the author in person, if they are still alive and you can find them.

If a book is out of print and/or the author is dead, you can turn to WATCH – Writers, Artists and their Copyright Holders – an online database of literary and other creative estates run jointly by Reading University and the Harry Ransom Humanities Research Center of the University of Texas at Austin: http://tyler.hrc.utexas.edu/. Other alternatives are the Authors' Licensing and Collecting Society (www.alcs.co.uk), the Association of Authors' Agents (www.agentsassociation.co.uk) and several others. See the Society of Authors' *Quick Guide to Permissions* as above.

Keep records of all quotations you use that are longer than a few words.

How much you can quote without permission has never been definitively settled. 'Fair use' or 'fair dealing' for critical purposes, for example in a review, article or biography, is generally accepted to be up to 800 words in total from a prose work, with a maximum of 400 words in a single extract, so long as the extract is used for comment on works and not on persons. But it is safest to ask for permission, and essential in all cases to credit the work clearly and quote accurately. Again, see the Society of Authors' *Quick Guide to Permissions*.

(The Society also provides guides to libel, indexing and other vexed questions for a small fee.)

Fees can be charged for permissions, sometimes quite high ones, and permission can be refused. In these cases, you can paraphrase, provided that you credit the source, and make it clear that this is your own summary.

MIDGE'S NOTE

It's vital that you develop a thorough system of note-taking that allows cross-referencing and includes precise details of where you found your information (book details, interview date or archive reference). Your research might take you years, and you could travel miles in the process. If you can't understand the notes you made in a museum in Caracas, it's unlikely that you will be able to retrace your steps. I make notes on my laptop and then copy them on to old-fashioned index cards under individual names and topics. So for my book on POWs, for example, I have an index card labelled 'chess' which tells me which books and archives have information on chess, and cross-refers to another index card called 'hobbies'. I have two sets of index cards – one for POWs in Europe and one in the Far East. You can buy computer software that will do something similar.

Writing

1: Short pieces as starting points
by Sally Cline

In Chapter 2 'What is literary non-fiction?', we suggested that small prose bites can be a good starting place for writing full-length non-fiction.

The usual length for an essay, reflection or memory piece would be less than 1,000 words, sometimes as short as 200 words. Begin with a 200-word mini-essay. Then move on to longer pieces. Each time, remember that you can make use of rhythm, metre, imagery and other literary techniques to balance your straight narration. Your focus should be on tight, clear theme, topic or plot.

TOP TIP

Sharp writing. Extreme concision. Experimentation. Illumination and surprise.
A medley of these can result in vivid prose, and also entertain your readers.

EXERCISE: MEMORY 1

Think back to your first year in a job. Recall the most important person, image, object, task or event that you have never forgotten. Write a short colourful description and the reason for the unforgettable memory. Use 350 words. You can do this with a partner. Each one tells their tale in turn, then both of you write the short piece.

EXERCISE: MEMORY 2

Take the same memory and think about what kind of book it might be the opening of.

A memoir? An autobiography? A literary non-fiction book on office life, employment, friendship, power politics?

Now write the first four pages of your book. About 1,000 words.

Brief Prose Reader, an interesting, and small, book, offers helpful essays for thinking, reading and writing.[1] In each chapter the *Reader* helps writers to

---

TOP TIP

Never let the prose style, however short the piece, overshadow the substance.
Content should be rich and enduring even in a brief piece.

EXERCISE: CHILDHOOD 1

In her memoir *An American Childhood* Annie Dillard wrote:

'Like any child, I slid into myself perfectly fitted, as a diver meets her reflection in a pool. Her fingertips enter the fingertips on the water, her wrists slide up her arms. The diver wraps herself in her reflection wholly . . . '[2]

Use this as your opening paragraph. Now write a 400–500-word prose essay/reflection continuing the image and developing the content.

EXERCISE: CHILDHOOD 2

1) Decide how your very short reflection on childhood could be contained within a full-length prose work. Is it to be

- A memoir?

- An autobiography?

- A nature or landscape book?

- A piece of travel writing? A book on psychiatry or social history?

2) What changes should you make to accommodate your choice of genre? Write down a plan of the book, with the genre, a synopsis and chapter headings. Consider where the short piece should come.

- At the start?

- In Chapter 2?

- Near the end?

---

1. K. Flachmann, M. Flachmann, K. Bernander, C. Smith, *Brief Prose Reader. Essays for Thinking, Reading, and Writing*, Prentice Hall, New Jersey, 2002.

2. Annie Dillard, *An American Childhood*, Harper & Row, New York, 1987, p. 11.

improve their ability to write briefly but at an increasingly sophisticated level. It contains integrated learning tools that develop writers' critical thinking as well as their reading skills.

Adjectives and adverbs

In a short piece, cut down on adverbs (e.g. quite, fairly, etc). Instead, use more verbs. If you want pace, make them active verbs (I walked, she hit, they flinched). If you want long, slow, elegant sentences, use the passive tense or the 'ing' form (e.g. I was paying great attention).

Writer Ian Seed produces masterly short pieces. Read this one:

> Lost in the wet mist, I met a hermit who led me to his hut. The hut was bare, just two stone benches. He wanted me to lie down and sleep, though I hadn't eaten all day.
>
> 'Tomorrow we shall find food,' he promised, and held my hand to comfort me.
>
> I dreamt of crows flying, blood dripping like rain from their beaks. When I awoke, there was a hole in my throat, into which I was able to insert a finger.[1]

The clever touch is the end sentence with its change of tone, atmosphere and action. Even more stylish is the preceding sentence about his dream, which gives clues to the end, but the reader may not pick them up until the conclusion.

Seed's short prose is called 'Betrayal'. It contains only 82 words in three paragraphs. There are only two adjectives and no adverbs.

EXERCISE

1) Use the title 'Betrayal'. Then write exactly 80 words in three paragraphs on that theme. Do not use any adjectives or any adverbs.

2) Write down how you might extend that theme into a full-length genre.

1. Ian Seed, 'Betrayal', from 'Four Short Prose Pieces', *Brevity Magazine: A Journal of Concise Literary Nonfiction* (online), Issue 37, Fall 2011.

An excellent way to practise brief pieces is to take an intimate scene, within a family, inside a neighbour's house, in a pub or a cafe, at a nightclub. Think of the dynamic that will move that scene from static to active, then write it in one paragraph, making sure it is fully rounded with an end that either resolves the situation or reverses the readers' expectations.

Here is another short piece by Ian Seed called 'Insect':

> *Walking by the council houses in the falling snow, I thought I saw someone waving to me from a downstairs window. Yet when I got close enough to press my face against the frosty glass, I realised I had been mistaken; there was only a family watching television. Looking more closely still, however, I saw myself walking on the screen. The youngest daughter was crying because the way I dragged my crushed leg behind me reminded her of an insect.*[1]

Where would you say a tension first enters the prose? Where does it first become deeply disturbing?

Last hints

- Close reading of poetry can help you write short prose pieces. The way poets condense and use imagery in order to heighten their effects is exactly what you need.

- Hints and brief speculation in narrative work well.

- Another useful device is showing 'what the narrator doesn't know'. This offers readers surprise and insight.

1. Ian Seed, 'Insect', *Brevity Magazine*, Issue 37, Fall 2011.

2: Description

by Midge Gillies

In literary non-fiction you should be *painting the picture*. You might be inviting your reader to feel the heat of the desert, to see the stillness of a bird of prey, or to look into the face of a murderer.

As long as you've done your research, you can use many of the tools available to the writer of fiction. Like the novelist, you should be attempting to *show* rather than *tell*. So, for example, rather than *telling* the reader it was hot, *show* them just how hot it was, by describing the effect on the colonel as he sat sipping his cocktail and wiping his hands on the napkin that arrived on the silver tray next to his drink.

Writers of non-fiction have the added advantage of knowing their material so intimately that they have a whole battery of telling details at their disposal. When, in *The Wild Places*, Robert Macfarlane describes how, during the Irish Famine, no one was strong enough to dig graves, he adds the chilling detail that bones are still turned up today from burial pits.[1]

You can gather material for descriptions from:

- Oral histories and interviews
- Books
- Photos and film
- Visiting a place
- Using your imagination – as long as you're honest with the reader

EXERCISE: Using sound and movement

Describe two different people coming up the stairs. How do you know who it is just by listening? Do they take two steps at a time, or shuffle along slowly? Does their stick rattle the banister or their hand brush the wall? Do they hum to themselves or gasp for breath?

1. Robert Macfarlane, *The Wild Places*, Granta, London, 2012, p. 178.

EXERCISE: Using metaphor to describe a person

This is a variation of an old parlour game, but it's a useful way to start thinking metaphorically.

One person waits outside the room while the others choose a famous figure, for example, David Beckham. The person comes back in and asks questions.

'If this person were an animal, what type of animal would they be?'

The answer might be a 'gazelle', because of its speed and grace.

'If this person were a dessert, what type of dessert would they be?'

The answer might be 'chocolate profiteroles', because of their glamour and sophistication.

Think of other similar questions, and apply them to a character in your non-fiction story.

EXERCISE: Using colour in description

Photocopy an interesting colour image – for example, a scene of devastation after a fire or a hurricane, a funeral in Iraq – in black and white. Ask the group to guess the colours in the original. Finally, allow them to see the colour photo. They may be surprised at what they find. This is a good exercise in focusing observation.

EXERCISE: Learning to see in a different way

Take a friend who's either much older or much younger – even a small child – with you on a walk that's familiar to you. Ask them to give you a running commentary on what they see. Does their selection depend on factors such as their height, their age, their interests, even what kind of mood they are in? For example, a child might notice a rusting tractor; an elderly person might be astonished by the unfamiliar crops in a field; someone in a bad mood might see only rubbish; someone who's in love might marvel at the colour of the leaves.

3: Interviewing
by Sally Cline

People say everyone has a story to tell. And indeed they do. Some of those stories will enrich your book, whether it is a travel book, a memoir, a book about feminism, a study of fear or a biography of a well-known magician with an untold secret.

Some of those stories are nearly impossible to wrench out. But good interviews can make the impossible possible.

Interviewing for all types of literary non-fiction
Not all types of non-fiction books demand interviews. Nature books, for instance, rely on description and analysis, although even then you might want to talk to someone who has lived in a particular area or knows a particular landscape well. Sadly you can't interview the wild boar who have been invading farms in New York State, but talking to a farmer who has been invaded would definitely give your writing an edge.

Travel books, biographies and other kinds of literary non-fiction, however, are enhanced by interviews and can often not be written without them.

TOP TIP

Think carefully about where you sit when you interview someone. To help you build up a strong rapport, they need to be able to see you clearly. This is especially important if they are elderly and may have hearing difficulties, or be suspicious of strangers. Your recorder should also be carefully placed to pick up their voice, but not near any loud background noise (such as traffic from an open window).

Three interview techniques

1. Hard-edged journalistic technique. This uses prepared closed questions. It requires limited specific answers.

2. Soft journalistic technique. Uses prepared but open questions allowing flexibility to the interviewee to move in several directions.

3. Non-journalistic technique. Here the interviewer has prepared the general subject area for questioning, but after a few minutes of questions lets the interviewee wander off track. This will relax them and you may make important discoveries for which you could not have prepared questions.

TOP TIP

If you are doing many interviews, you might want to invest in a digital recorder. This device is about the size of a matchbox and your subject will soon forget it's there. The sound quality is superb and you can connect the machine directly to the USB port of your computer. This will make it easier to save the file and to transcribe it later. Most will record for more hours than the longest interview would ever last, so you don't need to worry about coming to the end of the tape. You can also connect it to a telephone, although, of course, you must tell your interviewee that you're recording the conversation.

SALLY'S NOTE

I learned my interviewing technique first as a journalist using hard-edged techniques. Often today I get told off in pubs for giving complete strangers the same treatment!

Twenty years later I relearned my interviewing skills. As a social science researcher, I found the softly softly method often works much better, especially if you are talking to interviewees about difficult subjects. That needs an understanding, flexible approach.

Which method to use?

Use the method that best suits your subject and above all your interviewee.

Get into twos.

One of you is interviewee Ben Gibson, a grandfather whose daughter-in-law Alice, recently separated from his son James, refused to let him continue to see his beloved eight-year-old grandchild Betty.

The other person is the interviewer, Freda, a social worker assigned to the case. She comes to interview Ben.

• 1st Use the hard-edged journalistic technique.

Write out your first six questions. Then try them out in an interview.

• 2nd Use the soft journalistic technique.

Write out your first six questions. Then try them out in a practice interview.

• 3rd Use the non-journalistic open technique.

Decide between you which worked best and why.

TOP TIP

When using questions, always try to find the right balance between empathy and detachment.

Interview preparation

1. **Decide the purpose of the interview.** Write it down in one sentence. Do a literature search and background reading.

2. **Make sure you are interviewing the most relevant person.**

   • If you are writing an art history book about medieval manuscripts, interview an authority on the topic or a museum curator. Also try to find some independent scholars.

   • If you are writing about widowhood, make sure your interviewees come from several social classes and diverse age groups. Try interviewing children of widows to get a different perspective.

3. **Request your interview.**

- You can use phone, email, letter or fax. Ensure you leave enough time if using letters for a response.

- Suggest a 30-minute to 60-minute interview.

- Always offer to go to your interviewee's home, office, nearby location. They are doing you a favour. But, for your own safety, remember to make sure someone knows where you are.

- Learn as much as possible about your interviewee. Be knowledgeable about the subject under discussion.

4. **Prepare for the interview.**

Decide which interview technique to use. Make a list of questions. Ensure they are narrow, not broad. They should not be able to be answered with yes/no. Show you know the territory. E.g. If interviewing a city councillor who has failed to get disabled loos put into a city centre site, try this opener:

'In an article you wrote three months ago you rightfully, expressed horror at your fellow councillors' negative reaction to your proposed plan. What development has there been since then?'

The word 'rightfully' will show that you are on your interviewee's side. This will help your interview.

5. **Conducting the interview.**

- Ask, in advance, if you can use a tape or digital recorder.

- Always use a battery-operated one. Take spare batteries. Try out your tape recorder in advance. I would always take a spare tape recorder.

- Also take notepad and pencils so that you can make key notes while the tape is on.

- Before arriving, review your research.

- Go over your questions. Recheck the tape recorder.

- Ensure you are clear about the purpose of the interview.

• You will have chosen one interview style for your opening ten minutes. You may decide to switch to a second style after that. Have three sets of questions handy.

• Get there five minutes early.

• After a good start, you could hand the mic to your interviewee. They will then feel much more in control and much more comfortable. They will relax.

• Young people are more at ease with technology. You may find a slight resistance among older people. Try to offer them reassurances. Let them interview you first. This usually produces a laugh.

• If you don't understand an answer, politely ask them to put it another way.

• Always ask for examples.

• Never give your own opinions. You are there to listen.

• Listen carefully and show how carefully you are listening. This is important.

• Stay so that if a new direction is being offered you can decide whether or not to take it.

6. **What to do after the interview.**

• Transcribe the interview. Record date, place, time and interviewee's full name and address for your records.

• Write and thank the interviewee.

• Write up your notes.

• Ask if you can go back again. People open up slowly over time.

TOP TIP: QUESTIONS 1

Don't use a double-barrelled question, i.e. a question that lurks inside another question – e.g. 'Do you agree that university parking is a problem and should administrators do something about it?' Here you have two questions and the first is ambivalent.

TOP TIP: QUESTIONS 2

Always be clear – e.g. 'What do you think about Cambridge University parking?' It is not clear what your question is driving at.

TOP TIP: QUESTIONS 3

Don't use biased questions, i.e. those that will lead interviewees to respond in a particular way – e.g. 'Don't you think parking near the colleges is a major problem?'

EXERCISE

Do this in pairs. You are writing a book about food and its relation to health.

Your interviewee is a chef who is manager of a supposedly top restaurant denounced in last week's newspapers as having rats in the kitchen.

1st You are the interviewer. Write your letter to the chef (woman or man), asking for an interview.

2nd Your partner is the chef who writes back an affirmative answer but with some conditions.

3rd The interviewer decides on the method, then writes out the first six questions.

4th As a pair, conduct the interview.

What if your interviewee tells lies and you spot them?

- If you are good at the art of conflict management and your interviewee is up for it, use a direct challenge.

- Be aware that may be your last question!

- If you hate conflict, then drop the point for the moment. Let the interviewee relax, then return later to the same point.

- Do this several times if necessary.

- Always leave some time between attempts.

TOP TIP 1

You often get the best information once you've closed your notebook or switched off the tape recorder. If the interviewee says something startling, don't be afraid to make a note or to switch on the tape recorder again.

TOP TIP 2

If an interviewee is reluctant to talk about the core of your subject, do persist. You cannot, of course, force someone to speak. In your book when you sum up that interview you should be objective, but you may also indicate that person's reluctance to talk. Analyse what that might mean. Make your reader curious.

What happens if several interviewees disagree?

- Write down everyone's account.

- If there is a core of agreement among them, use it.

- Different versions reveal different viewpoints and raise issues of truth and the limited nature of techniques such as interviewing.

- Including several different versions will add to the fascination of your material.

Do you show interviewees the use you have made of their answers in your final draft?

There are two possible answers to this.

- Some interviewers agree to send their interviewees the material that concerns them before publication.

- Others, knowing that interviewees may try to stop publication, do not show them material in advance.

SALLY'S METHOD

As a biographer I never agree to show my interviewees everything I use. Nor do I give them the power of veto.

But I try to play fair. I give them a broad, accurate outline of what I want their interview for. They know the questions because they are right there answering them. At the end I tell them how I shall probably use the material. I tell them at the start that I must retain control of my book.

I always write and thank them immediately afterwards.

Most importantly, I never give interviewees the power of veto. I tell them at the start that I must retain control of my book.

4: Using quotations and dialogue
by Midge Gillies

Flick through any book of literary non-fiction and you will see the prose broken up by speech, whether in the form of dialogue or quotation. Dialogue is rarer, and used mainly in memoir, travel and other first-person writing. Memoirists in particular frequently include remembered dialogue, in a tacit pact with the

A small boy was abducted from a city playground. It was February and snowing. There were about a dozen children on the swings and roundabouts. Six or eight parents stood about shivering, trying to be cheerful.

A community playworker was supposedly in charge. In fact, several witnesses said that she had left the playground and gone to the cafe a few minutes away to fetch a take-out coffee.

The local police force was called in but the child was never found.

Four of you will role-play the interviews.

- One will be the playworker
- One the detective assigned to the case
- One the mother of the missing boy
- One a reliable witness (male) who had been watching the kids play

Take turns to be the detective who interviews the other three.

Each of you, as interviewer, uses a different method.

At the end compare results.

reader that it can only be as accurate as the writer's memory, but will not be wholly invented. If dialogue is not just a matter of your own memory, but, for example, from a radio or television exchange, you will probably have to ask permission from the copyright holder(s). (See **Copyright** below.)

Quotation is key in all literary non-fiction. You will probably have several sources you want to quote from, such as letters, diaries, newspaper reports, interviews, your subject's work (if they are a writer) and other books.

Quotation has several advantages:

- It can give greater insight into a person and show their different voices. How a statesman writes or speaks to his wife or lover will be different from his public speeches or ministerial memos.

- Quoting from a letter, diary or interview can vary the pace and texture of your writing. Adding comments from different sources in the build-up to an event can heighten the tension; including someone's witty remark can lighten the tone.

- You may need to use someone's own words as evidence if you are making a controversial claim, for example, about their whereabouts just before an assassination.

- Quoting original sources will give your writing authenticity and immediacy – for example, if you can quote an interview with the survivor of a shipwreck, or the last words of a famous actor.

Copyright

If it becomes clear that you want to quote extensively from a source for which you need permission, write to them to ask their permission and how much they charge. (See **Research** section.) If they refuse, or charge you an impossible amount, you may have to rethink how you deal with those parts of the book.

TOP TIP 1

Don't just quote from a source for the sake of it. Even if you've found a document no one has ever seen before, it still has to earn its place in your book. Ask yourself why you need to quote from it and whether it would be better paraphrased. If it does earn that place, however – if it is vivid and strong – it can be worth its weight in gold.

TOP TIP 2

Don't just consider traditional sources such as letters and diaries. You might want to quote from emails, texts, phone messages or simple scraps of paper. Churchill's scrawled notes in which he reveals how he planned what became his most memorable wartime speeches, for instance, are fascinating. They show not only how he chose his words, but also how he arranged the lines in a way that helped him to deliver them in his famously stirring oratorical style.

EXERCISE

Think of a famous event such as Martin Luther King's 'I have a dream' speech. Make a list of all the sources you would like to consult, if you were trying to re-create that moment on the steps of the Lincoln Memorial in Washington in August 1963. As well as King, who else would you like to quote?

Make similar quotation lists for other historical moments – the birth of Christ, the assassination of the Romanovs, the death of Diana, Princess of Wales. Remember that minor players can be as interesting as major ones.

5: Truth versus facts
by Sally Cline

Just because you're writing non-fiction doesn't mean that everything you write will always be true. Some people lie about their age (as I found when the marriage certificate for the seventeen-year-old music-hall star Marie Lloyd added a year to her age); others aren't at home when the census man comes knocking. Officials make mistakes, records get destroyed in fires and lost in wars. All the writer can do is to make sure their facts are as accurate as possible, and to present them in an honest way.

It is tempting to assume that human memory will always let the side down, but I have learned not to be dismissive of something someone has told me which doesn't fit into what I think I know. My own father told me that he had been held in a certain POW camp in occupied Poland which I later found out was in Germany. But later still I discovered that it had in fact been moved. So the camp had been in both places.

Even if there are elements of a story that you know can't be true, don't assume that the whole account is false. Sometimes you have to follow your gut instinct about whether or not someone is telling the truth. I still regret leaving out a detail in a profile of a Jewish businessman I wrote as a young and inexperienced news reporter. The man, who was believable in all other respects, told me that as a young boy in the Second World War he had been interned at Lingfield Race Course in Surrey. This sounded just too fanciful; I didn't have time to check what he was saying and I left it out of my piece. I later discovered that his story was completely accurate.

No one likes to admit they don't know the whole story but some of the best books of literary non-fiction are based on skilful guesswork. In Claire Tomalin's brilliant *The Invisible Woman*, an investigation into the story of Nelly Ternan, the actress and elusive mistress of Charles Dickens, she says quite simply:

> *At a guess, she has been living in France. It is only a guess. This is to be a chapter of guesses and conjectures, and those who don't like them are warned.*[1]

After such honesty, we only trust her more.

EXERCISE: MEMORY

Think of an event that you went to with a friend within the last month. (It could be a play, a party, even a writing class.) Without discussing it with each other, both of you write down everything you remember. Now compare the two versions. Can you agree that either has made any factual errors? Does reading another account help to jog your own memory? If they are different, what do the differences tell you?

---

1. Claire Tomalin, *The Invisible Woman*, Penguin, London, 1991, p. 135.

Acknowledgements

Sally and Midge would like to thank

The Arvon Foundation and especially Ruth Borthwick for their support.

Rachel Calder, our wonderful, hard-working, unflappable agent.

David Avital, our new enterprising editor at Bloomsbury, and before him Jenny Ridout, our enthusiastic former editor. Thanks also to Inderjeet Tillier, who was so helpful in the early stages of the book, and Claire Cooper, our production editor, who has been sensitive and meticulous in the book's latter stages

Glenn Jobson, for his skill, patience and understanding.

Our dazzling guest contributors, who have been such an inspiration and joy to work with.

Sally's acknowledgements

My most important thanks go to my co-author Midge, who is funny, flexible, clever and calm. When all about are losing wits, she stays serene! Carole Angier, my Co-Series Editor, for all her support and hard work. To Rosemary Smith, who again handled proofreading, research queries, editing material and this author, with her usual brilliance, the word 'thanks' is insufficient.

I am grateful to The Royal Literary Fund, especially Steve Cook and Eileen Gunn, for their Advisory Fellowship and their support.

Yet again I thank my family and friends: I thank my daughter Marmoset for constant commitment, care and clever ideas; Vic Smith for months of bubbling affectionate interest and support; Chris Carling and Martha Campbell for wise reading and rereading early drafts.

Thank you to Tracy and Richard Baker in Sennen, Cornwall, and Susan and Larry Gilg in Austin, Texas, for months in their peaceful, sunny retreats.

My gratitude to Colette Paul, John Gardner, Frankie Borzello, Katharine McMahon, Alan French, Jonathan and Joan Harris, Sally Lawrence, Kathy Bowles, Margi Tenney, and especially Michelle Spring, who was never too busy writing Arvon Vol. 2 to cheer me on for Vol. 3.

Three women have made my part of the book possible. Angie North has maintained my house and life when I am abroad working, and offered constant, steady encouragement when at home. Jill (Ruby) Dawson has sustained me professionally and has been an inspiration. Ba Sheppard's realistic, sane and kind advice and her inexhaustible faith in the books has kept me going for 34 years.

Midge's acknowledgements

I would like to thank Sally for asking me to be her co-author. The journey has led me to many new and exciting books and writers; Sally has always been the most generous and hard-working of colleagues and the kindest of friends. Together, Sally and Carole Angier have made the perfect series editors – attentive, wise and always willing to listen.

I am immensely grateful to the Society of Authors for practical advice and encouragement.

Yet again I thank my family for their patience and support: my husband, Jim Kelly, my daughter, Rosa Kelly, and my mother, Renee Gillies. And again I thank my mother for her typing skills.

Friends Andrew Balmford, Sarah Blakeman, Jenny Burgoyne, Veronica Forwood and Bridie Pritchard provided their usual sanity and sustenance. Michelle Spring and Jill (Ruby) Dawson continue to inspire.

CITY AND ISLINGTON
SIXTH FORM COLLEGE
283-309 GOSWELL ROAD
LONDON EC1V 7LA
TEL 020 7520 0652

Permissions

The authors and publisher would like to thank the following for their kind permission to reproduce quotations:

Extract in Tips and Tales from 'A Literature of Place' by Barry Lopez in *Portland Magazine*, Summer 1997, by permission of the author. Copyright 1996 Barry Holstun Lopez.

Quotations from *Living Dolls* by Natasha Walter by permission of the author.

Select bibliography
and further reading

Note: where a book has appeared in more than one section, it has been listed only in the first.

Part 1: Literary non-fiction

2. What is literary non-fiction? by Sally Cline

Ackroyd, Peter. *Dickens,* Sinclair Stevenson, London, 1990; HarperCollins, New York, 1990.

Brown, Ian. *The Boy in the Moon: A Father's Journey to Understand His Extraordinary Son,* St Martin's Press, New York, 2011.

Cameron, Stevie. *On the Farm: Robert William Pickton and the Tragic Story of Vancouver's Missing Women,* Alfred A. Knopf, Canada, 2010.

Capote, Truman. *In Cold Blood: A True Account of a Multiple Murder and its Consequences,* Random House, New York, 1965; Penguin Classics, London, 2000.

Cather, Willa. *Death Comes for the Archbishop,* William Heinemann, London, 1927.

Cline, Sally. *Couples: Scene from the Inside.* Little, Brown, London, 1998; Overlook, New York, 1999.

————. *Radclyffe Hall: A Woman called John,* John Murray, London, 1997; Overlook, New York, 1999; Faber and Faber, London, 2010.

————. *Zelda Fitzgerald: Her Voice in Paradise,* John Murray, London, 2002; Arcade, New York, 2003; Faber and Faber, London, 2010.

Cunningham, Michael. *Flesh and Blood,* Penguin, London, 1996.

Didion, Joan. *The Year of Magical Thinking,* Harper Perennial, London, 2006; Vintage, New York, 2007.

Ehrenreich, Barbara. *Smile or Die: How Positive Thinking Fooled America and The World,* Granta, London, 2010; published in the US as *Bright-Sided: How the Relentless Promotion of Positive Thinking Has Undermined America,* Picador, New York, 2010.

Fiennes, William. *The Music Room*, Picador, London, 2009; W.W. Norton & Co., New York, 2009.

Foran, Charles. *Mordecai: The Life and Times*, Alfred A. Knopf, Canada, 2010.

Hall, Radclyffe. *The Well of Loneliness*, Virago, London, 2008.

Hemingway, Ernest. *Death in the Afternoon*, Vintage Classics, London, 2007.

Hoare, Philip. *Leviathan or, The Whale*, Fourth Estate, London, 2008.

Hollinghurst, Alan. *The Line of Beauty*, Picador, London, 2005; Bloomsbury, New York, 2005.

Huggan, Isabel. *Belonging: Home Away from Home*, Bantam, London, 2004.

Hustvedt, Siri. *The Shaking Woman or a History of My Nerves*, Sceptre, London, 2011.

Johnston, Wayne. *Baltimore's Mansion: A Memoir*, Knopf, Canada, 1999; Anchor Books, London, 2000.

King, Ross. *Defiant Spirits: The Modernist Revolution of the Group of Seven*, Douglas & McIntyre/McMichael Canadian Art Collection, Canada, 2010.

Lounsberry, Barbara. *The Art of Fact: Contemporary Artists of Nonfiction*, Greenwood Press, New York, 1990.

Mailer, Norman. *The Armies of the Night, History as a Novel/The Novel as History*, New American Library, New York, 1968.

Mantel, Hilary. *Wolf Hall*, Fourth Estate, London, 2009; Henry Holt, New York, 2009.

Raban, Jonathan. *Coasting: A Private Voyage*, Vintage, London and New York, 2003.

Sebald, W.G. *The Emigrants*, New Directions, New York, 1997; Vintage, London, 2002.

—————. *The Rings of Saturn*, New Directions, New York, 1999; Vintage, London, 2002.

—————. *Vertigo*, New Directions, New York, 2001; Vintage, London, 2002.

Symons, A.J.A. *The Quest for Corvo*, Penguin, London, 1966; New York Review, New York, 2001.

Thompson, Hunter S. *Hell's Angels: The Strange and Terrible Saga of the Outlaw Motorcycle Gangs*, Random House, New York, 1967.

Winchester, Simon. *Atlantic: A Vast Ocean of a Million Stories: The Biography of an Ocean*, Harper, New York, 2010; Harper Press, London, 2011.

Winterson, Jeanette. *Oranges Are Not the Only Fruit*, Pandora, London, 1989.

Wolfe, Tom. *The Kandy-Kolored Tangerine-Flake Streamline Baby*, Farrar, Straus & Giroux, New York, 1965; Mayflower, London, 1968.

————. *The New Journalism*, Harper and Row, New York, 1973.

Periodicals

Joan Didion. 'Why I Write', *New York Times Magazine*, 5 December 1976.

Park, Robert E. 'The Natural History of the Newspaper', *American Journal of Sociology* 29 (November 1923), 273–289.

Xiaocong He, 'A Masterpiece of Literary Journalism: Joan Didion's *Slouching Towards Bethlehem*', *Sino-US English Teaching*, Vol. 3, No. 2 (Serial no. 26), February 2006.

3. Challenges of literary non-fiction by Midge Gillies

Berendt, John. *Midnight in the Garden of Good and Evil*, Vintage, London, 1997.

Deakin, Roger. *Waterlog, A Swimmer's Journey through Britain*, Chatto & Windus, London, 1999.

Gillies, Midge. *The Barbed-Wire University, The Real Lives of Allied Prisoners of War in the Second World War*, Aurum Press, London, 2011.

Grant, Colin. *I & I: The Natural Mystics: Marley, Tosh and Wailer*, Jonathan Cape, London, 2011.

Hicks, Carola. *The Bayeux Tapestry: The Life Story of a Masterpiece*, Vintage, London, 2007.

Junger, Sebastian. *The Perfect Storm: A True Story of Man against the Sea*, Fourth Estate, London, 1998; Harper Perennial, New York, 2007.

Lopez, Barry. *Arctic Dreams: Imagination and Desire in a Northern Landscape*, Picador, London, 1987; Vintage, New York, 2001.

Macfarlane, Robert. *The Wild Places,* Granta, London, 2010.

Maitland, Sara. *A Book of Silence*, Granta, London, 2009.

Murakami, Haruki. *What I Talk About When I Talk About Running*, Vintage, London, 2009.

Shapiro, James. *1599: A Year in the Life of William Shakespeare*, Faber and Faber, London, 2006; HarperCollins, New York, 2006.

Skloot, Rebecca. *The Immortal Life of Henrietta Lacks*, Crown Publishing, New York, 2010; Pan, London, 2011.

Sobel, Dava. *Longitude: The True Story of a Lone Genius Who Solved the Greatest Scientific Problem of His Time*, Fourth Estate, London, 1996; Walker Publishing, New York, 2007.

Summerscale, Kate. *The Suspicions of Mr Whicher or The Murder at Road Hill House*, Bloomsbury, London, 2009.

Swift, Daniel. *Bomber County*, Hamish Hamilton, London, 2010; Farrar, Straus & Giroux, New York, 2011.

Thubron, Colin. *To a Mountain in Tibet*, Chatto & Windus, London, 2011.

4. Reflections on travel writing by Midge Gillies

Bailey, Rosemary. *Life in a Postcard: Escape to the French Pyrenees*, Bantam, London, 2002.

Blixen, Karen. *Out of Africa*, Penguin Classics, London, 2001.

Boswell, James and Johnson, Samuel. *A Journey to the Western Islands of Scotland* and *The Journal of a Tour to the Hebrides*, ed. Peter Levi, Penguin Classics, London, 2006.

Bryson, Bill. *Notes from a Small Island*, Black Swan, London, 1996.

Buford, Bill (ed.). *Granta Travel Writing 10*, Penguin Books/Granta, London, 1984.

Chatwin, Bruce. *In Patagonia*, Vintage Classics, London, 2003.

————. *On the Black Hill*, Vintage Classics, London, 2008.

Cherry-Garrard, Apsley. *The Worst Journey in the World*, Vintage Classics, London, 2010.

Cobbett, William. *Rural Rides*, Penguin Classics, London, 2005.

Dalrymple, William. *In Xanadu: A Quest*, Flamingo, London, 1999.

Defoe, Daniel. *A Tour through the Whole Island of Great Britain*, Penguin Classics, London, 2005.

Finkel, David. *The Good Soldiers*, Atlantic Books, London, 2010.

Junger, Sebastian. *War*, Fourth Estate, London, 2011; Twelve, New York, 2011.

Lee, Laurie. *As I Walked out One Midsummer Morning*, Penguin, London, 1973. *Cider with Rosie*, Vintage Classics, London, 2002.

Leigh Fermor, Patrick. *Between the Woods and the Water*, John Murray, London, 2004.

————. *A Time of Gifts*, John Murray, London, 2004.

Macaulay, Rose. *Fabled Shore: from the Pyrenees to Portugal*, Arrow Books, London, 1959.

Markham, Beryl. *West with the Night*, Virago, London, 1984.

Morris, May (ed.). *The Illustrated Virago Book of Women Travellers*, Virago, London, 2006.

Newby, Eric. *Love and War in the Apennines*, Hodder & Stoughton, London, 1971.

———. *A Short Walk in the Hindu Kush*, Picador, London, 1981.

Sinclair, Iain. *London Orbital*, Penguin, 2003, London.

Slater, Nigel. *Toast: The Story of a Boy's Hunger*, Harper Perennial, London, 2004.

Stark, Freya. *Ionia: A Quest*, John Murray, London, 1954.

———. *A Winter in Arabia*, John Murray, London, 1940.

Theroux, Paul. *The Great Railway Bazaar*, Penguin Modern Classics, London, 2008.

Tóibín, Colm. *Bad Blood: A Walk Along the Irish Border*, Vintage, London, 1994; Picador, New York, 2001.

West, Rebecca. *Black Lamb and Grey Falcon: A Journey Through Yugoslavia*, Macmillan, London, 1941.

Wheeler, Sara. *Cherry: A Life of Apsley Cherry-Garrard*, Vintage, London, 2002.

———. *Terra Incognita: Travels in Antarctica*, Vintage, London, 1997.

5. Reflections on food writing by Sally Cline

Bourdain, Anthony. *Kitchen Confidential. Adventures in the Culinary Underbelly*, Bloomsbury, London, 2001.

Cadbury, Deborah. *Chocolate Wars: From Cadbury to Kraft: 200 Years of Sweet Success & Bitter Rivalry*, Harper Press, London, 2010.

Cline, Sally. *Just Desserts: Women and Food*, André Deutsch, London, 1990; Diane Publishing, New York, 1990.

———. *Lillian Hellman and Dashiell Hammett: Memories or Myths?* (forthcoming, Golden Books).

———. *Women, Celibacy and Passion*, André Deutsch, London, 1993; Carole Southern Books, New York, 1993; Optima, London, 1994.

Collingham, Lizzie. *Curry: A Tale of Cooks and Conquerors*, Vintage, London, 2006.

Fisher, M.F.K. (with Introduction by Prue Leith). *With Bold Knife and Fork*, Vintage, London, 2001.

Hall, Radclyffe. *Adam's Breed*, Virago Modern Classics, London, 1986.

Hellman, Lillian and Feibleman, Peter. *Eating Together: Recipes and Recollections*, Little, Brown, Boston, 1984.

Hickman, Trevor. *Historic Cheeses: Leicestershire, Stilton and Stichelton*, DB Publishing, Derby, UK, 2009.

Hirst, Christopher. *Love Bites: Marital Skirmishes in the Kitchen*, Fourth Estate, London, 2010.

Jaffrey, Madhur. *Eastern Vegetarian Cookery*, Jonathan Cape, London, 1983.

Lawson, Nigella. *Nigella Express*, Chatto and Windus, London, 2007.

Loohuizen, Ria. *The Realm of Fig and Quince*, Prospect Books, Totnes, UK, 2010.

Roden, Claudia. *The Book of Jewish Food: An Odyssey from Samarkand and Vilna to the Present Day* (new edition), Penguin, London, 1999.

Slater, Nigel. *The Kitchen Diaries*, Fourth Estate, London, 2005.

Wright, John. *The River Cottage Edible Seashore Handbook*, Bloomsbury, London, 2009.

6. Reflections on nature and landscape by Midge Gillies

Baker, J.A. *The Peregrine*, New York Review Books Classics, New York, 2005.

Blythe, Ronald. Akenfield: *Portrait of an English Village*, Penguin, London, 1969.

Buxton, John. *The Redstart, New Naturalist Monograph No.2*, Collins, London, 1950.

Clare, John. *Selected Poetry*, Faber and Faber, London, 2004.

Cocker, Mark. *Crow Country*, Vintage, London, 2008.

Cocker, Mark and Mabey, Richard. *Birds Britannica*, Chatto & Windus, London, 2005.

Deakin, Roger. *Wildwood: A Journey Through Trees*, Penguin, London, 2008.

————. *Notes from Walnut Tree Farm*, Penguin, London, 2009.

Dillard, Annie. *Pilgrim at Tinker Creek*, Harper Perennial Modern Classics, New York, 2007; Canterbury Press, Norwich, 2011.

Fitter, R.S. *London's Natural History*, Collins, London, 1945.

Mabey, Richard. *Flora Britannica*, Chatto & Windus, London, 1996.

————. *Food for Free*, Collins, London, 2007.

————. *Gilbert White: A Biography of the Author of The Natural History of Selborne*, Profile Books, London, 2006.

————. *Nature Cure*, Pimlico, London, 2006.

————. *Weeds: A Cultural History*, Profile Books, London, 2010.

Macfarlane, Robert. *Mountains of the Mind: A History of a Fascination*, Granta, London, 2008.

Melville, Hermann. *Moby-Dick*, Vintage Classics, London, 2007.

Potter, Jennifer. *The Rose*, Atlantic Books, London, 2011.

Sprawson, Charles. *Haunts of the Black Masseur: The Swimmer as Hero*, Vintage, London, 1992.

Spufford, Francis. *I May Be Some Time: Ice and the English Imagination*, Faber and Faber, London, 1997.

Swift, Graham. *Waterland*. Picador, London, 2010.

Thompson, Flora. *Lark Rise to Candleford*, Penguin Modern Classics, London, 1973.

Thoreau, Henry. *Walden*, Princeton University Press, 2004; Oxford Paperbacks, UK, 2008.

White, Gilbert. *The Natural History of Selborne*, Penguin Classics, London, 2006.

Periodicals

Lopez, Barry. 'A Literature of Place', *Portland Magazine*, Summer 1997.

7. Reflections on feminism by Sally Cline

Angelou, Maya. *I Know Why The Caged Bird Sings*, Virago, London, 1984.

Atwood, Margaret. *Bodily Harm*, Jonathan Cape, London, 1982; Simon & Schuster, New York, 1982.

————. *Curious Pursuits: Occasional Writing 1970-2005*, Virago, London, 2005.

————. *The Handmaid's Tale*, Anchor Books, New York, 1998 (first published 1985); Vintage Classics, London, 2010.

————. *Moving Targets: Writing with Intent, 1983–2005*, House of Anansi, Toronto, 2004; Carroll & Graf, New York, 2005.

—————. *Second Words: Selected Critical Prose*, House of Anansi, Toronto, 1982.

Banyard, Kat. *The Equality Illusion: The Truth about Women and Men*, Faber and Faber, London, 2010.

Beauvoir, Simone de. *The Second Sex*, Vintage Classics, London, 1997.

Bidisha. *Beyond the Wall: Writing a Path through Palestine*, Seagull Books, Hove, 2012.

Brownmiller, Susan. *Against our Will: Men, Women and Rape*, Pelican, London, 1986.

Cline, Sally. *Reflecting Men at Twice their Natural Size* (co-author Dale Spender). André Deutsch, London, 1987; Henry Holt, New York, 1987; Fontana, London, 1988.

Dworkin, Andrea. *Intercourse*, Basic Books, New York, 2006.

Faludi, Susan. *Backlash. The Undeclared War Against Women*, Chatto & Windus, London, 1991, 1992; Vintage, London, 1993.

Friedan, Betty. *The Feminine Mystique*, Penguin Modern Classics, London, 2010.

Gray, John. *Men are from Mars, Women are from Venus*, HarperCollins, New York, 1992; Harper Element, London, 2002.

Greer, Germaine. *The Female Eunuch*, Paladin, London, 1976.

Gupta, Rahila. *Enslaved: The New British Slavery*, Granta Books, London, 2007.

Kassindja, Fauziya, with Layli Miller Bashir. *Do They Hear You When You Cry*, Delacorte Press, New York, 1998.

Lentricchia, Frank and McLaughlin, Thomas (eds). *Critical Terms for Literary Study*, University of Chicago Press, Chicago, 1995.

Lorde, Audre. *The Cancer Journals,* Aunt Lute Books, San Francisco, 2007.

Middlebrook, Diane. *Her Husband: Ted Hughes and Sylvia Plath, a Marriage,* Little, Brown, London, 2004.

Millett, Kate. *Flying,* Knopf, New York, 1974.

—————. *Sexual Politics*, Virago, London, 1977 (originally published 1970).

Moran, Caitlin. *How To Be a Woman*, Ebury Press, London, 2011; Harper Perennial, New York, 2012.

Orbach, Susie. *Bodies*, Picador, New York, 2009; Profile Books, London, 2010.

Rich, Adrienne. *On Lies, Secrets and Silence: Selected Prose 1966–1978*, W.W. Norton, New York, 1995.

————. *Of Woman Born*, W.W. Norton, New York, 1976, 1986.

Spender, Dale. *Man Made Language*, Routledge & Kegan Paul, London, 1980.

Tannen, Deborah. *You Just Don't Understand: Women and Men Talking*, Virago, London, 1991.

Walter, Natasha. *Living Dolls: The Return of Sexism*, Virago, London, 2011.

Periodicals

Pokorny, Brad. Review of *Do They Hear You When You Cry*, Baha'i Library On Line.

Potts, Robert. 'Light in the Wilderness', *Guardian*, 26 April, 2003.

Tangelder, Johan D. 'Reformed Reflections: The Power of Language', www. reformed reflections.ca/faith-and-life/power-of-language.html, accessed 9 September 2011.

8. Reflections on history by Midge Gillies

Arthur, Max. *Forgotten Voices of the Second World War*, Ebury Press, London, 2005.

Bair, Deirdre. *Simone De Beauvoir: A Biography*, Vintage, London, 1991.

Beard, Mary. *Pompeii: The Life of a Roman Town*, Profile, London, 2009.

Beer, Gillian. *Darwin's Plots* (3rd edition), Cambridge University Press, 2009.

Beevor, Antony. *Stalingrad*, Penguin, London, 2007.

De Waal, Edmund. *The Hare with Amber Eyes: A Hidden Inheritance*, Chatto & Windus, London, 2010.

Forster, Margaret. *Hidden Lives: A Family Memoir*, Penguin, London, 2001.

————. *Precious Lives*, Vintage, London, 1999.

Fraser, Antonia. *The Gunpowder Plot: Terror & Faith in 1605*, Mandarin, London, 1997.

Gardiner, Juliet. *The Thirties: An Intimate History*, Harper Press, London, 2010.

Gillies, Midge. *Marie Lloyd: The One and Only*, Victor Gollancz, London, 1999.

————. *Waiting for Hitler: Britain on the Brink of Invasion*, Hodder & Stoughton, London, 2007.

Hartley, L.P. *The Go-Between*, Penguin Modern Classics, London, 2004.

King, Stephen. *On Writing, A Memoir of the Craft*, New English Library, London, 2001.

Kurlansky, Mark. *Cod: A Biography of the Fish That Changed the World,* Penguin, New York, 1998; Vintage, London, 1999.

Kynaston, David. *Austerity Britain 1945–1951,* Bloomsbury, London, 2007.

Light, Alison. *Mrs Woolf and the Servants: The Hidden Heart of Domestic Service,* Penguin, London, 2007.

McKenna, Neil. *Fanny and Stella: The Scandalous Lives and Extraordinary Trials of Two Victorian Cross Dressers,* Faber and Faber, London, 2012.

Moorehead, Caroline. *A Train in Winter: A Story of Resistance, Friendship and Survival,* Chatto & Windus, London, 2011.

Nicholson, Virginia. *Millions Like Us: Women's Lives in War and Peace 1939–1949,* Viking, London, 2011.

Sellar, W.C. and Yeatman, R.J. *1066 and All That,* Methuen, London, 1998.

Souhami, Diana. *Gertrude and Alice,* Rivers Oram/Pandora List, London, 1993.

Summerscale, Kate. *The Queen of Whale Cay: The Eccentric Story of 'Joe' Carstairs, Fastest Woman on Water,* Fourth Estate, London, 1997; Viking Adult, New York, 1998.

Terkel, Studs. *The Good War: An Oral History of World War Two,* Pantheon, New York, 1984.

Thurman, Judith. *Secrets of the Flesh: A Life of Colette,* Bloomsbury, London, 1999.

Tomalin, Claire. *The Invisible Woman: The Story of Nelly Ternan and Charles Dickens,* Penguin, London, 1991.

Waters, Sarah. *The Little Stranger,* Virago, London, 2009.

Winchester, Simon. *The Surgeon of Crowthorne: A Tale of Murder, Madness and the Love of Words,* Viking, London, 1998; published in the US as *The Professor and the Madman: A Tale of Murder, Insanity, and the Making of the Oxford English Dictionary,* Harper Perennial, New York, 2005.

9. Reflections on sexuality, friendship and death by Sally Cline

Alvarez, Al, *The Savage God: A Study of Suicide,* Weidenfeld & Nicolson, London, 1971.

Appignanesi, Lisa. *All About Love: Anatomy of an Unruly Emotion,* Virago, London, 2011; W.W. Norton, New York, 2011.

Blair, Tony. *A Journey*, Hutchinson, London, 2010; Knopf, New York, 2010.

Broyard, Anatole. *Intoxicated By My Illness*, Clarkson Potter, New York, 1992.

Campbell, Alastair. *Maya*, Hutchinson, London, 2010.

Chabon, Michael. *Manhood for Amateurs*, Harper, New York, 2009; Fourth Estate, London, 2011.

Cline, Sally. *Lifting the Taboo: Women Death and Dying*, Little, Brown, London, 1995; Abacus, London, 1996; New York University Press, 1997.

Dillon, Millicent. *A Little Original Sin. The Life and Work of Jane Bowles*, University of California Press, Berkeley, 1998 (first published 1981).

————. *You Are Not I. A Portrait of Paul Bowles,* University of California Press, Beverley, 2000.

Gray, John. *The Immortalization Commission. Science and the Strange Quest to Cheat Death*, Allen Lane, London, 2011.

Hemingway, Ernest. *The Sun Also Rises*, Scribner, New York, 2003.

Johnson, Rachel. *Shire Hell*, Penguin, London, 2008.

King, Laurie and Spring, Michelle. *The Arvon Book of Crime Writing*, Bloomsbury, London and New York, 2012.

Love, Patricia. *Hot Monogamy: Essential Steps to More Passionate Intimate Lovemaking*, Plume, New York, 1995.

Mailer, Norman. *The Castle in the Forest*, Random House, New York, 2007.

Mars-Jones, Adam and White, Edmund. *The Darker Proof* (second revised edition), Faber and Faber, London, 1988.

Patchett, Ann. *Truth and Beauty*, HarperCollins, USA, 2004.

Phillips, Adam. *Monogamy*, Faber and Faber, London, 1996.

Powell, Julie. *Julie/Julia Project: Bon Appetit Blog*, e-Pub Bud Books.

————. *Julie and Julia: 365 Days, 524 Recipes, 1 Tiny Apartment Kitchen*, Little, Brown, New York, 2005.

Roth, Philip. *The Humbling*, Houghton Mifflin Harcourt, New York, 2009; Jonathan Cape, London, 2009.

Somerville, Rowan. *The Shape of Her*, W & N, London, 2010.

Sontag, Susan. *Illness as Metaphor and Aids and its Metaphors*, Picador, 2001.

————. *Regarding the Pain of Others*, Picador, New York, 2004.

Tennyson, Hallam. *Alfred Lord Tennyson: A Memoir by his Son*, Vol. 1, Macmillan, London, 1897.

Titchmarsh, Alan. *Mr MacGregor*, Pocket Books, London, 1999.

Woolf, Virginia. *A Room of One's Own*, Penguin Modern Classics, London, 2002.

10. Reflections on the mysteries of mind and body by Sally Cline

Jamison, Kay Redfield. *Touched With Fire: Manic-Depressive Illness and the Artistic Temperament*. Free Press Paperback, Simon & Schuster, New York, 1993.

——————. An Unquiet Mind. *A Memoir of Moods and Madness*, Alfred Knopf, New York, *1995*; Picador, London, 1997.

Sacks, Oliver. *Awakenings*, Picador, London, 1973.

——————. *The Man Who Mistook His Wife for a Hat*, Picador, London, 1986.

——————. *The Mind's Eye*, Picador, London, 2010.

Styron, William. *Darkness Visible*, Picador, London, 1991.

Wolpert, Lewis. *Malignant Sadness: The Anatomy of Depression*, Faber and Faber, London, 1999.

Woolf, Virginia. *The Death of the Moth and Other Essays*, Harcourt Brace Jovanovitch, New York, 1942.

Part 2: Tips and tales – guest contributors

Davies, Stevie. *Unbridled Spirits: Women of the English Revolution, 1640-1660*, Women's Press, London, 1998.

Kessler-Harris, Alice. *A Difficult Woman: The Challenging Life and Times of Lillian Hellman*, Bloomsbury, London and New York, 2012.

Sellers, Susan. *Vanessa and Virginia*, Two Ravens Press, Isle of Lewis, 2008.

Part 3: Write on

Planning

Beauvoir, Simone de. *Memoirs of a Dutiful Daughter*, Penguin Classics, London, 2006.

Beckett, Andy. *When the Lights Went Out: Britain in the Seventies*, Faber and Faber, London, 2010.

Blackburn, Julie. *The Three of Us*, Vintage, London, 2009.

Brendon, Piers. *The Dark Valley: A Panorama of the 1930s*, Pimlico, London, 2001.

Chang, Jung. *Wild Swans: Three Daughters of China*, Harper Perennial, London, 2004.

Cline, Sally and Angier, Carole, *The Arvon Book of Life Writing: Writing Biography, Autobiography and Memoir*, Bloomsbury (Imprint Methuen Drama), London and New York, 2010.

Clinton, Bill. *My Life*, Vintage, New York, 2005; Arrow, London, 2005.

Dillard, Annie. *An American Childhood*, Harper & Row, New York, 1987.

Dylan, Bob. *Chronicles: Volume 1*, Simon & Schuster, New York, 2004; Pocket Books, London, 2005.

Epstein, Helen. *Where She Came From: A Daughter's Search for her Mother's History*, Plume, New York, 1998.

Flachmann, K., Flachmann, M., Bernander, K., and Smith, C. *Brief Prose Reader. Essays for Thinking, Reading, and Writing*, Prentice Hall, New Jersey, 2002.

Frey, James. *A Million Little Pieces*, Anchor Books, New York, 2003; John Murray, London, 2004.

Galloway, Janice. *This Is Not About Me*, Granta, London, 2009.

Gandhi, Mahatma. *The Story of My Experiments with Truth*, Beacon Press, Boston, MA, 1993; Penguin Classics, London, 2001.

Gordon, Lyndall. *Mary Wollstonecraft: A New Genus*, Little, Brown, London, 2005; HarperCollins, New York, 2005.

Hughes, Kathryn. *The Short Life & Long Times of Mrs Beeton*, Fourth Estate, London, 2005.

Mandela, Nelson. *A Long Walk to Freedom*, Little, Brown, London, 1994; Back Bay Books, New York, 1995.

Masters, Alexander. *The Genius in my Basement*, Fourth Estate, London, 2011.

Morton, Andrew. *Diana. Her True Story – In Her Own Words*, Michael O'Mara Books, London, 1998; Pocket Books, New York, 1998.

Murray, Jenni. *Memoirs of a Not So Dutiful Daughter*, Black Swan, London, 2009.

Obama, Barack. *Dreams from My Father*, Broadway, New York, 2004; Canongate, London, 2008.

Pelzer, Dave J. *A Child Called 'It'*, HCI Books, Florida, 1995; Orion, London 2012.

Proulx, Annie. *Bird Cloud: A Memoir*, Scribner, New York, 2011; Fourth Estate, London, 2011.

Sellers, Heather. *You Don't Look Like Anyone I Know: A True Story of Face Blindness and Forgiveness*, Riverhead Books, New York, 2010.

Sher, Abby. *Amen, Amen, Amen: Memoir of a Girl Who Couldn't Stop Praying (Among Other Things)*, Scribner, New York, 2011.

Spinelli, Jerry. *Knots in My Yo-Yo String*, Knopf, New York, 1998.

Spurling, Hilary. *Burying the Bones: Pearl Buck in China*, Simon & Schuster, London, 2010; Simon & Schuster, New York, 2011.

Thompson, Craig. *Blankets*, Top Shelf Productions, USA, 2003.

Vidal, Gore. *Palimpsest: A Memoir*, Abacus, London, 1996.

Vilar, Irene. *Impossible Motherhood: Testimony of an Abortion Addict*, Other Press, New York, 2009.

Periodicals

Seed, Ian. 'Betrayal', from 'Four short prose pieces', *Brevity Magazine: A Journal of Concise Literary Nonfiction* (online), Issue 37, Fall 2011.

————. 'Insect', *Brevity Magazine: A Journal of Concise Literary Nonfiction* (online), Issue 37, Fall 2011.

Research

Bevan, Amanda. *Tracing Your Ancestors in The National Archives, The Website and Beyond*, The National Archives, London, 2006.

Drabble, Margaret (ed.). *The Oxford Companion to English Literature*, Oxford University Press, 2006.

Christian, Peter. *The Genealogist's Internet*, The National Archives, London, 2009.

Christian, Peter and Annal, David. *Census: The Expert Guide*, The National Archives, London, 2008.

Codlin, Ellen (ed.). *The ASLIB Directory of Information Sources in the United Kingdom*, ASLIB, 1982–1984.

Crockford's Clerical Directory (published annually), Church House Publishing, London, 1858–

Debrett's Peerage & Baronetage 2011, ed. Charles Kidd. Debrett's Ltd., Richmond, Surrey, 2011.

Grannum, Karen and Taylor, Nigel. *Wills and Probate Records*, The National Archives, London, 2009.

Hoffman, Alice. *Research for Writers*, A. & C. Black, London, 2003.

Kershaw, Roger. *Migration Records: A Guide for Family Historians*, The National Archives, London, 2009.

The New Grove Dictionary of Music and Musicians, ed. Stanley Sadie. Oxford University Press, 2001.

Oxford Dictionary of National Biography, ed. H.C.G. Matthew and Brian Harrison, Oxford University Press, 2004.

Palgrave Macmillan Dictionary of Women's Biography, ed. Jenny Uglow and Maggy Hendry, Maggie. Palgrave Macmillan, London, 2005.

Pearsall, Mark. *Family History Companion*, The National Archives, London, 2007.

Phillimore Atlas and Index of Parish Registers, ed. Cecil Humphery-Smith. Phillimore, Andover, 2003.

Spencer, William. *Air Force Records: A Guide for Family Historians*, The National Archives, London, 2008.

Army Records: A Guide for Family Historians, The National Archives, London, 2008.

Whitaker's Almanack 2012 (published annually), Bloomsbury, London 2011.

Who's Who (published annually), A&C Black, London, 2011.

Writers' & Artists' Yearbook 2012 (published annually), A&C Black, London, 2011.

The Writer's Handbook 2011, ed. Barry Turner, Palgrave Macmillan, London, 2010.

Index

arvon

The Arvon Foundation is a registered charity which strives to promote the transforming power of writing. Through public courses, partnerships and work with young people, Arvon has helped thousands of individuals to begin a creative journey of self-discovery and imagination through writing.

The Arvon Foundation sprang to life in 1968 as a reaction by two poets, John Moat and John Fairfax, to what they saw as a dogmatic and lifeless approach to teaching poetry. Their solution was to encourage young people to find their voices by removing them from their everyday lives and enabling them to live and work with two published writers for a week. The infectious energy and idealism of Moat and Fairfax

Photo: Phil Grey

took off and captured the imagination of young people, teachers and writers, laying the basis for what has become a thriving and prestigious national enterprise.

Today Arvon runs four historic writing houses in the UK, where published writers lead week-long residential courses with individuals at all stages of their writing lives. Public courses are offered in a diverse range of genres, from novel writing, advanced poetry and radio fiction to food writing and comedy. Many highly regarded writers have at one time attended an Arvon course: Andrew Motion,

Photo: Paul Floyd Blake

Hilary Mantel, Lemn Sissay, Pat Barker, Roger McGough, Alan Hollinghurst and Sian Hughes among them. No qualifications or previous experience are required; Arvon is for anyone with a desire to write.

Arvon's ongoing commitment to open access is reflected in its grants programme, which provides financial support to enable those on low or no income to attend a course. Young people remain a vital part of the organisation's work and hundreds of under-18s participate in bespoke courses every year. Partnerships with groups such as the Medical Foundation for the Care of Victims of Torture and The Princess Royal Carers Trust continue to bring a diverse range of writers to Arvon.

www.arvonfoundation.org

The Arvon Foundation Ltd is a registered charity number No. 306694.

Supported by
ARTS COUNCIL ENGLAND